35.00

Integrated Circuit Mask Technology

Integrated Circuit Mask Technology

David J. Elliott
Strategic Planning Manager, Microelectronic Products
Shipley Company, Newton, Massachusetts

McGraw-Hill Book Company
New York   St. Louis   San Francisco   Auckland
Bogotá   Hamburg   Johannesburg   London   Madrid
Mexico   Montreal   New Delhi   Panama   Paris
São Paulo   Singapore   Sydney   Tokyo   Toronto

Library of Congress Cataloging in Publication Data

Elliott, David J.
   Intregrated circuit mask technology.
   Includes index.

   1. Integrated circuits—Masks.   I. Title.
TK7872.M3E44   1985   621.381'73   84-4383
ISBN 0-07-019261-8

Copyright © 1985 by McGraw-Hill, Inc. All rights reserved. Printed in the United States of America. Except as permitted under the United States Copyright Act of 1976, no part of this publication may be reproduced or distributed in any form or by any means, or stored in a data base or retrieval system, without the prior written permission of the publisher.

1 2 3 4 5 6 7 8 9 0   DOC   DOC   8 3 2 1 0 9 8 7 6 5 4

ISBN 0-07-019261-8

The editors for this book were Roy Mogilanski and Ruth L. Weine, the designer was Elliot Epstein, and the production supervisor was Thomas G. Kowalczyk. It was set in Baskerville by Monotype Composition Company, Inc.

Printed and bound by R. R. Donnelly & Sons, Inc.

This book is dedicated to Jane, Ben, and Holly.

Contents

Preface · xiii
Acknowledgments · xv

1 PATTERN DESIGN AND DATA PRODUCTION · 1
  Introduction, 1
  Historical Overview, 2
  Computer-Aided Design Approaches, 6
  Design Rules, 7
    Impact of Lithography on Design, 9
    Pattern Elements and Their Electrical Result, 9
    Diffused Regions, 10
    Ion-Implant Regions, 10
    Polysilicon Regions, 10
    Contacts, 11
    Metal Layers, 11
    Design-Rule Limitations, 12
  Pattern Layout, 13
    Hand-Drafting, 13
    Array Technique, 17
    Silicon Compilers, 18
    Automatic Placement and Routing, 20
      The Routing Step, 20
    Hierarchical Design, 20
    Symbolic Logic, 23
    Fixed-Grid Layout, 24
    Building-Block Design and Layout, 26
  Device Modeling, 28
  References, 31

2 MASK-QUALITY GLASS — 33

Introduction, 33

Glass Melting and Forming, 34
   Suitable Optical Transmission, 37
   Low Thermal Expansion, 38
   Stabilization Time, 40
   Material Costs, 40
   Low Defect Levels, 42
   Cleaning and Handling Resistance, 44

Glass Composition, 45

General Properties of Soda-Lime, Crown Borosilicate, Barium-Aluminum Silicate, and Quartz Glasses, 46
   Soda-Lime Glasses, 46
      Green Soda-Lime Glass, 46
      White Soda-Lime Glass, 47
   Borosilicate Glass, 48
   Quartz Glass, 49

Optical Transmission of Glass, 50

Glass Cleaning, 50
   Ultrasonics versus Pinholes, 54
   Blank Protection prior to Metallization, 55

Blank Hardness, 58

Mask Inspection, 59

Glass Flatness, 59
   Warpage, 63
   Plastic Flow, 63
   Vacuum-Chuck Distortion, 64
   Gravitational Sag, 64

Plate Size versus Thickness, 67

Edge Beveling, 67

3 COATING FOR MASK BLANKS — 69

Introduction, 69

Mask-Blank Coating Types, 70
   Emulsion Mask Characteristics, 70
      Advantages of Emulsion Masks, 70
         Low Cost, 70
         High Photosensitivity, 70
         Good Image Resolution and Contrast, 71
         Reversal Processing, 71
         Enhanced Image-Edge Effects, 73
      Weak Points of Emulsions, 74
   Diazo Resin Coatings, 75
   Resists as Mask Coatings, 76
   Iron Oxide Coatings, 77
   Chromium, 81
      Low-Reflectivity Chromium, 81

Glass-Blank Cleaning prior to Deposition of the Masking Layer, 83
Glass-Blank Deposition Techniques, 83
   Chemical-Vapor Deposition, 84
   Vacuum Deposition, 87
   Evaporation, 89
     Crucible Evaporation, 89
     Filament Evaporation, 89
     Flash Evaporation, 90
     Induction Evaporation, 90
   General Vacuum Deposition Criteria, 91
References, 91

4 SUBSTRATE IMAGING   93

Introduction, 93
Imaging, 95
Electron-Beam Imaging, 98
   Rapid Turnaround, 100
   Optical versus Electron-Beam Processes, 100
   Raster versus Vector Scan, 102
Electron-Beam System Capabilities, 104
   Throughput, 105
   Electron Optics versus Light Optics, 106
   Electron Sources, 107
   Facilities Requirements, 107
Writing Strategies, 109
Reticles, 114
MEBES, 116
   Data Format, 116
Vector-Scan Writing in Production, 117
Variable-Shaped-Beam Writing, 122
Contact Printing, 123
   Exposure Parameters, 125
   Hard- and Soft-Contact Printing, 127
Processing Photoresists and Electron Resists, 128
   Exposure Control, 129
   Resist Developing, 131
   Imaging Sequence for a Positive Optical Resist, 133
   Developer Control, 134
   COP Negative Electron Resist, 138
   PBS Positive Electron Resist, 138
   Other Electron Resists, 139
   Backscatter in Resist Films, 139
   Multilayer Resist Process, 140
   AZ-2400 as an Electron Resist, 142
   Electron-Beam Resist Troubleshooting, 142
   Electron-Beam Resist Selection, 143

Pattern Generation, 146
 Pattern-Generator Capabilities, 147
 Plate Stability, 149
 Staging, 149
 Control System, 150
 Plate Handling, 150
 Exposure Energy versus Line Width, 152
 Modulation Transfer Function, 153
 Depth of Focus, 155
 Reflectance versus Resolution, 157
 MTF versus Resist and Developer Parameters, 159
 Parametric MTF Improvement, 161

Photorepeaters, 161

Reticle Production, 164

Spectral Reflectance, 167

References, 167

5 ETCHING   169

Introduction, 169
Surfaces to be Etched, 170
Resist Images as Masks, 171
Image Hardening, 173
Post-Bake Parameters, 174
Thermal Flow, 174
Resist Shrinkage, 174
Etch-Resistance Testing, 176
Postexposure Baking, 176
Postdevelopment Exposure, 177
Wet Etching, 178
 Chrome Etching, 179
 Etch Profiles, 180
 Wet Etchants for Chrome, 181
 Iron Oxide Etching, 186
 Equipment for Wet Etching, 186
 Wet versus Dry Etching, 187
Dry Etching, 188
 Advantages of Dry Etching, 188
 Overview, 190
 Etch Duration versus Temperature, 191
 Etch Rate versus Pressure, 192
 Etch Rate versus rf Power, 192
 Etch Rate versus Oxygen Gas Concentration, 193
 RF Power versus Etch Rate for Mixture of CCl_4 and Air, 194
 Pattern Width of Master Mask versus Copy Mask, 195
 Etch Time versus Line-Width Change, 195
 Undercut Profiles, 197

Overetching, 200
Reverse Etching, 201
Resist Removal, 202
   Resist-Removal Criteria, 203
   Wet-Chemical Resist Removal, 203
   Dry-Chemical Resist Removal, 204
References, 207

6 PATTERN MEASUREMENT   209
Introduction, 209
Optical Microscopy, 212
   Image-Shearing Microscopes, 216
   Photosensing Devices, 217
   TV Scanning Microscopes, 218
   Laser Measurement, 219
Scanning-Microscope Measurement, 222
Thickness Measurement, 231
   Interferometry, 231
   Stylus Profilometry, 233
   Prism-Coupler Measurement, 236
   Ellipsometric Measurement, 237
   Channel Spectra, 238
Applications for Pattern Measurement, 239
References, 241

7 MASKS IN PRODUCTION   243
Introduction, 243
Inspection, 243
   Defects, 244
   Registration Errors, 245
   Critical-Dimension (CD) Checking, 245
   Mask-Quality Checks, 246
   Overall Inspection Criteria, 246
Definitions and Sources of Defects, 247
Mask Quality and Yield, 251
Examples of Mask Defects, 252
Inspection Technique, 255
   Optical Comparator Method, 256
   Image Enhancement, 257
   Adjacent-Die Comparison Method, 258
Pellicles for IC Mask Protection, 259
   Transmission Properties of Pellicles, 262
   Midultraviolet Technology and Pellicle Use, 264
   Pellicle Particle Protection, 265

Mask Defects and Repair, 268
   Defect Removal by Laser, 269
   Repair of Transparent Defects, 270
      Repair Equipment, 272
   Patching Clear Defects, 274
   Ink-Dot Repair of Defects, 275
   Washing Procedure for Repaired Reticles, 275

Mask Cleaning in Production, 276
   Forces Affecting Particle Contamination, 276
   Cleaning after Deposition, 277
   Dry Cleaning of Masks and Reticles, 277
   Chemical Cleaning, 278
   Cleaning Low-Expansion Glass, 281

References, 281

INDEX 283

Preface

This book details the major fabrication steps and many process techniques used to produce high-resolution masks for integrated-circuit fabrication. Processing parameters for the equipment and chemicals used are presented, giving emphasis to practical details and techniques. Many of the physical parameters, the principles and laws governing the behavior of light and electrons, and the other mask process reactions are explained so as to provide a reference framework for mask makers. The aim of this book is to provide a useful source of practical information on mask-making to facilitate better communication of this subject and to improve the quality of the mask-manufacturing processes.

The forces that drive mask technology are reviewed in this book, especially the lithography factors. The charts below summarize both the pattern resolution trends and the lithography technologies used to produce various levels of resolution and wafer throughput.

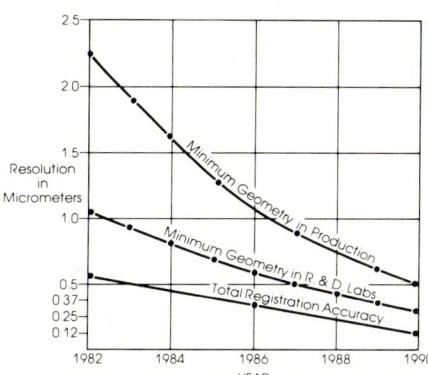

CHART 1 Integrated circuit feature size and registration control trends (*Semiconductor Information Services, Woburn, Mass.*)

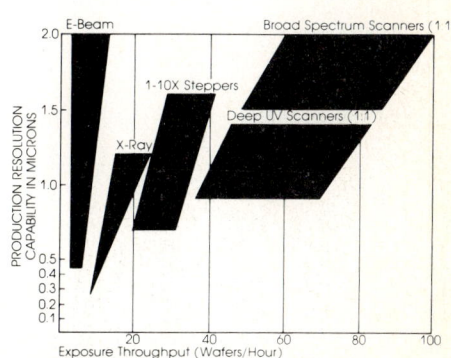

CHART 2 Wafer exposure system; resolution versus throughput. (*Semiconductor Information Services, Woburn, Mass.*)

Most experts view lithography as the driving force of both mask and wafer fabrication technology. Special attention has therefore been given in this text to the imaging step in IC fabrication.

David J. Elliott

Acknowledgments

I would like to acknowledge both Karen Stackpole for her work in preparing the manuscript and the many individuals from our industry worldwide whose technical contributions made the writing of this book possible.

1
Pattern Design and Data Production

INTRODUCTION

The use of computers to provide new device designs has become a matter of fact, and recent very large-scale integration (VLSI) integrated-circuit design has leaned heavily on new and more powerful computing capability. Next-generation components will require even more complexity and utilize more computer time. Computer-aided design (CAD) has grown at an incredible rate, reaching into many fields, including architecture, chemical-experiment design, mathematical modeling, aeronautics, organizational studies, and medicine, to name a few.

The use of CAD in VLSI design is now widespread and extensive, and is considered by many experts to be one of the most well-developed applications of CAD. There are several aspects of VLSI CAD, including

1. Current VLSI CAD capabilities and trends
2. Device modeling
3. Logic simulation, device analysis, and time studies
4. Interconnection strategy
5. CAD relationship to lithographic processes
6. CAD relationship to testing chips and designs
7. Future role of CAD in new devices

The level of integration seems to be a common measure of the rise in integrated-circuit (IC) complexity. Early integrated circuits had up to 10 logic gates, and next evolved into medium-scale integration (MSI) integrated circuits that typically had between 10 and 100 logic gates. Beyond MSI came large-scale integration (LSI) with between 100 and 1000 gates. The current VLSI integrated circuits carry over 1000 gates, and people are already discussing the next layer of integration as being ultralarge-scale integration (ULSI).

HISTORICAL OVERVIEW

Integrated-circuit fabrication using photolithography started in the early 1950s with pioneering work at Fairchild Semiconductor and Texas Instruments. The basic steps used to conceive, design, test, fabricate, and chip test are essentially the same ones as were used 30 years ago. The method for handling each step has changed considerably, but basic changes have not been introduced. In summary form, these steps are as follows:

1. Define and optimize the IC fabrication and interconnection processes.
2. Electrically define circuit elements.
3. Design logic schematic.
4. Convert logic design to mask patterns (geometries).
5. Electrical test simulation of design to detect flaws.

These steps originally involved many hours of engineering time, since all were performed manually. The pattern dimensions were arrived at by evaluating several different geometries and measuring the yield of each test chip. Final pattern geometries were heuristically derived. After building a chip that met initial yield requirements, tests for rejects, electrical properties, and other parameters were run. The final result of this largely trial-and-error approach was a set of specifications for the electrical parameters and design rules (physical parameters) to match. Tolerances for each geometry were specified as they are today, to keep a maximum yield level.

A given customer, in the 1960s, would begin by putting together a drawing of the chip, called a "logic schematic." This sketch would then be built using discrete-component technology, a process called "breadboarding." Assuming all went well after this step, a layout designer would create the mask-pattern dimensions by drawing a set of mask geometries on paper, one for each level of the process. These drawings were then traced onto Rubylith, a red plastic material made by Ulano that served as the photographic master from which optical reductions were made. The Rubylith patterns were inspected for accuracy against the original drawings of the layout designer, a laborious task. Once again, after making any necessary corrections, the Rubylith masters were "shot" with a large reduction camera and reduced over 100 times to make the final emulsion masks. The devices were then built from the mask sets, and only after chips were complete could manufacturers get an idea of how their products performed.

In the next decade, as device complexity increased, these manual steps became so cumbersome and labor-intensive that shorter, more effective methods had to be devised to preserve overall process economies. The sheer volume of Rubylith sheets needed in a process area was "eating" an inordinate amount of costly facility real estate. The problem was solved by digitally encoding all the IC pattern geometries. The machine that accomplished this task became known as the optical pattern generator. The actual method involved taking the final drawings and converting them into data tapes. This was done by placing an electromechanical digitizer over the drawings and tracing the circuit pattern.

The major advancement made possible by digitizing the art work was computer handling of the IC pattern data. Now the computerized artwork could be run through a design-rule-check (DRC) program to test for open or short circuits or other design flaws. Once a flaw in the IC pattern artwork was detected, it could be easily changed via the digitizing system. In the earlier example, where Rubylith was used, an entirely new piece of artwork would have to be scribed to correct an error.

Once a series of designer drawings had been converted to digital signals that could be manipulated, corrected, and tested, the job of portraying the images on a screen was tackled. The amount of time saved by digitizing artwork was helpful, but many hours still were needed before a given design could be actually tested for defects. A key shortcut was to use the cathode-ray-tube (CRT) screen for laying out all the IC graphics. In the 1970s, interactive graphics, with the use of computers and screens, helped design engineers actually build prototype arrays much faster. For example, a memory section with many identical elements could easily be generated on the interactive graphics systems. This type of equipment would replicate a given common cell many thousands of times on a given device pattern and arrange or configure the pattern, electronically and rapidly. Prior to the advent of interactive graphics, all such configurations would require hand-drawing. All gate-array and memory-array cells had to be placed individually in the IC artwork. The electronic manipulation of interactive graphics saved hundreds of hours of artwork generation time.

By the mid 1970s, several major problems in IC artwork generation had been solved, namely, the digitizing of engineering drawings and the interactive layout process, both allowing for real-time changes and corrections to original design without replotting or recutting artwork. Further time savings were accrued by rapidly placing the thousands of identical pattern elements in an array with the use of interactive graphics terminals. Despite these advancements, all IC geometries for all mask levels needed to be "placed in silicon" before actual testing of the device could occur. The need existed, then, for an IC design simulator. The level of device integration was such that individual ICs could not be tested on the chip, and had to be simulator tested.

The next innovation was software to simulate the circuit functions. Many different programs were developed to perform IC simulation, resulting in good verification of the layout designers' work. In addition, the interactive graphics equipment could print out a drawing of the final digitized tape after modifications. An important benefit of this software was the ability to automatically verify the match between design layout metallization or interconnections and the balance of the design. An example of an operator working on an interactive CAD system is shown in Fig. 1-1.

In the 1970s, chips could not be modified, as they are today, to correct a defect or modify the result of a design error. This made it especially important to ensure the accuracy of the complete IC design before sending the artwork into manufacturing. However, ensuring accuracy with computer assistance is a far cry from using a computer to generate an entirely new IC design. Several innovations were needed before the automatic IC CAD system could be put into place. These

FIG. 1-1 CAD system with interactive graphics. *(VIA Systems, Inc.)*

innovations were assisted by the development of standard cell arrays and gate arrays. From this, Stevens and Hashimoto developed a computer algorithm called the "channel router," which was used to design ICs. Further algorithms were developed to provide the metallization or interconnection patterns for a large number of possible circuit designs.

The increased use of automatic-placement computer programs was helped by newer and simpler design styles. The gate arrays, for example, and other designs with standard cells in a regular pattern were more easily designed because of the repeatability of the units. The gate array, or standard slice, shortened the total design time and did not sacrifice precious silicon real estate in the process. Thus, free-form layout began to give way to automatic design and test programs. All new designs, for the first time, had to be testable *before* they were rendered in silicon. Thus, the responsibility for testing was moved from the postfabrication part of the process to the very beginning. Today, untestable designs are not even considered for possible use.

The overall job of producing first a design and second the data from which masks will be made is complex and involves many individual steps. The basic building blocks used to reach the point of reticle production are shown in Fig. 1-2. Automated design has become mandatory because of the rapid increase in device complexity and the

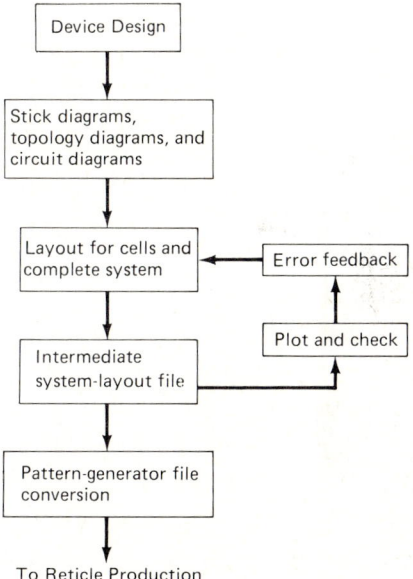

FIG. 1-2 Primary steps in design and data production.

commensurate increase in design time required. A typical 16-bit microprocessor chip requires in excess of 50 worker years of design time alone. The Intel 8086 reportedly required 13 worker years for just the layout phase. An increase in the sophistication of software and hardware has resulted in at least the capability to design even more complex chips than the 32-bit microprocessor. As shown in Fig. 1-3, the design tests are now split into several separate categories, each a separate entity.

COMPUTER-AIDED DESIGN APPROACHES

The design of an integrated circuit is a joint task wherein people utilize computers to perform the necessary functions. The trend toward greater interaction between people and computers has been facilitated by additional software for use with interactive graphics systems. Systems are used where a single operator can completely lay out the electronic parameters for a given VLSI design. The more complex systems save

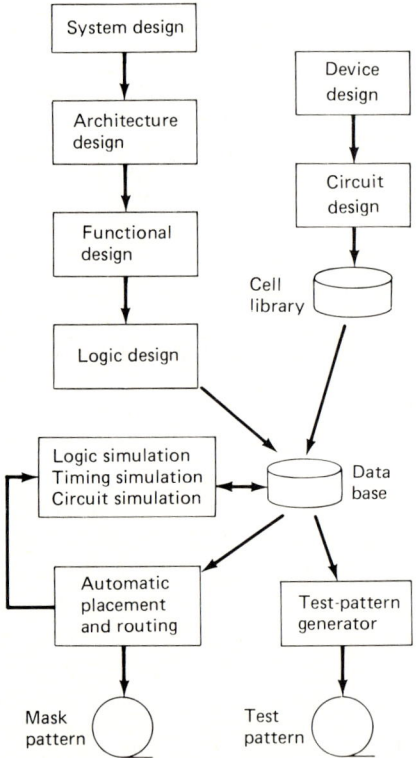

FIG. 1-3 Outline of design tasks. *(Diagram by courtesy of T. Sudo.)*

considerable design and layout time. Since the price of design time increases considerably every year for a given VLSI structure, CAD hardware and software is an expensive but cost-efficient proposition.

The first question one could ask in settling down to generate a new IC design is: What are the first considerations? The end use of the chip generally predetermines the general type [bipolar or metal-oxide semiconductor (MOS)] of technology to be used. Bipolar and MOS circuits both follow similar fabrication sequences, so a more basic question must be asked: What are the rules for VLSI chip design? This turns out to be a "chicken-and-egg" story, since the fabrication processes used to implement an undefined design provide a set of rules for the designer to follow. Thus, in a sense, the advance in IC fabrication-process technology made increased alternatives possible for the VLSI designer. We will consider the role of these designer's rules first and then explore the world of the designer and the tools used to generate a given IC configuration.

DESIGN RULES

The designer of VLSI ICs obviously cannot create a series of mask-level patterns that contain geometries that are beyond the limits of the fabrication process. Also, the design must take into consideration the basic limits and parameters for the proper electrical functioning of various circuit elements (transistors, interconnections). Thus, a complete understanding of device lithography and device physics is necessary for arriving at the geometrical design rules or limitations for creating a new design. Figure 1-4 shows design-rule drawing examples.

Design rules are defined as those physical constraints on the circuit geometries imposed by device physics and pattern lithography processes. These rules give the designer the minimum geometrical boundaries for line widths, overlay tolerances through the entire mask set, and the rules for extensions of given circuit elements on the chip.

Device physics changes only as the substrate material and overlaid materials (deposited oxides, silicides, metals, dopants) change. The electrical parameters for silicon and silicon oxides are fairly well mapped, along with the semiconductor materials commonly used—including polysilicon, silicon nitride, and aluminum and alloys of aluminum. New metal silicides, gallium arsenide, and new polymer dielectrics are examples of changes in material technology that affect the designer's activities. These materials possess different electrical properties and react differently in the fabrication process than the other materials mentioned. Also, the scaling rules will most likely change for new materials, and these limits must be defined. Material technology changes

8 INTEGRATED CIRCUIT MASK TECHNOLOGY

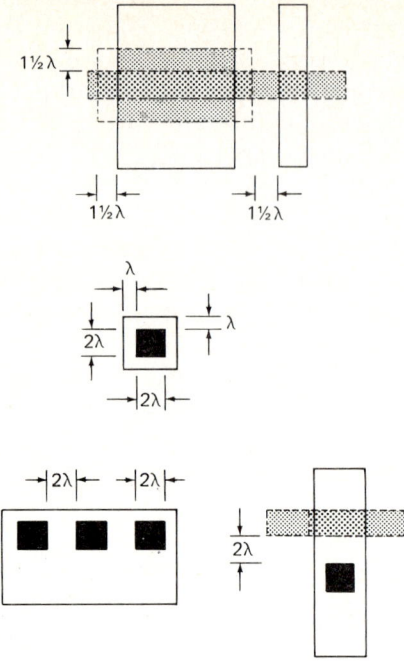

FIG. 1-4 Examples of design-rule drawing. *[Ref. 3.]*

constantly as new demands on circuit density create the need for smaller and faster integrated circuits.

New methods for applying materials to substrates also change the design rule possibilities. For example, laser doping or configured ion deposition allows for changes in the thickness of oxide or other dielectric layers, which in turn change circuit topology. Topology is a major constraint in VLSI design, and new technology improvements are the sole means for improving design. In fact, design often drives the downstream technologies. An example is isoplanar design schemes, where one specific objective was reduction of step heights to ease the burden on lithographers. Other designers' innovations have significant impact on the lithographic process. In some cases, design schemes do not favor lithography, especially when designers have a poor understanding of photoresist-imaging and etching parameters. The designers of ICs, and more recently VLSI chips, must necessarily understand all the geometrical constraints imposed by downstream processing, including ion-implant profiles, reflections from polysilicon and aluminum and their effect on pattern widths, minimum spacing due to optical and electrical proximity effects, and all the physical phenomena that affect geometries where microstructures are involved.

Impact of Lithography on Design

Designers seek to place as much information as possible within the chip area. Lithographers have worked hard at getting the imaging and etching processes under the control necessary to maintain the ever-shrinking line widths and spaces. Lithography, more than any other single factor, has provided the designer with more and more silicon real estate every year. The combination of better resist-imaging tools, higher-resolution resists, and dry-etching technology have provided the means to shrink geometries and thus leave more silicon available for additional circuitry.

In IC design, the limits of the distances between various features are really determined by the resolution of the fabrication process. If the IC fabrication process can provide 2-μm resolution, then mask-design rules can be set for this minimum distance. This distance must be maintained between lines over a given mask level and also from level to level throughout the entire mask set. All geometrical features are then held to the tolerance established by the capabilities of the photolithography or electron-lithography steps.

Because of the large number of variables, the design constraints or minimum working distances are often difficult to maintain during mask and wafer fabrication. The glass or silicon substrate is subject to movement as room or process-environment ambient temperatures change. Resist sensitivity sometimes varies from one lot to the next, causing pattern sizes to shift in the resist-imaging step. Alignment of mask to wafer is not always perfect, and of course, this problem accumulates with each successive mask layer. Sometimes these shifts off the pattern centers will cancel each other out. Etching will vary, and overetched geometries end up smaller than those normally etched. All factors considered, there are ample opportunities for fabrication steps to cause geometry variations that violate the design specifications.

Pattern Elements and Their Electrical Result

In considering the design rules to follow for a given circuit, the designer first looks to the basic mask levels. We will study each of the typical levels for an MOS process and relate the design rule to the consequence of violating that rule. The relationship between pattern sizes and electrical working parameters essentially determines what a chip does. All processes, from design through mask inspection and use on a production line, are ultimately tied to this basic relationship. Diffused regions, polysilicon layers, ion-implant regions, contact sizes, metal spacing, and pad area are examples of sections that have distinct electrical requirements that in turn are directly related to the pattern size.

Diffused Regions

Diffused regions always have a minimum spacing that is determined by both lithography and electrical requirements. In the design stage, placing two diffused regions too close could cause serious problems. For example, there are depletion layers associated with the junctions of the diffused regions. When spacing is not sufficient, the depletion layers will overlap, resulting in current flow where none was desired. Diffused-region separation has been shrinking along with all other device parameters. A 4- to 6-μm line width for a diffused region is typical, but safety margins sometimes cause this figure to be more like 5 to 8μm.

The width of the depletion layer is variable and current flow occurs there. The depletion layer will be thin when the surrounding region is at ground. However, when low voltage exists on the diffused regions, the regions can be more closely spaced. Another way of reducing spacing between diffused regions is to provide a high doping level at the surface of the wafer between diffused regions. This, in turn, reduces the possibility of overlapping depletion layers.

Ion-Implant Regions

Design rules for ion-implant regions depend on the type of device. If the implant is to become a transistor gate, its spacing parameters will be different from a device where the ion-implant region is placed close to but is separate from an enhancement-mode transistor-gate region. In the first case, the design should provide for extension of the ion-implanted area so that it overlaps the entire gate area. The actual distance it extends beyond the gate is also specified in the design rules. A 3- to 5-μm separation is typical for ion-implant regions next to an enhancement-mode gate region. The same dimension is appropriate for an ion-implant-region overlay on a gate region.

Polysilicon Regions

Line widths of polysilicon are not associated with depletion layers and generally can be placed closer together than diffused regions. The reflectiveness of the polysilicon *is* a factor in spacing widths in design rules. The reflections from polysilicon during resist patterning affect the dimensions formed in the resist. If the designer is familiar with the fabrication process, he or she will know about the reflection phenomenon and its relationship to proper design rule layout. Polysilicon lines run as small as 3 to 4 μm. Design considerations for polysilicon lines overlapping on other areas must be given. For example, the overlapping of a polysilicon line and a diffused line can cause an unwanted capacitor. The amount of spacing required to prevent this overlap is very small and probably can be the minimum resolution dimension for that chip. Polysilicon-gate dimensions are also very critical to specify. For example, polysilicon lines running over a diffused area will form a transistor. If the polysilicon-gate area is too small and does not extend a sufficient distance beyond the diffused area, a short circuit will occur. Figure 1-5 shows the translation of the design rule into the chip structure.

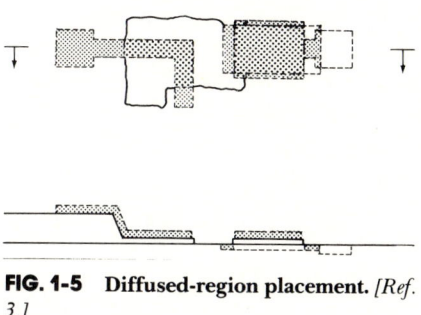

FIG. 1-5 Diffused-region placement. *[Ref. 3.]*

Contacts

The contact mask establishes ohmic contact between a metal layer and polysilicon or a diffused layer. The design rules for contacts will specify the diameter of the contact. If the contact area is too small, there may be problems getting good electrical connection to the bottom layer. Contacts that are too large may make electrical connection to another unintended layer. Other rules for contacts apply to placement inside the IC pattern. For example, contacts cannot occur over certain gate regions *if* the gate regions are too thin. When the gate or polysilicon thickness is sufficient, then contacts can be designed that are placed only partway into the polysilicon layer. Figure 1-6 shows contact placements.

Metal Layers

Interconnection-level metal or metallization is the covering that goes over all previously etched oxides, nitride, polysilicon doped glass, and other materials. The design rules for metal are given somewhat favorable treatment since they are expected to cover steps higher than any previous

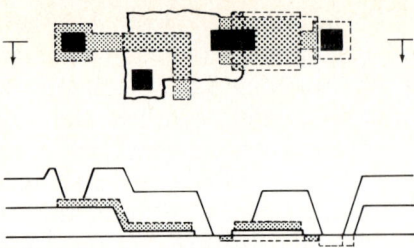

FIG. 1-6 Contact placements. *[Ref. 3.]*

level. Design rules or line widths for aluminum metallization are typically somewhat larger than line widths used elsewhere in the process. Linewidth constraints also arise because of the reflectivity of the metal, resulting in additional unwanted exposure between line-space pairs that are too close together. The more sensitive a given resist is to the exposing wavelength, the more likely the chance that this "cross-trace" or "bridging" exposure phenomenon will occur. Figure 1-7 shows the metal-layer pattern placement.

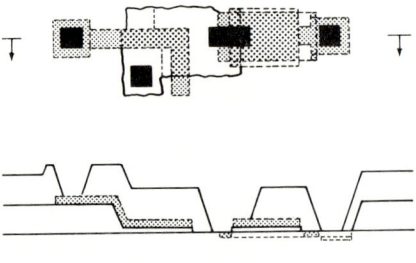

FIG. 1-7 Metal-layer pattern placement. *[Ref. 3.]*

Aluminum metallization is also required to completely encircle the contacts. Metal sizing for both contact coverage and current-carrying capability throughout the chip to the pad areas is critical. In some circuits, small nicks or edge defects will occur, and since the design rule for the metal level was wide enough or sufficiently large, the circuit will continue to function. These kinds of safety margins are wisely placed in the metal-level design rules.

Design-Rule Limitations

Overall electrical parameters are derived through careful study of the design rules and the establishment of electrical values that fit the chip specifications. They must also fit the capabilities of the lithographic process, as we have seen in the foregoing discussion. The smaller the designs for IC devices become, the closer they approach the physical, electrical, and lithographic limitations of the technologies used to produce the circuits. While lithography has advanced considerably, the limits of the materials are not changing. For example, the current-carrying capability of aluminum becomes marginal as dimensional scaling continues downward. Many parameters either do not scale in a linear fashion or acquire nonscalable "behaviorisms" that preclude shrinking beyond a certain point. New semiconductor materials, such as metal silicides, will be needed to carry the flag of smaller dimensions down into the submicron region.

PATTERN LAYOUT

Once a design concept has been formed and the application for which the chip is intended has been properly identified, the pattern-layout phase is tackled. Pattern layout is a costly step since computers can still be used only for parts of the layout process. A large amount of technical engineering time must be spent in conjunction with the computer aids. As VLSI chips become more complex in structure, layout processes must turn more directly to computerized techniques and rely less on hand-drafting.

The number of methods used for mask-pattern layout increases constantly. We will discuss the primary methods and compare them with one another. The trend seems to be one of using a pattern layout that closely matches the type of IC to be fabricated. Gate arrays, microprocessors, and memory chips all have distinct differences, each calling for a different design, layout, and data-production approach.

Hand-Drafting

VLSI chip patterns are often hand-drafted at the layout stage. In hand-drafting, the oldest and most commonly used technique, the circuit patterns are hand-drawn as a composite of the mask set. VLSI complexity has made hand-drafting difficult since the size of the original artwork tends to keep increasing in order to maintain the accuracies of the circuit at final size.

New graphics equipment has been developed to improve the resolution of filmwork used in hand-drafted layouts. Superficially, the persistence of hand or manual techniques in such a sophisticated application seems contradictory. However, computer programs are still unable to "pack" the circuitry as tightly within the silicon real estate as hand-directed methods can. Computers use basic blocks of silicon area for various parts of the chip. Inevitably, pockets of space are left where the blocks do not quite fit together. In hand-drafting, every available "spot" of silicon on the chip is used as long as it conforms to the design rules.

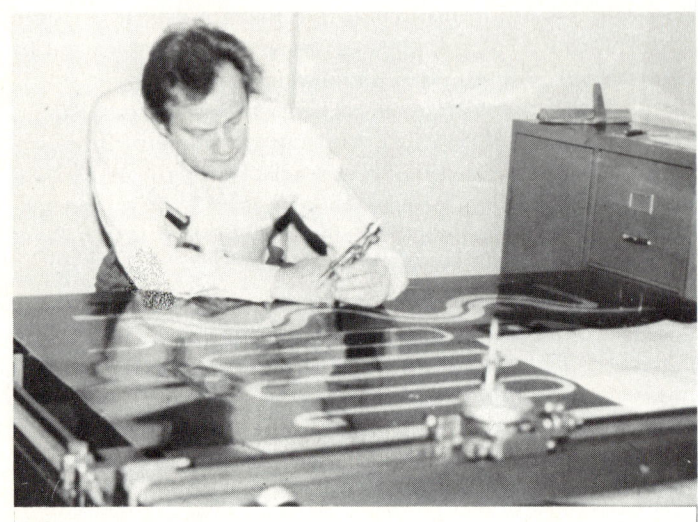

FIG. 1-8 **Rubylith preparation on a coordinatograph.** *(Photronics Labs, Brookfield, Conn.)*

The scale of the drawings for VLSI chips is typically 1000 to 2000 times the final chip size. Simpler IC devices are drafted at 200–600× final size. The lower-density chips, which often represent large production runs, are physically inscribed onto a lithographic film that has two layers: a base of polyester or similar plastic, and a covering colored plastic film layer that is lifted away after the pattern has been inscribed. Figure 1-8 shows this operation in progress. Rubylith is a material commonly used for the process. The operation takes place on a coordinatograph or other precision device for mechanical drawing. This technique involves physically cutting the red or orange top film layer and then physically peeling it away from the clear base layer.

The red color that remains to form the pattern is a mask for the wavelengths of light used to subsequently expose the silver halide emulsions on high-resolution glass plates that become the 10× reticles. An improved alternative to manual Rubylith cutting and peeling is automatic inscription or cutting that is driven by a digital code of the mask pattern. The use of a digitizer simply permits the hand-drawing of the design to be digitally coded and then inscribing by the automatic Rubylith cutting machines. The final step is still one of physically and manually removing the red upper layer of film. Wherever manual operations are used in such a complex mechanical task, error incidence is high. Part of the reason for this is the redundancy and tedium of such a task. Figure 1-9 shows an operator checking artwork on the copy board.

Higher-density designs must be drafted onto more stable plastic films at still larger magnifications. The drawings are placed manually onto Mylar at $1000-2000\times$ magnification. This task requires a solid grounding in design rules and overall IC fabrication processes by the designer, who must then digitize or code them onto a large sheet (2–3 ft on a side). This is performed with accuracies of 0.1 mm for a 1.0-m drawing. The digital pattern is then fed into a computer, where the designer can make some changes or corrections. Overall, the preparation of such a complex drawing at $2000\times$ is very labor-intensive and can also result in errors.

The cost of the production of a complex drawing or layout for IC artwork has opened up the way for hardware in the form of interactive graphic terminals. Such equipment allows a designer to take a simple sketch, sit down at a computer terminal and screen, and achieve the same result as the hand-cut layout at $2000\times$. The difference is in the time saved by the interactive system where designer and machine can communicate and build the layout on the screen. The computer in an

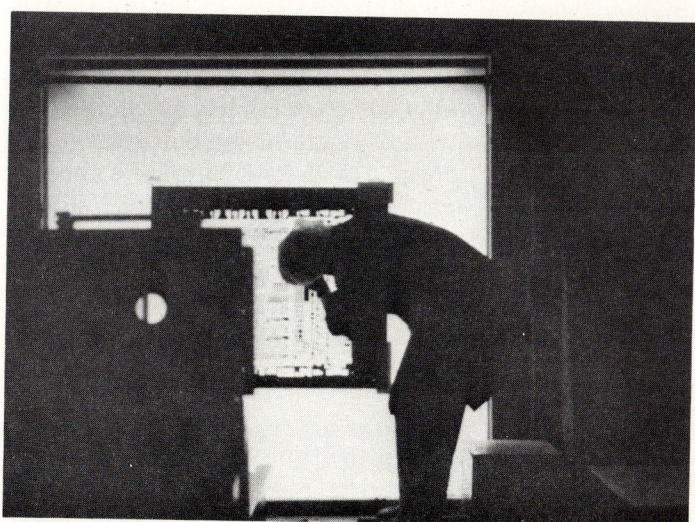

FIG. 1-9 Operator checking artwork on a copyboard. *(Photronics Labs, Brookfield, Conn.)*

interactive graphic system will be fed design rules and electrical-parameter information, and will check the designer's work against these values as the procedure continues. Figure 1-10 illustrates an interactive design system.

FIG. 1-10 Operator working on a CAD system. *(Photronics Labs, Brookfield, Conn.)*

Software has even infiltrated the area of hand sketches in the form of description language to create IC patterns. This is essentially a procedural programming language that defines many basic IC structures or elements. It is a powerful tool, but it is limited by being a batch or "block" technique. This immediately puts it into the same category as other computer-aided design methodologies in that the packing density frequently suffers from block-style layout. This is perhaps analogous to packing ice cream. More product is hand-squeezed into an equivalent area (quart) because nobody has yet devised a machine that will place the same amount of ice cream in the same volume. And yes, you do pay more for hand-packed ice cream, just as hand-drafted IC layouts are quite expensive.

In all cases, hand-drafted layouts are digitized for VLSI devices. The digital information can then be placed, at $100\times$, onto an emulsion plate via a variable-aperture photoplotter. The $100\times$ master is then photo-reduced to a $10\times$ reticle, using a lens that is corrected for several aberrations. Hand-drafting continues to be a primary method for IC pattern layout.

The hand-drafted and the semiautomated design approaches both use a photoplot of the digitized artwork. This graphic aid is useful for recordkeeping and for double-checking the pattern data. Figure 1-11 shows a photoplotter with a printout emerging.

FIG. 1-11 Photoplotter printing out a design. *(Photronics Labs, Brookfield, Conn.)*

The balance of design styles to be discussed in this chapter are those using a fair degree of computer assistance. These methods are used for different types of VLSI designs, and the method is often selected to match the particular needs of the chip architecture. Most of these design techniques use some degee of human interaction, as completely automatic computer design is still in the future.

Array Technique

The need for very rapid turn-around time on custom and semicustom ICs generated the idea for gate and transistor arrays. Gate arrays and transistor arrays are characterized by having wafers processed completely through all the mask levels and stopping at the interconnection metal levels. Transistor arrays are basic gates formed by interconnecting transistors. The final interconnection of the gates completes the circuit. In the gate array, the building blocks (gates) are already formed, and the task is simply to wire together the gates.

There are two basic steps for chip layout using the array technique. The first is the simulation of the design logic needed to produce the circuit layout. The second step is to work with either an interactive display or an automatic system that does the job of routing, placement, and partitioning.

18 INTEGRATED CIRCUIT MASK TECHNOLOGY

In the past, gate and transistor arrays were noted for their loss of silicon real estate. New software tools containing "stronger" or more sophisticated algorithms have been developed to reduce the space. Current CAD systems contain the tools to generate high-density arrays. The array approach does provide rapid turn-around time but still sacrifices some circuit area by virtue of the fundamental arrangements needed to form an array. The amount of human intervention required for this approach is held to a minimum, mainly for correcting a small segment of the circuit that has not properly been wired.

Silicon Compilers

The Bristle Blocks program developed at California Institute of Technology was an early example of a silicon compiler system. The concept is one of automating the definition of the macrofunctions and microfunctions of an integrated circuit from inception to final layout. If this can be done, the time required for design will be shortened considerably, and the circuit layout that comes out of a compiler should be of very high quality.

A silicon compiler is analogous to a high-level, abstract computer language as compared to, say, a lower-level language that spells out all the details. The description of the circuit given to the compiler is more abstract than that used for manually designed circuits. In manual design, for example, the designer would need to specify the gates, a function performed automatically by the compiler. In the compiler, various elements of the program are processed in an attempt to fit the description given by the person inputing the data. The silicon compiler takes the functional circuit description and essentially synthesizes the pattern, including descriptions of the major blocks provided by automatic definition.

The input for a silicon compiler can be in the form of a flow diagram (see Fig. 1-12). In this case, we use the example of a programmable logic array (PLA) and move from the functional level to the layout level, using a silicon compiler. The flowchart has been converted into a circuit

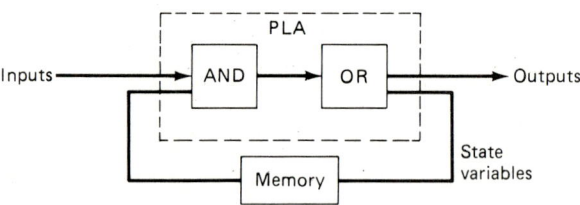

FIG. 1-12 Flowchart for a PLA.

diagram in Fig. 1-13, and then into the actual pattern in Fig. 1-14. The placement and routing of the circuit is all performed automatically with a chip assembler. The chip assembler also draws the final layout shown in Fig. 1-14.

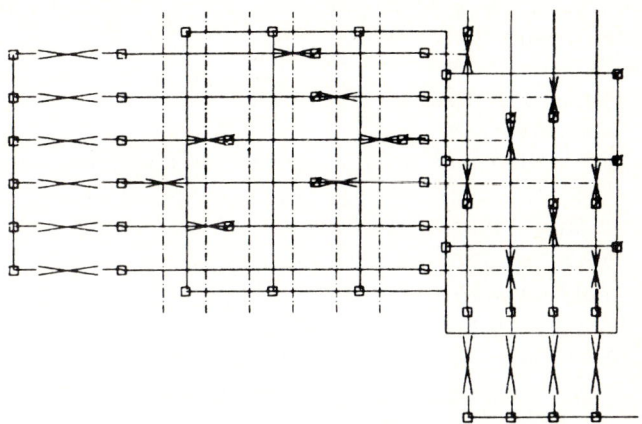

FIG. 1-13 Circuit diagram of silicon compiler. *[Ref. 5.]*

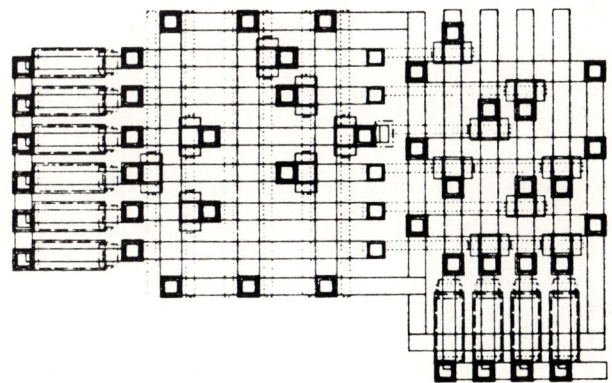

FIG. 1-14 Pattern data for silicon compiler. (Drawn from diagram in Fig. 1-13.) *[Ref. 5.]*

The primary advantage of silicon compilers is their ability to automate the process of implementing a given design that is specified in relatively abstract terms. Their primary disadvantage is the inability of the compiler to use all the available silicon real estate. An example of a very successful application of a silicon compiler would be turning a high-level system specification for a signal processor into a finished mask-set definition in

2 worker-days. Minimizing human intervention is another advantage of the silicon compiler.

Automatic Placement and Routing

In this design approach, the gates, transistors, and other circuit functions are first placed and then interconnected automatically. The guidelines for this level of automation are the design rules, and the objective is, of course, minimal use of silicon real estate.

Circuit placement is difficult to fully automate because it is difficult to define with standard computer algorithms. There are many different approaches used to place circuit elements; the most popular are the constructive and heuristic techniques. Heuristic (or trial-and-error) approaches begin with one or more modules or blocks placed, and others are added and optimized in building-block fashion. As the placement of elements continues automatically, the designer intervenes periodically to make adjustments and modifications. In some cases, the designer may place certain elements ahead of time and then let the placement program continue.

The Routing Step

The routing of the circuit is performed in two general steps. The first step is global routing, where electrical connections to the separate or distinct areas of the chip are assigned. Global routing must take into account the silicon space that exists between the various chip-element blocks. These channels need to be wired in a certain order for an optimal pattern, and associations between all of the different chip sections must be considered.

Local routing is the second step. This is often performed on an interactive graphics system so that the designer can intervene to make certain decisions regarding allocation of input/output (I/O) pads, modification of overloaded channel connections, or addition of an element to a mask level—such as a new interconnection. Automatic placement and routing is still in a semiautomatic stage for many chip designs, but other designs, depending upon the simplicity of their structures, can be fully placed and routed without any designer intervention.

Hierarchical Design

This method of design is structured in the sense that basic and sizable blocks of the chip, which represent functional subsystems, are first laid out. Once their boundaries are established, the next step is to define the subsections within each major block or subsystem. Finally, the smallest sections of the chip, the actual gates and transistors, are designed. Figure 1-15 shows the result of the first step, a global "floor plan" of the chip. Note that there are also global connections, or buses, drawn at this stage. The blocks at this level are the various memory sections—read-only memory (ROM), random access memory (RAM)—and other standard units such as the arithmetic and logic unit (ALU) and the programmable logic array (PLA). There is generally an upper-limit figure indicating how many elements may be manipulated at this stage. This number may vary between 20 and 50 as a general rule.

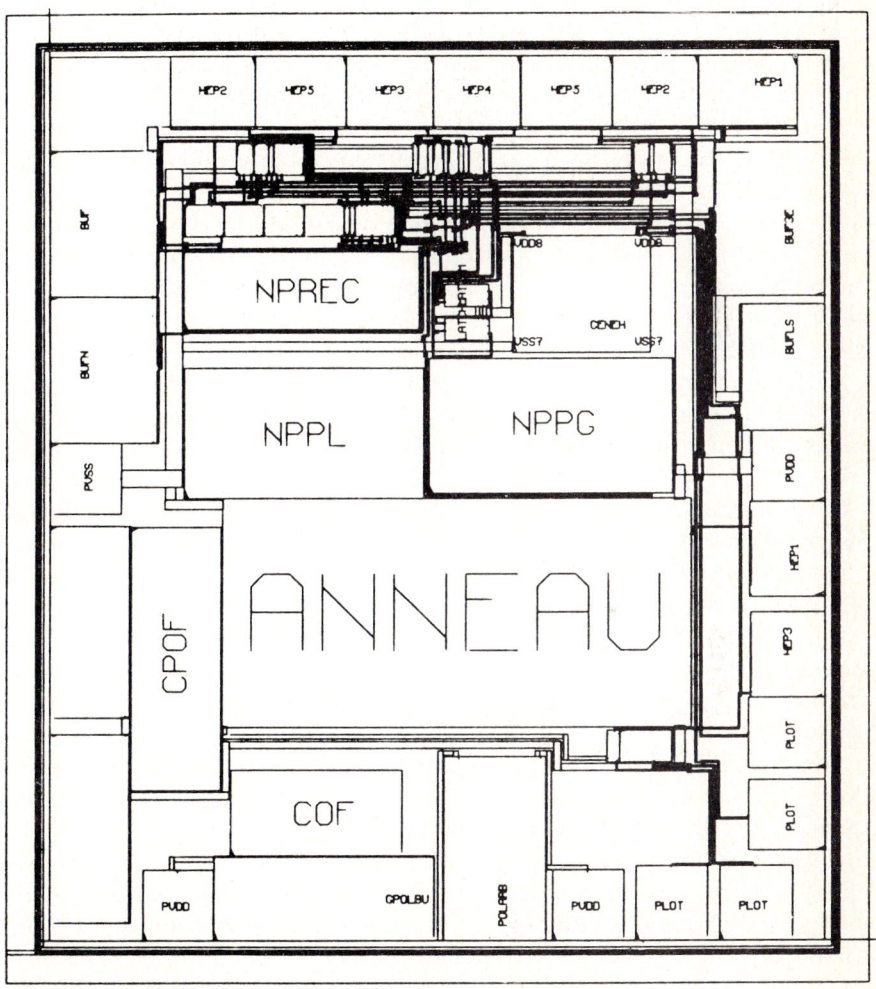

FIG. 1-15 Hierarchical design "floor plan." *[Ref. 5.]*

The term "hierarchical" is used since the chip is designed from the top down, down to the lowest or smallest fundamental unit. At the global level or block level where hierarchical design begins, the experienced designer will know not only about how much of the wafer area to allow for various major circuit elements but also how to predict the communication of data between the major block elements. The floor plan should be relatively efficient if the designer understands the relationships between circuit elements.

The functional circuit elements within the larger blocks are then designed. These are generally tailored to the end use or application for which the chip is intended. In some cases, the initial functional circuit elements are manually designed, and once a pattern is established for a given redundant structure, the computer will automatically complete the job. The automatic interconnection of functional elements is a standard CAD function, especially when the initial optimization is performed manually on a small scale. One of the advantages of this hierarchical-design style is the orderliness of the chip pattern that results. Compared to conventional, manually designed circuits that contain random and tangled interconnections, chip designs using hierarchical techniques are quite orderly. Very complex chips can be designed easily by several people with this style, as major blocks within the chip are given to different parts of the design team.

A fundamental benefit of hierarchical design is the freeing of the creative designer from the monotonous tasks of checking distances between elements and rearranging elements to see if they fit properly. The designer should be left to the more creative job of conceptual IC pattern design or adaptation of concepts to new applications. Mechanical tasks associated with the design of a complex IC are many and should be left to the computer. Perhaps the most significant benefit of computer technology in general will be the taking over of noncreative and essentially mechanical jobs by computers, leaving people time to solve the more complex problems of our society that require intuition, creativity, and other uniquely human qualities that cannot yet be relegated to computers.

The data base for hierarchical design contains all the instructions for the entire circuit. This permits checking and cross-checking (for consistency) the work being performed between major chip sections. Once the data base has laid out the circuit blocks, the designer needs to get an idea as to the size and shape of the major circuit sections, a job performed by the evaluators. This approach also uses other chip software, including the chip assembler and the chip planner. The chip assembler defines the position of the blocks within the chip, and the chip planner lays out the floor plan of the chip as the design moves from the top down. The chip-planning program is generally an interactive job, sometimes with the aid of a program for placement of the blocks. Placement is critical, since the arrangement of the blocks will have a large impact on the connection patterns. The connection patterns typically consume 50 percent of the total chip area and are obviously a key consideration. The chip assembler, working from the bottom up, puts the functional elements into each block as it is completed by the placement program. The assembler places the connections that are consistent with the design rules and other chip specifications. Also aiding in the process are automatic routers that can run buses and other elements.

Hierarchical design is useful for the design of very complex chips, since by its very nature it breaks down the task into simpler units and handles each unit separately. Even with the advent of silicon compilers, hierarchical design concepts will be selected for many VLSI chip designs owing to the orderliness this approach provides.

Symbolic Logic

Symbolic-logic methodologies for circuit design and layout have been in use for some time. Symbolic methods rely upon the abstraction of many design and layout functions into symbols or characters that represent various functions. Symbolism acts to simplify the long and arduous task of mask design and layout. Engineers with little design experience can relate to the use of symbols and successfully complete a chip, a task not possible if done with strictly manual operations.

Symbolic IC design and layout techniques use several approaches to actually define the mask patterns. One approach is the "sticks" method, where designers are free to use topological descriptions that do not fall into restrictive grid patterns or other confining shapes. This sort of free-form design uses graphical symbols that are placed in relation to each other and do not fall into a larger block as in hierarchical design. One example of the sticks method, developed by Thompson-EFCIS in Grenoble, France, is shown in Fig. 1-16.

This example is from the Sticks package provided by Calma, and the three sections show how a circuit diagram can be automatically compacted. Compaction is done in accordance with design rules and adds a powerful aspect of the final chip. The figures in Table 1-1 indicate the

TABLE 1-1 *Design-rules geometry versus chip performance factors*

Design rules, μm	6	5	4
Maximum/typical density, gates/mm^2	310/220	450/320	700/500
Speed, ns	5	3.5	2
Speed-power product, pJ	1.3	1.0	0.6

24 INTEGRATED CIRCUIT MASK TECHNOLOGY

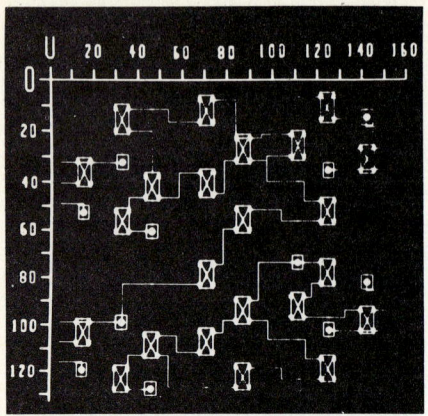
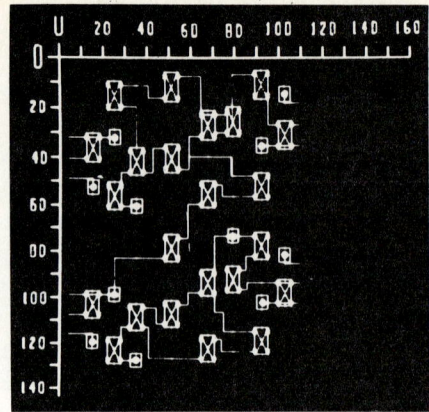
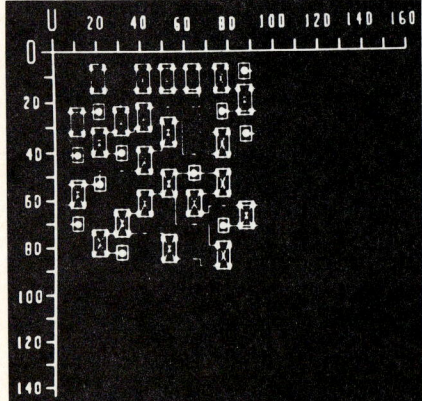

FIG. 1-16 "Sticks" program used for circuit compaction. *(Calma)*

changes in device performance that take place when geometries are shrunk. A change in the design rules from 6 to 5 to 4 μm makes a significant change in the number of possible gates, the speed of the device, and the speed-power product.

Symbolic design and layout cuts out all the time required to specify the dimensions and other geometrical parameters. Figure 1-17 shows the symbolic representation of a portion of a device and the translation of the symbols into mask-pattern data. Note the relative simplicity of the symbols compared to the detail in the pattern data generated from the symbols.

Fixed-Grid Layout

The other main type of symbolic design and layout is the fixed-grid method. The fixed grid takes the circuit area and divides it into a

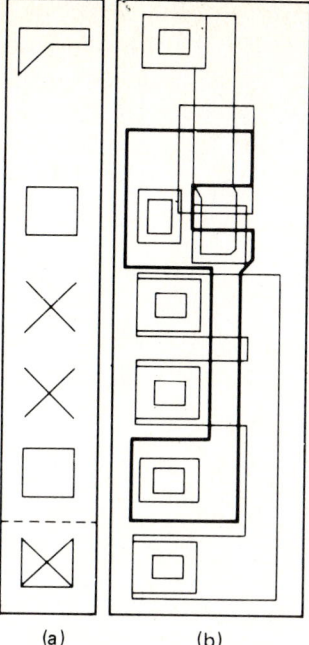

FIG. 1-17 Comparison of circuit symbology (a) and pattern data (b).

uniformly spaced matrix. The size of the grid is determined by the design rules and generally represents a minimum geometry or feature size to be used with the process. A symbol is used to define the series of mask patterns that occur at a fixed grid location throughout the mask set. The symbols are then placed on the grid, and each section is laid out until the entire chip is designed. The use of an interactive graphics system allows the designer to get good feedback, and the chip is laid out. There are commercially available systems that take a character-based design and will place it on the grid. Hewlett-Packard has developed an interactive graphics system (IGS) that performs in this way. Some programs will take the symbolic layout and check it for design-rule violations. One such system, called SIDS (symbolic interactive design system), gives the operation an on-line design-rule check and a trace option that checks for electrical conductivity.

Symbolic layout makes the design of complex circuits easier by simplifying the design-rule parameters. This in turn saves time, but at some cost in device density. One approximation of the tradeoff that occurs with this design methodology indicated a 15 percent loss in circuit density and a 63 percent reduction in layout time. This is probably a good economic tradeoff. Part of the silicon loss can be compensated through compaction, available in both the fixed-grid and the sticks methods. An example of the fixed-grid input and output program is shown in Fig. 1-18. Note the relatively equal spacing in x and y planes in the logic plan and the compaction in the final pattern data.

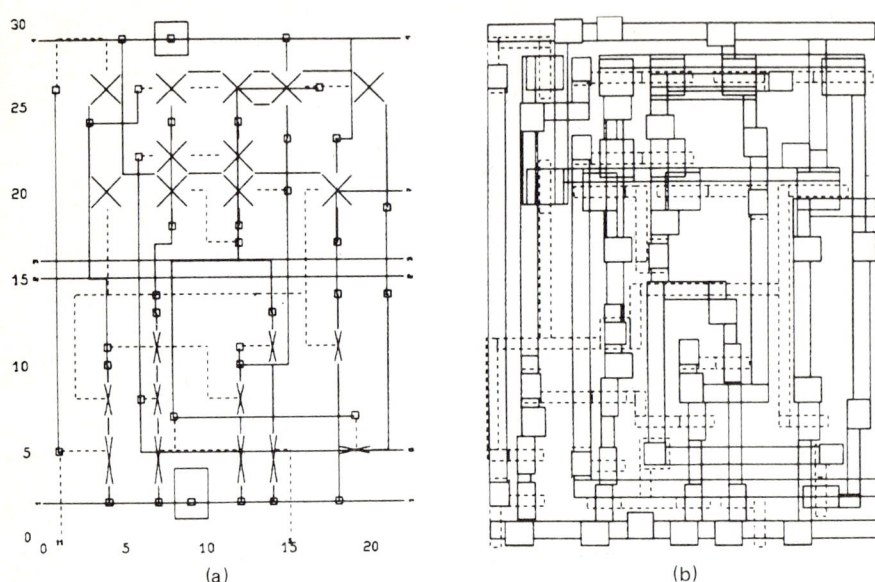

FIG. 1-18 Input (*a*) and output (*b*) of the symbolic program using TRICKY. *(Thompson-EFCIS.)*

Building-Block Design and Layout

Building-block methods rely on the use of standard libraries of stored cells. These libraries are stored according to a whole spectrum of applications. A graphic illustration of the approach is shown in Fig. 1-19. The building-block method is fast and is suited for logic circuits. As shown in the figure, the layout starts with a series of blocks surrounded by channels that are used for the interconnections. Automatic placement and routing routines are then run, providing an efficient method for tasks that typically take much longer with interactive or semiautomatic techniques. Of course, there are also manual checks and interactive aspects with this approach, but they are minimized by using more standardized circuit types, such as medium-sized logic chips.

The basic steps begin with the definition of the cell library that can

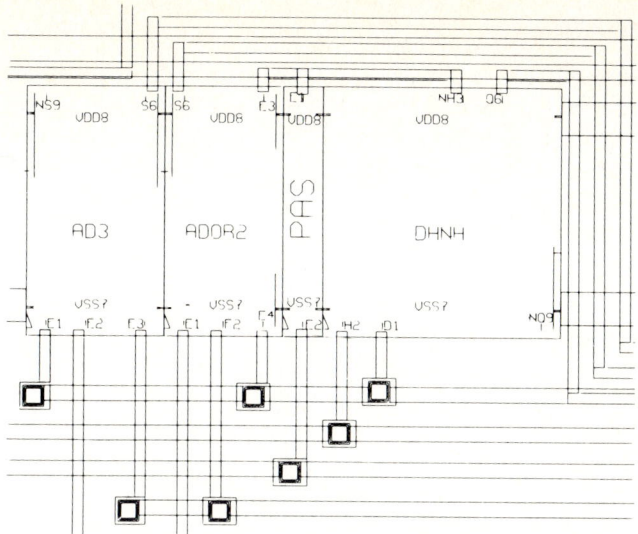

FIG. 1-19 Building-block design-style layout. *[Ref. 5.]*

be run parallel to the steps outlined above where the blocks are defined. The cell library contains the definition of the size, shape, and topology of standard cells. The other parameters defined and placed in the library include the electrical features, graphic features, and mask-geometry features. Once the library is complete, the layout step begins. Cells are taken from the library and placed in the desired format. At this stage, a CAD program is used that will help determine the optimal placement and the position of the interconnection wires. There are a variety of programs available that range from completely automatic to interactive ones that permit the designer to make modifications and finish off with manual corrections of unsuccessful routings.

Building-block design and layout is fast because it uses the same circuit description at the logic level and at the layout and test-pattern-generation level. When nonstandard cells or functional units designed elsewhere are added to the building-block design, time is lost, but flexibility is gained. The challenge of software designers is to provide algorithms that accommodate this need, allowing the designer to take the best of one design approach and combine it with inherent advantages of others. Higher-level software and more advanced and more automated CAD systems are moving in this direction, taking the job of chip design and layout and assigning most of the work to the computer. The designer is left to do the more interesting job of matching various cell or chip elements to very specific applications.

DEVICE MODELING

Device modeling is a relatively new field that helps circuit designers to better predict the behavior of their designs. The use of device modeling also serves to show how a given IC will operate *before* the cost of producing a mask set is assumed. Semiconductor device modeling is essentially a numerical simulation of a given IC topology, an example of which is shown in Fig. 1-20.

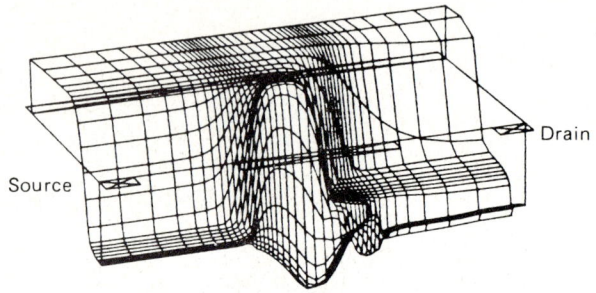

FIG. 1-20 Three-dimensional diagram from device-modeling study. *[Ref. 7.]*

Several mathematical equations are used to model IC device behavior. These formulas (electromagnetic field equations) match the behavior of electrons in the working device and hence are considered valid in modeling. In fact, almost all semiconductor devices operate under laws of electronic behavior that are quite predictable. Since some of the equations are nonlinear and some of the behavior in the IC *is* linear, additional models that incorporate approximations of device behavior are used. The resulting three-dimensional model shown in the figure will allow designers to study the internal workings of the device they have tentatively structured. The example given in Fig. 1-20 is log-scaled hole density, resulting from a simulation including avalanche generation.

Designers will be able to better design circuits with the understanding of device operation given through modeling. The substitution of process parameters for fabrication, using simulator software, is becoming a relatively inexpensive task. The problem still facing device modelers is the large amount of computer time or resource needed in modeling. This often forces the designer and modeler to use a more simplified program that tells less about the device than should be known. In the future, it is expected that with additional computational power and more sophisticated programs that include circuit, process, and device parameters in a single program, modeling will be a powerful tool in the hands of VLSI design engineers.

PATTERN DESIGN AND DATA PRODUCTION   **29**

The major trends affecting the mask-design disciplines are shown in Fig. 1-21. The continued increase in device density is projected through

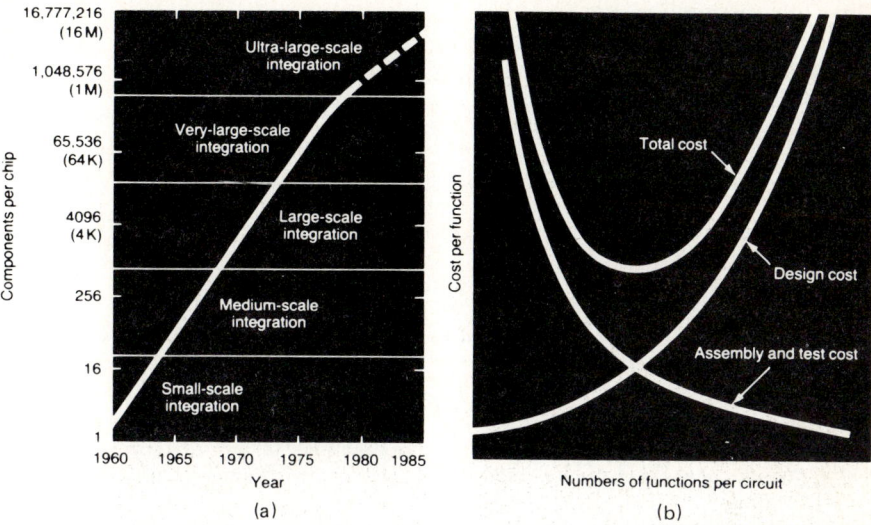

FIG. 1-21 Major trends affecting mask fabrication: (*a*) components per chip versus year, and (*b*) cost per function versus density. *[Ref. 8.]*

1985. The evolution of chips with up to at least 4 million components is expected. The design for such a chip will require a large number of well-developed CAD programs, most of them totally automatic. The chart showing cost of chip design indicates the rising expense of design, another reason why totally automated VLSI design systems must be used in the future.

The range of integrated-circuit design tools is broad, including everything from totally manual design methods to fully automated techniques. Figure 1-22*a*, *b*, and *c* outlines the variety of methods that include both ends of the design spectrum. The primary thrust has been to provide the chip designer with design tools that are an *aid* in laying out complex chips. Thus, computer technology has been called upon to do just that: aid the designer. The tasks performed by the computer are the more routine and redundant ones that are easiest to program. In the future, the thrust will be to let the computer take over the more imaginative jobs in chip design. This area is already getting considerable attention and is referred to as design automation (DA).

One example of an advanced design system is the Zyp program, which is a combination of original software, current CAD tools, and cell

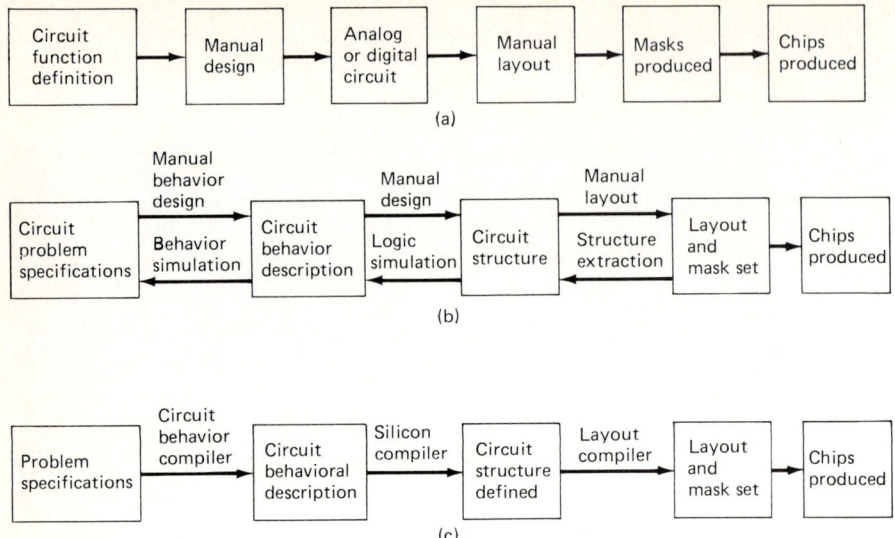

FIG. 1-22 Evolution of integrated circuit design functions: (*a*) traditional design (1960–1975), (*b*) computer-aided design (1975–1990), and (*c*) design automation (1990–   ).

libraries connected to form a complete and "friendly" design system. The cell libraries already contain the buffers, gates, flip-flops, inverters, ROMs, RAMs, and binary comparators. In addition, analog building blocks such as operational amplifiers, voltage references, and comparators are in the cell library sections. When the designers sit down with this type of system, they simply draw the logic diagram or other form of specification and then begin composing by referring to standard sections or libraries in the Zyp system (Fig. 1-23).

Following cell selection, the designer feeds the information into a computer, along with a network of the desired interconnections. The remaining steps are verification, artwork-generation software, placement and routing diagrams, and data-base tapes on which the masks are based. The use of any of these design systems depends on the application, and semicustom circuits will have different payback schemes than full-custom chips. Factors to measure are turn-around time, design iteration risk, cost of software and design tools, and silicon area usage. The overriding concerns that will determine the most cost-effective approach are circuit complexity and production volume. The standard-cell approach, as used in the Zyp system, is quite cost-effective over a wide range of chip complexities and production volumes. Advancements in design software will continue to make the overall process less expensive from the standpoint of value received versus cost applied. The trend to

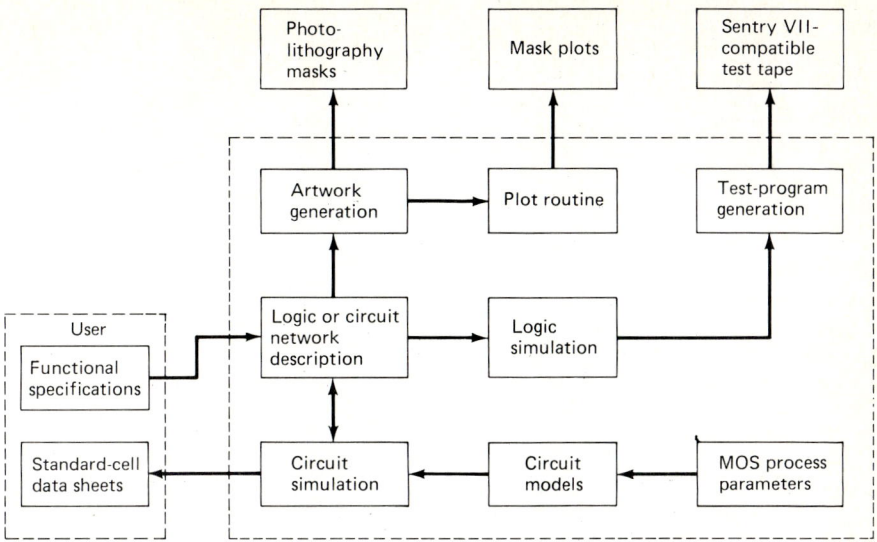

FIG. 1-23 Outline of Zyp system for advanced IC design. *[Ref. 10.]*

use design automation will certainly accelerate costs initially, but eventually it will reduce the cost component in total VLSI chip economics.

REFERENCES

1. Barbe, D. F. (Ed.): *Very Large Scale Integration*, Springer-Verlag, New York, 1982, chap. 4.
2. Colclaser, Roy A.: *Microelectronics Processing and Device Design*, Wiley, New York, 1980.
3. Mead, Carver, and Lynn Conway: *Introduction to VLSI Systems*, Addison-Wesley, Reading, Mass., 1980.
4. Horne, D. F.: *Dividing, Ruling, and Mask Making*, Crane, Russak, New York, 1974.
5. Avenier, J. P.: "Digitizing, Layout, Rule Checking—The Everyday Tasks of Chip Designers," *IEEE Proceedings* **71**(1), January 1983.
6. Feuer, M.: "VLSI Design Automation: An Introduction," *IEEE Proceedings* **71**(1), January 1983.
7. Engl, W., H. Dirks, and B. Meinerzhagen: "Device Modeling," *IEEE Proceedings* **71**(1), January 1983.
8. Posa, John G.: "Superchips Face Design Challenge," *High Technology*, January 1983, p. 34.
9. Groves, Bill: "Do It Yourself VLSI," *Digital Design*, September 1982, p. 60.
10. Lee, B., and Casey Jones: "CAD Tools Must Change to Meet the Needs of VLSI," *Electronics*, Nov. 17, 1981.
11. Miller, Dean, and Jeff Rubin: "Structured Logic-Design is Fast and Affordable," *Electronics*, Nov. 17, 1981.

2
Mask-Quality Glass

INTRODUCTION

The semiconductor industry continues to place increasing demands on the manufacturers of mask-quality glass. Smaller IC geometries mean greater sensitivity to any irregularities in the glass used to make masks. Wafer lithographers have shifted from contact to off-contact and soft-contact and then projection as a means to pattern wafers. New lithography techniques are headed in the direction of beam writing, including electron-beam, focused ion beam, laser beam, and other approaches. Masks and the requirements for making them, however, have not changed radically. All the current wafer-patterning strategies call for glass or quartz-based mask blanks. Only a small percentage of wafer-patterning applications are now run *without* using masks. These are occasional critical mask levels that are electron-beam (e-beam) written.

Masks are here to stay, and the major challenge is keeping the quality of the glass blank (and the imaged chrome) parallel with the lithography advancements made in all other areas. Mask-quality glass must be continually upgraded according to the technology shifts taking place in the wafer process areas. These break down as shown in Table 2-1.

TABLE 2-1 *Effect of technology changes on glass quality*

Wafer technology changes	Demands created for mask-quality glass
Wafer diameter increasing.	Better flatness needed to make the same geometries.
Shorter wavelengths now used to image resists (mid to deep uv, 365–250 nm).	Mask materials must not absorb the energy (wavelengths) needed for resist exposure.
Smaller pattern sizes.	Lower glass expansion values needed.
Increased dimensional control required for a given pattern element size.	Increased control over glass defects or irregularities.

In this chapter we will deal with the mask blank. This is the glass substrate before coating or metallization; all the steps that lead up to the point where the blank will be coated with iron oxide, chromium, silicon, or other maskable material will be discussed. The primary objective of this discussion will be the identification of the major parameters that produce a high-quality mask blank. High-quality masks simply cannot be produced without high-quality blanks.

Defects in mask-blank manufacturing are discussed along with glass properties, blank-manufacturing process control, and trends in technology that affect mask makers and users. Overall, the primary trend influencing all these subjects is smaller IC dimensions. Smallness requires control, and as pattern elements approach macromolecular dimensions, control with the aid of specialized software is needed.

There are limits to the amount of control that can be exercised over a given process or material. At some point, the process must be changed completely, and this usually takes place when a basic process material is changed. For example, patterning wafers at shorter wavelengths than 436 or 365 nm called for optics and mask materials that transmit a high percentage of the available energy at shorter (approximately 300 nm) wavelengths. New mask materials (quartz) had to be brought into the process, and new processes developed to advance mid- and deep-uv (ultraviolet) technology. Further, resists originally were not available that responded well to these shorter energy bands. New resists were then developed and, along with them, shorter light sources.

Mask-blank technology has had a similar evolutionary pattern. Original early processes were tuned finer and controlled more tightly to meet the needs of the IC design rules. Finally, lithographers turned to glass with better stability, increased chemical resistance, and higher overall purity and began again to process-refine.

The steps we will discuss find their beginning in a very natural setting: beach sands and geologic structures within the earth's crust. The raw materials for glass-blank manufacturing are dug from the earth, as is raw material for nearly every other industrial process. Critical to the future of highly uniform mask-blank manufacturing is a guaranteed supply of fairly uniform and consistent silicon dioxide. Purity levels of raw materials needed to be carefully screened, and several sources had to be made available.

GLASS MELTING AND FORMING

Sand and silica are reduced to a molten mass and refined, and impurities are removed until an acceptable level of quality is reached. Frequently, raw glass sheet is made at this point. Borosilicate glasses are, for example, produced in quantity and then melted. The processes that lead up to the production of a raw glass plate are shown in Fig. 2-1. The melting of different types of glasses is a complex and highly specialized operation. Borosilicates are melted at Corning Glass, for example, in special platinum-lined furnaces that were originally used to produce high-purity optical glass. Additional modifications leading to improved capabilities have kept Corning both a pioneer and world leader in mask-blank manufacturing.

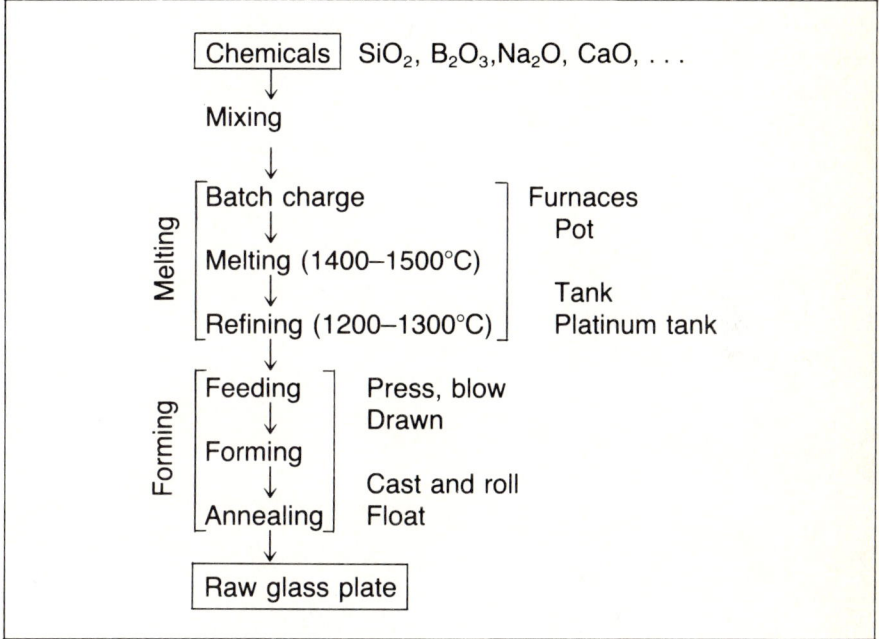

FIG. 2-1 Glass melting and forming.

By means of computers, melting furnaces are able to maintain close control over the physical and chemical properties of the glass. One example of composition control is the reduction or even elimination of alkali in mask-quality glass. Alkali present in a glass increases its dimensional instability. Reduced alkali reduces the blank thermal-expansion coefficient. The chemical and physical resistance of the glass is also increased as alkali content is decreased. Ion migration is also reduced with lower alkali content.

An advantage of lower alkali is better wear resistance or better weathering. Weathering causes alkali to emerge or leach from the blank and deposit on the blank, causing a visible film or stain. Another problem with alkali in the glass is a reaction that occurs at the interface of the glass and the chromium layer. Alkali ions are moved toward this interface when the blank is subjected to elevated temperatures and high-energy electric fields (electron-beams, plasma process chambers for blank pretreatment, etc.). The alkali ions react readily to weaken the chrome, and pinholes form in these areas after etching.

The melting process and its various control mechanisms result in the raw glass sheet shown in Fig. 2-2. The material shown in this photograph is LE-30, a low-expansion borosilicate glass from Hoya. The contents of this chapter will follow an outline parallel to the actual process for blank production. This process can vary with manufacturer, with inspection and cleaning operations being inserted at different points according to the maker's choice. A typical outline is

1. Melting
2. Raw glass sheet
3. Cutting
4. Smoothing
5. Polishing
6. Cleaning
7. Surface inspection
8. Flatness check
9. Final glass substrate

Each step is characterized by special equipment and each manufacturer develops its own techniques to optimize the process. Magic is

FIG. 2-2 Raw glass sheet.

usually said to be a fundamental part of resist lithography, but occasionally it spills over into other microelectronic operations. As long as creative humans are involved in manufacturing operations, we can expect a certain amount of occult art to exist in the process. No two people do the same job in exactly the same manner. We should not expect them to, since not even our machines can give us high levels of reliability. The industry continues to change, and glass needs change at the same time. The glass used for VLSI processes must stand up to several functional criteria. This is essential in light of the near-zero defect levels that are needed to maintain high chip yields in production. The main criteria for mask-quality glass are discussed in the following sections.

Suitable Optical Transmission

Masks are used in a variety of wafer-exposure systems, operating at several different wavelengths. Masks must transmit strongly in the wavelength region where the resists are sensitive. Contact printers and proximity aligners generally use a broad band of wavelengths, incorporating most of the mercury spectrum. Scanning projection printers operate at a minimum of three distinct bandwidths. For example, Perkin-Elmer Micralign projection printers can be used in the following areas: UV-4: 340 to 400 nm; UV-3: 280 to 340 nm; UV-2: 240 to 280 nm.

Optical step-and-repeat exposure systems typically expose resists at the 436-nm wavelength or at a combination of 436- and 365-nm wavelengths. These systems are widely used since they can optically accommodate each individual die. Die-by-die alignment and focus override, to a large extent, the problems of wafer taper and nonflatness as well as variations in the exposure system itself. Step-and-repeat optical projection systems are now being outfitted with shorter-wavelength optics to further enhance resolution.

The ability of optical-exposure systems to resolve the highest resolution and provide line-geometry control needed for IC fabrication helps preserve the viability of glass-mask technology. Overall, mask-quality glass must deliver the necessary transmission needed to be compatible with both the output wavelengths of the exposure source and the absorption of the resist.

Figure 2-3 shows the relationship between percent transmission and wavelength for several types of mask glass. Borosilicate, white crown, and green soda-lime glass all transmit over 80 percent and 3500 Å (350 nm) and therefore are quite suitable for passing most of the principal exposure lines in the mercury spectrum. Quartz, desirable for thermal-stability reasons, has approximately 90 percent transmission down past the 200-nm region and is ideal for the deep-uv-imaging applications.

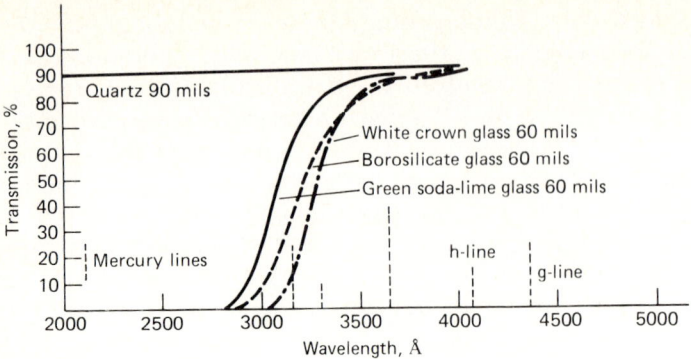

FIG. 2-3 Transmission versus wavelength for different glass types. *(Balzers)*

Low Thermal Expansion

Smaller IC geometries require increasingly stable mask materials. Thermal processing in the resist-imaging steps is still prevalent, requiring good glass stability. For example, resists exposed to electron-beam energy during exposure can heat the underlying glass to temperatures above 180°C. Glass plates, before being imaged, are often dehydration baked to promote good resist adhesion. After resist application, glass blanks are heated again for resist softbaking up to 110°C. Resist removal also requires, in some cases, immersion in heated resist strippers. Plasma etching before resist removal is yet another thermal process.

The main concern for in-process heat is in metal deposition *after* the imaged plates are ready for use in wafer-printing equipment. However, thermal shocks can deform plates prior to imaging, and some thermal effects are not easily relieved. The temperatures of these thermal processes, especially in phosphorus-doped glass or metallization, are not easily reduced, and therefore mask-quality glass for high-density IC chip designs must have good thermal stability.

The amount of thermal expansion and plate flatness that can be tolerated is a function of the IC geometry requirements. In lower-scale to medium-scale integrated circuits, dimensional specifications are looser than for large-scale and VLSI applications. The glass can then be selected on the basis of the application requirements. Generally, higher costs are associated with increased thermal stability in mask glass.

The relationship between runout in micrometers and temperature difference in degrees Celsius is shown in Fig. 2-4. Soda-lime glass shows the greatest amount of movement; it is also the lowest in cost. Plates ranging in size from 3 to 6 in undergo run-out above 1 μm for 1 to 3°C temperature differences. While much of this is relieved by allowing

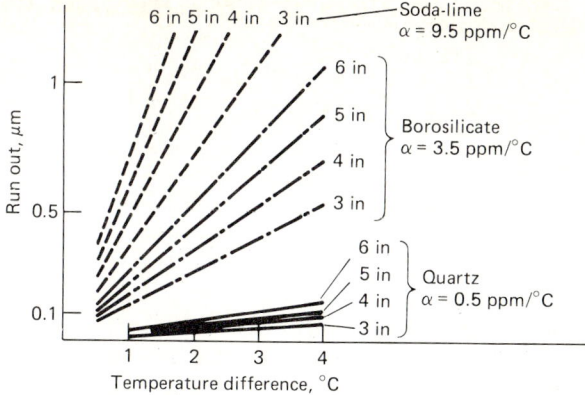

FIG. 2-4 Runout as a function of mask type, size, and temperature.

the glass to equilibrate, the time disruption for this to take place is often incompatible with production needs. Soda-lime and green glass are classified as high-thermal-expansion materials. Borosilicate glass keeps below 0.5-μm runout for temperature differences up to 2°C, in blank sizes up to 6 in. This level of thermal stability is much more compatible with the needs of production wafer processes containing 2-to 3-μm geometries. Borosilicate prices are considerably lower than quartz and not significantly greater than soda-lime. This makes borosilicate a good "workhorse" glass for mask fabrication. Borosilicate is classified as a low-thermal-expansion (LTE) material. Borosilicate is a good glass for masks to be used in projection aligners and e-beam exposure systems. In optical projection printing, ambient temperatures surrounding the mask change up to 5°C. This amount of temperature change in a process using a soda-lime glass would produce unacceptable dimensional changes on wafers.

Quartz is classified as an ultralow-thermal-expansion (ULTE) material. The runout is kept to less than 0.2 μm for up to 4°C temperature differences in plate sizes up to 6 in. The runout is less than 0.2 μm for temperature differences up to 2°C.

The thermal stability of quartz is tied closely to its low sodium content. Since quartz is called upon for deep-uv lithography, where its transmission properties are ideally suited, it satisfies the added need of improved dimensional stability to deliver finer resolution at deep-uv wavelengths.

Thermal stability is also a factor when one considers the variation in ambient temperatures in clean rooms. Figure 2-5 shows the relationship between the temperature change between exposures or clean-room

40 INTEGRATED CIRCUIT MASK TECHNOLOGY

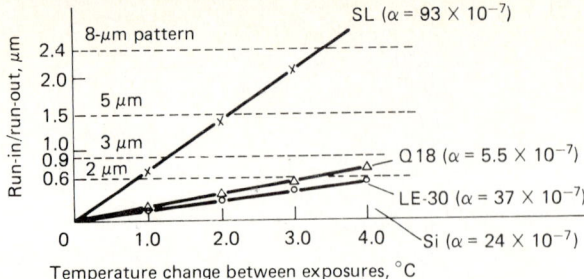

FIG. 2-5 Run-in/runout versus clean-room temperature for three glass types (pattern superimposed on a 100-mm wafer). Key: SL = soda-lime glass, Q = quartz, LE = low-expansion glass

temperature variation and the run-in or runout that takes place on a mask. Despite the use of various environmental-control equipment systems, clean-room temperature control can be difficult. The temperature can vary according to the number of people in the room, the heat generated by clean-room blowers that are not properly insulated from the rest of the room, rapid changes in temperature or humidity from the areas adjacent to the clean room, and numerous other factors. It should be apparent from the thermal data shown on glasses that extra capital invested in ensuring good temperature control will pay back rapidly in better chip yields. The heat generated by exposure systems and bake ovens also poses a problem of how to best arrange process equipment. Clean-room design should incorporate the thermal-control needs of the process and separate, where possible, thermal "generators" that can affect glass stability.

A summary of some major glass types that stand up to varying degrees of thermal processing is shown in Table 2-2.

Stabilization Time

Masks heated in the production line require various times to stabilize. The stabilization time versus run-in and runout is given in Fig. 2-6 for three types of glass blanks. The SL type is white crown glass (Hoya), and the LE-30 is a borosilicate glass, also from Hoya. The Q-18 and Q-25 glasses are Hoya quartz.

Material Costs

The price of these materials varies in direct proportion to their thermal stability. If we assign an arbitrary value of 1 as the price for green glass,

TABLE 2-2 *Categories of temperature-resistant glass*

Glass category	Thermal expansion, ppm/°C
High-thermal-expansion materials (HTE)	
Green glass, white crown glass, soda-lime glasses	9.5
Low-thermal-expansion materials (LTE)	
Alumina borosilicate and other low-alkali glasses	
Alkali content ≤2%, Hoya LE-30	3.5
Alkali content ≤0.12%, Corning 7059	4.5
Ultralow-thermal-expansion materials (ULTE)	
Corning N-ZEM*(N-365)	0.75
Corning N-ZEM (N-254)	0.75
Corning N-ZEM (N-185)	0.55
Synthetic quartz	0.51

* N-ZEM means near-zero-expansion materials. Number indicates absorbing wavelength.

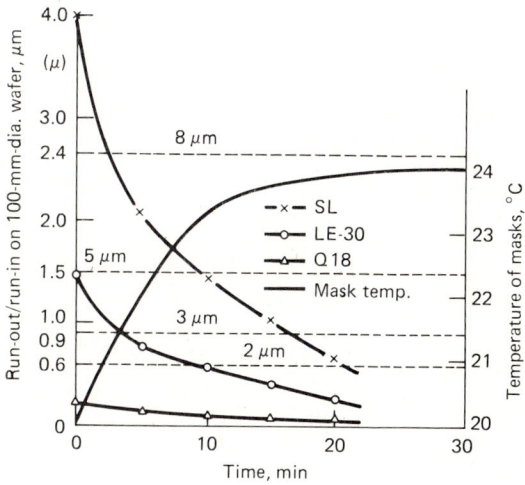

FIG. 2-6 Run-in/runout versus stabilization time for three types of mask glass.

then the price of white crown is approximately 1.5. On the same scale, the price of all the low-thermal-expansion materials would be 2.5 and that of the ultralow-thermal-expansion materials, including synthetic quartz, as high as 7 to 8.

Material cost is significant only when considered in relation to other individual costs of other materials in the process. Glass cost, when measured in value-added terms or as a percent of total masking or IC fabrication cost, is a very small number. The leverage of the glass blank as a yield improvement material is approaching that of the resist material.

Low Defect Levels

Masks with near-zero or zero detectable defects are needed for advanced IC fabrication. Defects in or on masks arise from a multitude of sources, and new origins of defects are found constantly. Since we are dealing in this chapter with the blanks (glass prior to coating or metallization), the number of defect sources is reasonably limited.

A defect in mask-quality glass should be loosely defined as anything connected to or part of the glass blank that could degrade or otherwise interfere with the process of pattern lithography. Defect levels have been tied to the amount of sodium in the glass, as shown in Figure 2-7. Note that the number of pinholes in the chromium layer is the measure of the defect, a problem since sodium at the chrome interface causes an etching reaction that results in a pinhole.

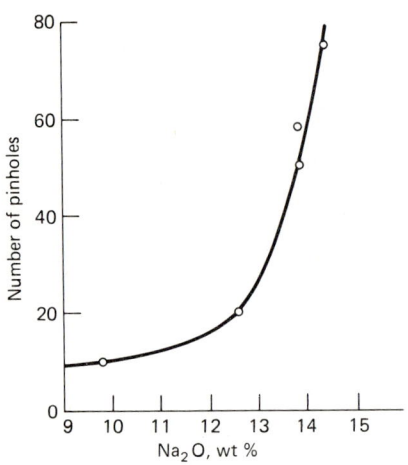

FIG. 2-7 Pinholes, caused by baking the glass, as a function of sodium content.

In essence, the objective of the mask is to provide accurate and repeatable transfer of image signals to resist-coated wafers. Thinking of the mask as a medium for image transfer, a defect can be regarded as *any* phenomenon disruptive to the medium.

Defects can be differences in the composition of the glass. Nonhomogeneous glass may change the absorption and transmission of wavelengths and/or light intensity. Changes in the intensity or transmission of nonuniform wavelengths will potentially change the imaging parameters. Glass composition can be affected by many individual factors, all of which come to roost in the melting furnace.

Changes in the operating parameters of the furnace and control of those parameters are critical to high-quality-glass manufacturing. Impurities, both in the raw materials and in the furnace environment, must be kept at minimum levels. Impurities such as sodium are easily accessed to the process, and strict controls are needed by both operators and equipment to prevent sodium and other contaminants from entering the melt.

Assuming the composition of the glass to be uniform, we can look to irregularities in the glass as another type of defect. Although on assay the glass will meet specifications for composition, bubbles, "seeds," or other nonuniformities in the structure may exist.

In the glass-making process, gases may become entrapped in the melt and end up in the sheet glass. These pockets change the refractive index of the glass where they occur. They also may be disruptive to the patterning process if they end up in a clear area, i.e., not buried under a structure of etched chrome.

Undissolved or unmelted portions of the original raw material sometimes end up in the glass. Structures of glass *within* the glass blank occur occasionally from other phenomena in the melting process. These nonuniformities will also cause optical aberrations that may be damaging to optical lithography.

Checking surface quality is another way of detecting and measuring defects in mask blanks. Surface defects, unlike "bulk" defects (in the glass), are often removed by cleaning or polishing techniques. Bulk defects near the surface can often be ground and polished out, assuming there still remains enough glass thickness to meet specifications. Bubbles, seeds, and other bulk irregularities are often removed by lapping and polishing. True surface defects can be removed by one of several cleaning methods, covered in the section of this chapter on blank cleaning.

Defects range from airborne particle contaminants to chemical stains left behind from earlier chemical treatments. Particles of abrasive material from the lapping, grinding, or other mechanical finishing operations are defect sources. Surface scratches, caused by poor rinsing or cleaning, are defects that can affect patterning processes. Scratches result from abrasive-material contamination in a much finer polishing operation. Defects on the surface can be particularly worrisome if they become entrapped during the metallization or coating step. Defects are removed from both sides of glass blanks. A common benchmark for the criticality of defects is their visibility through an optical microscope at $400\times$ magnification. Defects small enough to be undetected at this magnification do not generally cause serious pattern errors. However, smaller geometries (less than 2 μm) are naturally more sensitive to defects that might pass the $400\times$ optical inspection test. In the chapter on mask inspection techniques we will expand on more sophisticated techniques with advanced defect detectability, such as is possible with the KLA mask inspection system.

Defects on *both* sides of blanks are problematical. Backside defects cause reflections to the front surface and afterward are confused with frontside defects. All the surface and bulk defects discussed can cause opaque spots when illuminated in the optical printing system. This type of error is more serious than optical aberrations that change transmission characteristics only slightly.

Cleaning and Handling Resistance

The fourth primary criterion for mask-quality glass is resistance to cleaning and to the typical handling operations and equipment. Glass cut from raw sheet glass must be completely cleaned to remove chips and debris from the cutting operation. Glass cleaning involves the use of several different types of chemicals, including

1. Deionized (DI) water
2. Chromic acid
3. Ammonium hydroxide
4. Peroxide hydroxide solution
5. Methanol, trichloroethylene, and other solvents

In addition to chemical resistance, glass used for mask fabrication must have resistance to the handling and other mechanical forces encountered in processing. Ultrasonics are frequently used to dislodge particles in conjunction with cleaning acids, solvents, and detergents. Any new glass or glasslike materials considered for mask-making must be resistant to all these chemical and mechanical treatments. Glasses containing ingredients that might leach out of the surface could cause serious metallization adhesion problems or even disrupt optical transmission. Specifications for all mask materials must include complete cleaning and handling resistance criteria.

In summary, mask-quality glass must meet four major criteria in order to be acceptable for VLSI device fabrication. These critical functional properties are:

1. *Suitable optical transmission* for compatibility with resist
2. *Low thermal expansion* to preserve the exposure system's image-resolution and line-geometry control, despite necessary thermal environments in the process
3. *Low defect levels* to provide high-quality image transfer to the resist-coated wafer
4. *Good chemical and mechanical resistance* to sustain cleaning operations and mechanical handling in production equipment

GLASS COMPOSITION

We have discussed briefly the need for close control of mask-glass uniformity in order to fabricate high-quality masks. The approximate chemical compositions of the major types of mask glass are shown in Table 2-3. Silicon dioxide (SiO_2) is the major ingredient in all glasses, and quartz is almost pure SiO_2, with a combination of other oxides comprising the balance. Very small changes in the percent composition of glass ingredients can cause major changes in the functional properties. For example, small changes in the alkali content, on the order of tenths of 1 percent, will dramatically alter the ease of grinding and polishing the alumina glasses.

TABLE 2-3 *Characteristics of common types of glass*

Characteristic	Type of Glass			
	SLW (Soda lime)	SL (White crown)	LE-30 (Low-expansion)	Qz (Fused quartz)
Chemical composition, %				
SiO_2	73	70	60	100
B_2O_3	1		5	
Al_2O_3			15	
Na_2O	15	8		
K_2O	1	9		
CaO, MgO	10	12	20	
Others		1		
Physical properties				
Thermal expansion (10^{-7})	94	93	37	5
Transformation temperature, °C	542	533	686	1120
Refractive index, N_D	1.52	1.52	1.53	1.46
Young modulus, kg/mm²	7200	7340	7540	7410
Knoop hardness, kg/mm²	540	530	657	615
Electric resistivity ($\Omega \cdot$cm)	10^{12}	10^{15}	10^{15}	10^{18}
Specific gravity	2.50	2.56	2.58	2.20

GENERAL PROPERTIES OF SODA-LIME, CROWN BOROSILICATE, BARIUM-ALUMINUM SILICATE, AND QUARTZ GLASSES

A summary of several properties of soda-lime and quartz glass types is presented in Table 2-3. The water resistance of quartz is higher than that of soda-lime glass, although an exact figure has not been published. Note the wide variation among the various glasses in such critical properties as acid and base resistance. These are the major glass types, and new materials now under development promise functionality improvements for ULTE-grade masks.

Soda-Lime Glasses

Green Soda-Lime Glass

Green soda-lime glass is a workhorse material for hard-surface-blank production. Primary reasons for its popularity are abundant supply and relatively low cost. These reasons are complemented by the relative ease at which green soda-lime glass can be drawn into relatively flat and parallel sheets. Overall, the quality of the glass itself is high. Bulk defects such as volume inclusions are rare. Major surface defects are also few in number.

Green soda-lime glass from the melting furnace is pulled into large flat sheets. These are inspected for internal and external defects and then marked. The glass sheets are then cut into pieces; the selected areas of higher quality are used for masks. The relatively low cost of green soda-lime glass makes this "hunt-and-peck" approach economically feasible. Sections of the glass that are picked for their higher quality are then ground, smoothed, and finally polished.

Grinding operations are used to remove major defects in the surface of the glass or bulk defects near the surface. Special glass grinders remove enough material to leave ample plate thickness for subsequent smoothing and polishing to render a plate within necessary thickness specifications.

Glass smoothing or lapping is performed with special abrasives that are designed (in particle size) to remove all the surface irregularities left by the grinder. Figure 2-8 illustrates a typical smoothing operation.

After grinding, the plates are polished with an optical rouge that further evens out surface irregularities, thereby increasing the flatness of the glass. Care must be taken to remove all the abrasive particles from the smoothing operation. Any particles left on the plate from a previous grinding or lapping operation will cause considerable surface scratches.

FIG. 2-8 Glass-smoothing operation.

Green soda-lime glass is the least thermally stable of all mask-glass types. The sodium content is more than double that of the next stable type, white soda lime. Also, its cutoff frequency (transmission profile) begins at about 3700 Å, thereby absorbing some of the 365-nm line in the spectrum. This major "spike" is needed for faster resist exposure in all wafer exposure systems except step-and-repeat systems operating solely at 436 nm.

In summary, green soda-lime glass is highly useful for masks that are used to image IC geometries in the region above 3 to 4 µm. Geometries below 3 µm have line tolerances that are much more difficult to maintain when the less stable green soda-lime glass is used. While the majority of all ICs can still be produced with masks made of green glass, all new VLSI designs and all circuits with pattern elements below 3 µm are better processed with more stable glass masks.

The cleaning, surface inspection, and flatness inspection steps that follow are covered later in this chapter. All the major glass types discussed here are processed through these same steps just described.

White Soda-Lime Glass

White soda-lime glass, with less than half the sodium content of green glass, has better chemical resistance and increased transmission of wavelengths between 3300 and 3700 Å, where green soda-lime transmission has started falling off. However, the major advantage of the white soda lime over green soda lime is less sodium at the glass-chromium interface. The migration of sodium to this interface is caused by heat encountered in one of several process steps.

Borosilicate is classified as a low-thermal-expansion material. This singular major advantage weighs heavily in VLSI device fabrication. For example, on a 5-in plate a 2°C change in temperature can cause about 1.75 to 2.0 µm of runout with the less thermally stable soda-lime glass. Borosilicate and alumina-borosilicate glasses are now production-mask materials for this reason.

Advances in glass grinding, smoothing, and polishing will make the job of working borosilicate easier. Also, new inspection equipment will make the inclusions that occur in this glass type easier to detect. Screening of glass blanks in process with this new equipment will serve to upgrade the quality of mask blanks.

The geometries used on the more advanced IC designs can have line tolerances in the 0.2- to 0.3-µm region. Since borosilicate glass has higher dimensional stability and is generally of a higher purity level, it is a better choice for advanced mask designs. The lower sodium level is a special advantage for masks used with beam exposure equipment. The high temperatures caused by the scanning electron beam not only move the glass but also cause sodium to migrate to the surface, causing pinholes.

In resist baking (120°C maximum), e-beam resist exposure (approximately 200°C), and metal or chemical-vapor deposition (CVD) (approximately 120 to 300°C) the temperatures shown are typically encountered. The sodium that moves to the surface produces a sodium-chrome reaction that causes serious resist undercutting or "mouse-nipping." Thus, the lower sodium of white soda-lime glass solves a major problem. If processes are developed that can avoid all these higher temperatures (175°C or above is critical), green soda-lime glass will be suitable. The white soda-lime material is less easy to obtain, and the number of suppliers is fairly limited.

Borosilicate Glass

Borosilicate is one type of low-expansion glass that has become a primary mask-blank material for VLSI device fabrication. The bulk of VLSI processes are such that the blanks are subjected to high temperatures in both mask-making and mask use. Most of the masks used in wafer projection printing equipment are borosilicate. All masks for e-beam imaging (i.e., blanks that are coated with e-beam resist and placed into high-temperature e-beam systems) are also borosilicate. The primary advantage of better temperature resistance (low expansion) is balanced against the disadvantage of more difficult cutting.

Borosilicate glass is also more likely to have bulk defects such as inclusions. As discussed earlier, inclusions will stop the transmission of light where they occur, and if that place happens to be in a clear (etched) area, a lithography defect can occur. Borosilicate is more difficult to procure and costs for the material are higher.

Borosilicate glass is approximately 80 percent silicon dioxide and 20 percent boron dioxide. The transmission of borosilicate lies almost directly between white crown and green soda lime. Borosilicate glass appears to be able to fill the needs of VLSI mask fabrication down to device design rules of 1.5 to 1.8 μm. Resolution and critical-dimension tolerances below the 1.5-μm pattern-geometry size will require a more stable glass or glasslike material. Quartz is a more costly alternative, and there are several materials available that approach the stability, transmission, and other attributes of quartz. Additionally, improvements in the way of reduced process temperature and better process control will extend the useful life of white crown and borosilicate glasses.

Quartz Glass

Quartz is nearly 100 percent silicon dioxide with only small amounts of other constituent oxides. Quartz is classified as an ultralow-thermal-expansion (ULTE) glass. On a 6-in plate, the ambient temperature can change up to 3°C with a resulting runout of only 0.1 μm. In fact, the runout is so small that the process environment must change nearly 10°C before runout of 0.5 μm occurs.

The major applications of quartz are for ultrahigh-resolution devices, deep-uv lithography, and applications where extremely long mask life (due to undesirability in accessing the mask in the exposure aligner) is needed. Quartz is very low in sodium, thereby eliminating the mouse-nip problem. The very low sodium level is what gives rise to the high thermal stability.

Optical transmission of quartz is about 90 percent completely across the portion of the spectrum where resists are sensitive (absorptive) and where commercially available lamps emit. Quartz does, however, have the drawback of being very susceptible to fracturing and is expensive (between 3 and 5 times the cost of borosilicate glass). Another disadvantage is a very high susceptibility to bulk defects such as inclusions. Inclusions are "light blockers," and since quartz is used with particularly fine geometries, its sensitivity to inclusions relative to pattern defects is high.

The cost of quartz is not really a good barometer of its value. The real advantages of the thermal stability of quartz in terms of device yield are difficult to measure, but they exist. The high multiplying factors in IC economies tell us that only very fractional yield improvements will result in substantial dollar savings or increased IC chip output.

Also, the fact that quartz masks are usually used in projection printers means relatively long useful lifetimes for these blanks. Spreading both the assumed yield advantage and the lifetime of a quartz blank against its cost will result in a very low cost-per-wafer figure. On this basis, quartz blanks can be easily cost justified, especially for high-resolution, high-tolerance devices.

Quartz is also advantageous in the way of durability in cleaning solutions. Since masks must be periodically taken from the exposure systems and cleaned, cleaning resistance becomes a major parameter in determining mask life. Quartz has particularly high resistance to a variety of glass-cleaning solutions, especially when compared to the borosilicate, white crown, and green and white soda-lime glasses. As mid- and deep-uv lithographies become more widely used, quartz is the only material with extremely high optical transmission in the 200- to 300-nm wavelength region where deep-uv lithography resides.

OPTICAL TRANSMISSION OF GLASS

The optical transmission of glass is a key factor in mask fabrication. Resist exposure is the only step where substrates cannot be batch processed. For this reason, every attempt is made to expedite the exposure of each individual part in order to meet production demands. The available light energy for resist exposure is preciously guarded, and attempts to minimize absorption of critical wavelengths by the mask glass are important. The major mercury lines used in the wafer exposure equipment are measured against the percent transmission of those wavelengths by various glass types. All mask glass will absorb some of these critical spikes, but generally not more than 15 to 20 percent of the total energy. Even this amount is difficult to sacrifice when exposing relatively slow positive resists.

The wavelength transmission of three major glass types is shown in Table 2-4, including the data for the major wavelengths. One area of improvement for future glasses will be increasing the transmission at critical exposing wavelengths. Parallel development of more efficient light sources and faster resists will eventually reduce the pressure on the exposure step in mask and wafer lithography.

GLASS CLEANING

After the grinding and polishing operations, glass blanks are likely to have small glass flakes on the surface or edges. Glass flakes commonly come off of the edges of blanks, and glass manufacturers use proprietary methods to treat blank edges and minimize or eliminate flaking. Other

TABLE 2-4 *Glass type versus wavelength transmission*

Glass grade	Wavelength transmission, Å	Percentage, %
High thermal-expansion (HTE)	3660	80
	4050	85
	4360	90
Low thermal-expansion (LTE)	3660	80
	4050	85
	4360	90
Ultralow thermal-expansion (ULTE)	4050	90
	3660	85
	2540	70

sources of contamination include fingerprints, particles from the polishing slurries, stains from previous chemical treatments, and debris from the environment in general. Any of these contaminants can block the transmission of light, and extensive cleaning is used for this reason.

Cleaning techniques for glass are varied, ranging from many difficult chemical treatments to mechanical treatments. Types of cleaners include oxidizing acids, solvent-vapor degreasers, alkaline solutions, radio-frequency (rf) oxygen plasma, aqueous rinses, abrasive slurries, and mechanical washes or brushes.

Some of the glass and other particulates that contaminate glass-blank surfaces are tightly bonded by intermolecular forces (van der Waals). The amount of adhesion of these contaminants will in part determine the effectiveness of the cleaning method used. The van der Waals forces are a function of particle size, contact area, surface texture, and the chemistry of both the particle and the surface. There are also electrical forces resulting from the difference in contact potential. In addition to these, there are capillary forces that occur when liquid fills the space between the particle and the surface. Capillary forces are especially favored by relative humidity above 65 percent. The amount of adhesion of the various contaminants cited is measured in kcal/mol. The cleaning process must overcome these forces, which typically runs 0.5 to 10 kcal/mol.

Glass-cleaning techniques should be selected according to the application. In many situations, glass blanks that have been stored in a relatively dust-free and protected area may only need a dry-nitrogen blowoff. Nitrogen blow cleaning is effective for particles that are 50 µm or larger. Particles less than 50 µm in diameter will remain bonded. If particles are bonded by water evaporation, not even the forced dry-nitrogen stream will remove them. The problem with nitrogen and other forced-air cleaning methods is the loss of effectiveness caused by the boundary layer effect. This phenomenon occurs when the forced-air or forced-gas stream strikes the substrate and moves parallel to the surface. When this occurs, the pressure of the gas at the substrate surface is greatly reduced (by being diverted), thereby reducing the effectiveness of this cleaning method. As a result, particles are frequently left on the surface. The actual "dislocation force" created by the gas is often less than the adhesive force between the particle and the surface.

One cleaning technique that helps overcome the problem of loss of effectiveness is to provide an ionized field in the gas stream. Ionized forced-pressure-gas cleaning is more effective when the particle on the surface is similarly charged. In general, all forms of gaseous pressure cleaning are ineffective for removal of small (less than 50 μm) particles.

Pressurized water or chemical solutions have been useful for glass cleaning. The force of a liquid, under pressure, is greater than that of the much lighter gases. Pressurized-solution particle removal is good in the sense that most contaminants are dislodged from the surface, but there is the disadvantage that debris is simply moved around and redeposited elsewhere. The missing ingredient, researched and tested by people at Bell Laboratories, was mechanical brushes. The combination of scrubber brushes and high-pressure water provides all the action needed to chemically and physically clean a particle- or stain-contaminated surface. Numerous types of equipment are now commercially available to provide this type of cleaning. These particulates are the greatest source of defects on mask blanks. Particles left on the glass before metallization or other thin-film deposition will lead to undercutting or voids (pinholes) in the mask. While extra chrome or iron oxide can be laser-zapped or physically removed, voids are irreparable.

The typical equipment setup in a glass-cleaning production line is shown in Fig. 2-9.

Glass-blank cleaning should be performed under Class 100 clean-room conditions. The relative humidity and the air circulation and temperature should be monitored and controlled as well. Relative humidity of 45 percent, an air temperature of 21°C, and air movement in cubic feet per minute or volume turnover should be specified by clean-room engineers based on traffic in the area. All clean-room personnel must be completely clothed in clean-room attire and air-scrubbed before entering the area.

The water for glass cleaning should be controlled for temperature, resistivity, and particle size; water that has a resistivity of 18 MΩ at 21°C and that is absolute-filtered to 0.2 μm is suggested. All the parameters for the glass-cleaning operation can be microprocessor-controlled, including water flow rate and all the individual process steps.

FIG. 2-9 Production glass-cleaning line.

Resistance to the variety of chemical cleaning treatments is a key requirement for all the glasses used to make mask blanks. Chemical durability can be measured by a variety of tests. One commonly used test involves the weight loss of the glass after exposure to the chemical cleaning solution. Table 2-5 shows the results of this test for three major Hoya glass types.

Note the difference between quartz and the lower-thermal-resistance materials shown in Table 2-5. Since masks for step-and-repeat printing and scanning projection are not touched in production, the life of the masks is largely a function of their durability in chemical cleaning solutions. Other than chemical resistance, the only mechanical treatment a production mask (one used in projection printing) might encounter

TABLE 2-5 *Chemical durability of glass types*

	Glass type				
	SLW (White soda-lime)	SL (Soda-lime)	LE-30 (Low-expansion borosilicate)	Q-18 (Quartz)	Reference (Aluminum-barium borosilicate)
Weight loss, %, in deionized water at 100°C for 1 hr	0.050	0.058	0.015	0	0.043
Weight loss, %, in $\frac{1}{100}$ HNO_3 at 100°C for 1 hr	0.028	0.023	0.030	0.003	0.110

would be high-speed nylon-brush cleaning. One possible way to measure mechanical durability is to test for lapping and Knoop hardness.

The test data for major Hoya glass types are given in the following table.

Hardness	Glass Type			
	SLW	SL	LE-30	Q-18
Knoop hardness (100 g)	540	530	657	615
Lapping hardness (relative)	88	88	209	210

The lapping hardness is a better measure of abrasion resistance than Knoop hardness, which only measures the penetrability of a known weighted object. Since masks and mask blanks should never be hand-buffed or polished to remove surface dust, the life of a blank is considerable. The most important criterion at the mask-blank' stage, however, is complete removal of glass flakes before metallization or thin-film deposition.

A cleaning procedure designed to remove soils, glass flakes, dust, fingerprints, and lapping debris typically involves acids, solvents, and other detergent and surfactant proprietary chemicals.

Solutions that can be made in your own laboratory are often practical and less expensive. One procedure involves chromic acid solution followed by ammonium hydroxide, peroxide, and a methanol rinse, all interspersed with deionized water. The various soils on a glass surface will be removed by these solutions. The peroxide solution has a mechanochemical action wherein the cavitation energy of the bubbles serves to lift off or dislodge particles in the micrometer-size range. The parameters for this cleaning procedure are 53 min with maximum solution temperatures of 150°C. Always be careful to check any cleaning procedure for its maximum operating temperature and for chemical compatibility between the glass and the solutions used. All cleaning procedures should match the glass type.

Ultrasonics versus Pinholes

Ultrasonic cleaning for extended periods can have a negative effect on mask-quality glass. The data shown in Table 2-6 indicate the increase in pinhole density as a function of ultrasonic exposure. These data are for chromium-coated blanks, and the increase in pinholes for soda-lime and borosilicate glass is due primarily to the higher barium and boron content of these glasses. These elements in the glass contribute to weaker chrome adhesion (Table 2-6).

TABLE 2-6 *Pinholes per 4 cm² versus ultrasonic cleaning time*

Kind of glass	Ultrasonic applied time		
	0	3 hr	8 hr
Alumino-lime borosilicate (LE-30)	0	17	40
Alumino-barium borosilicate (7059)	1	212	1447
Soda-lime (SLW)	2	272	2935

Blank Protection prior to Metallization

Many blanks are coated with a protective solution that insulates the glass surface from environmental contamination. All operators handling blanks should wear plastic or rubber gloves. The sebaceous (oil) glands of the body (hands) always keep skin well-moistened with oil that often finds its way to glass surfaces. After putting on proper skin protection, operators can coat the blanks with the water-soluble film. In some manufacturing processes, this coating is applied before the glass is scored and broken and thus protects the glass *before* the small glass flakes from the edges have had a chance to deposit themselves elsewhere.

These water-soluble films can be removed by washing the blanks in warm water (40 to 50°C) in a mild neutral (pH 7.0 to 8.0) detergent solution. Commercial cleaning solutions are shown in Table 2-7. The suggested concentration for using these materials is very low: dilute to about $\frac{1}{4}$ to 1 percent or less in deionized water. The water should be processed through a final filtration in a Millipore Super Q, or equivalent system. The absolute-filter pore size should be 0.22 µm minimum, and water resistivity of greater than 10 MΩ is recommended.

When rinsing glass blanks, *do not* use still tanks or simple overflow systems. A good method is the "counterflow-cascade" technique wherein the water is moved in a direction opposite to the movement of the glass direction.

A procedure for cleaning glass blanks in order to remove the water-soluble film is as follows:

Step 1. Take glass blanks out of their container and insert in drain racks.

TABLE 2-7 *Commercially available glass-cleaning solutions*

Product	Producer
Triton X-100	Röhm and Hass, Philadelphia
Microclean	International Products Corp., Trenton, NJ
Orvus Paste (sodium lauryl sulfate)	Proctor and Gamble

Step 2. Soak for 5 min in a warm aqueous solution of surfactant combined with ultrasonics.

Step 3. Spray rinse with deionized water.

Step 4. Scrub gently with a clean-room sponge using the detergent surfactant solution.

Step 5. Spray rinse with Super Q water.

Step 6. Rinse in a counterflow-cascade tank with Super Q water. *Note:* Keep the glass plate completely wetted until it can be dried properly in a Class 100–Class 10 clean-room condition. This will avoid spotting on the plate.

Step 7. Dry the glass plate by one of the following techniques:
    a. Dip in a solution of isopropanol, and follow by placing the plate in a vapor of isopropanol.
    b. Dip in a fluorocarbon liquid, and follow by a fluorocarbon vapor dry.

Step 8. Spin dry the plates by dispensing Super Q water and nitrogen filtered through a 0.22-µm absolute membrane filter.

Step 9. Store parts in a clean cabinet.

Glass plates that are not coated with a water-soluble protective film may be cleaned by a different method. This technique is as follows:

Step 1. Immediately after polishing, soak in filtered tap water for a maximum of 10 min to prevent drying of polish compounds.

Step 2. Rinse with a high-pressure (greater than 40 lb/in^2) filtered-tap-water spray for 1 to 2 min.

Step 3. Immerse in a 40-kHz ultrasonic cleaner containing filtered tap water plus 0.2% Microclean (pH 7 to 8), raise the temperature up to 50°C (temperature increased from 20°C by ultrasonic energy) for 3 to 5 min.

Step 4. Scrub in a solution of filtered tap water plus 0.2% Microclean at room temperature (20°C) using a Scott Z foam sponge.

Step 5. Rinse in Super Q water (15 to 18 MΩ) in an overflow tank at $\frac{1}{2}$ gal/min overflow rate, at room temperature for 1 to 5 min. Steps 6 through 10 are programmed and timed by computer. Steps 6 through 11 are done under a Class 100 clean hood.

Step 6. Spray rinse at more than 5 lb/in^2 in Super Q water at room temperature for 3 min.

Step 7. Rinse in Super Q water (15 to 18 MΩ) in an overflow tank at $\frac{1}{2}$ gal/min overflow rate, at room temperature for 10 min.

Step 8. Immerse in a 40-kHz ultrasonic cleaner containing Super Q water (15 to 18 MΩ) plus 0.2% Microclean (pH 7 to 8) at a temperature of 50°C (temperature increased from 20°C by ultrasonic energy) for 10 min.

Step 9. Rinse in Super Q water (15 to 18 MΩ) in an overflow tank at $\frac{1}{2}$ gal/min overflow rate, at room temperature for 10 min.

Step 10. Spin rinse in a Fluoroware spin-rinser-dryer using Super Q water and dry nitrogen filtered through a 0.22-μm filter (12-min cycle).

Following step 10, the plates are subjected to 100 percent inspection. After visual and flatness inspection, plates are again washed under a Class 100 clean hood.

Step 11. Scrub in a solution of Super Q water plus 0.2% Microclean at room temperature (20°C) using a Scott Z foam sponge.

Step 12. Rinse and dry: repeat the sequence of steps 6 through 10.

Step 13. Package in Fluoroware boxes.

Following step 13, storage time may degrade wettability, as measured by water contact angle.* If it is necessary to clean plates in order to restore wettability, the following steps are suggested:

Step 14. Rinse in Super Q water (15 to 18 MΩ) in an overflow tank at $\frac{1}{2}$ gal/min overflow rate at room temperature for 3 to 5 min.

Step 15. Immerse in a 40-kHz ultrasonic cleaner containing Super Q water plus 2.0% Microclean (pH 9.5) at a maximum temperature of 50°C for 10 min.

Step 16. Rinse and dry as in steps 9 and 10, or follow usual prechromium-coating cleaning. (An alternative wettability improvement process is step 17.)

Step 17. Plasma clean at 50 to 100 W in oxygen atmosphere for 1 to 3 min.

Step 18. Since cleanliness, as measured by wettability water contact angle, degrades with time, sputter chromium as soon as possible after step 16 or 17.

Cleaning of glass substrates is an extremely sensitive procedure. The steps above are merely intended as a general outline for newcomers to the field. Modifications may be required to fit your specific situation.

---

* Per ANSI/ASTM C813-75, "Standard Test Method for Hydrophobic Contamination on Glass by Contact Angle Measurement."

58 INTEGRATED CIRCUIT MASK TECHNOLOGY

Glass cleaning at various stages of mask-blank preparation is extremely important in producing a high-quality product. All the various types of glasses can generally be cleaned in the procedures cited on the preceding pages. Cycle times and number of rinse steps may be varied, but certain aspects of all these procedures are critical to obtaining a high-quality surface and must not be avoided. For example, the removal of soils and stains necessitates the chromic acid and hydroxide combination followed by peroxide (dislodge particles via "chemical scrub"). Proper water removal without spotting always calls for the use of an alcohol rinse and an alcohol or fluorocarbon vapor to provide uniform drying. Extra counterflow rinses ensure complete chemical removal of other solutions (such as chromic ions) that could contaminate the glass. Cleaning is like process insurance; it *may* be possible to have too much, but getting caught without enough can be very expensive. The pressure of production calls for short cleaning cycles, and this can be done by using brushes, high solution pressure, and in-line or automatic batch-plate-handling equipment. Reduction of manual processing will help reduce operator-induced defects.

BLANK HARDNESS

The relative hardness of glass blanks and mask blanks plays a role in their life in a production line, including the number of defects that will occur and the number of cleaning cycles a mask will sustain. The harder the glass, the harder the chrome surface. Test data relating these parameters are given in Fig. 2-10 for white crown (SL), soda lime (SLW), borosilicate (LE-30), and quartz (Q-18).

Hardness is especially important in processes where contact printing is used. As the number of contacts increases, mask degradation increases. While quartz masks are more expensive, the cost of short mask life must be weighed against higher incremental blank cost.

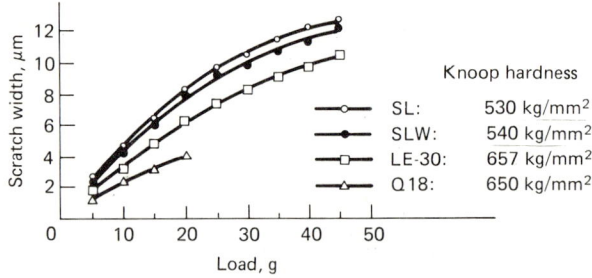

FIG. 2-10 Glass hardness test: scratch width plotted against load weight. Test made with a diamond stylus with a 5-μm radius at 60 mm/min.

MASK INSPECTION

The primary steps from raw-glass-plate production to the inspection step are outlined in Fig. 2-11. The raw plate is taken to the diamond cutter and then to the diamond flat generator, followed by thickness sorting. The grinding and smoothing steps use increasingly smaller abrasive compounds, finishing off with the polishing using cerium oxide powder. Even the small diameter of the cerium oxide powders can leave scratches in the glass surface. These microscopic scratches become a factor in lithography when pattern elements cross a microscratch. The light deflection or deviation in the chromium could affect the edge sharpness on a given pattern element. A typical inspection step on a production line is depicted in Fig. 2-12.

GLASS FLATNESS

The current trends in microlithography toward larger mask sizes begin to make demands on maintaining plate flatness. Larger glass blanks tend to run thicker than their smaller counterparts. For example, the

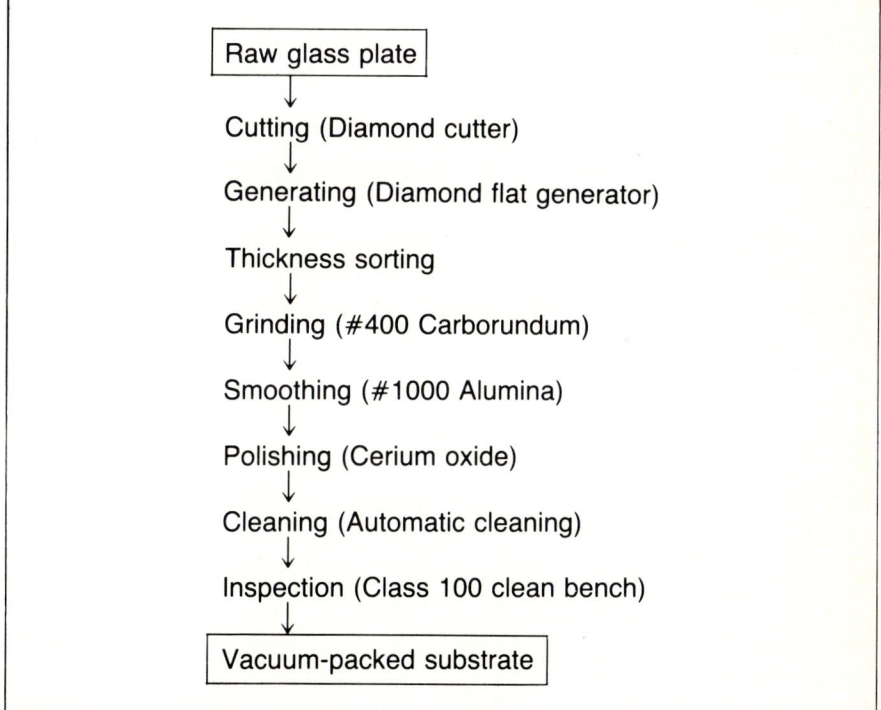

FIG. 2-11 Steps from raw glass plate to substrate.

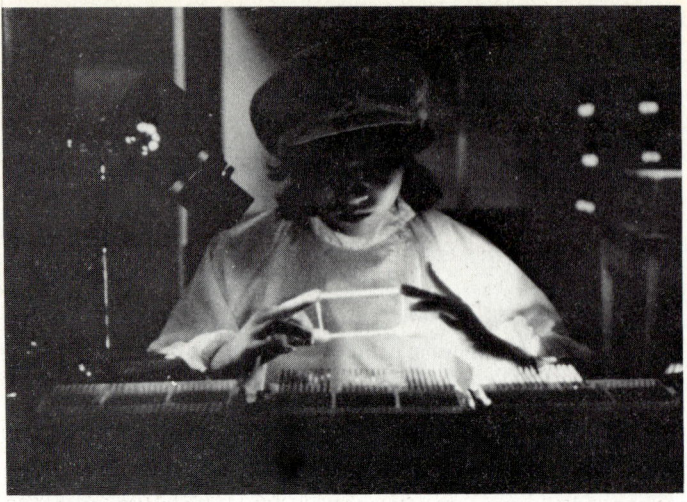

FIG. 2-12 Mask inspection during production. *(Hoya.)*

relationship between mask size and plate thickness can be plotted as shown in Fig. 2-13. Glass thickness is a major determinant of plate flatness. In calculating possible nonflatness for new process design, it will be remembered that gravitational sag is inversely proportional to the square of the plate thickness.

The two primary reasons for maintaining plate flatness are maintaining optimum resolution and controlling the changes (Δ) in line or geometry sizes. Microlithographers are faced with increasing dimension-control problems as specifications tighten against shrinking geometries. The use of full-wafer-exposure alignment systems means that the full field of pattern elements must be in focus *and* aligned while the wafer is being exposed. All the variations in the optical printing equipment, the plate and the wafer are combined over the entire pattern area. Heat from the wafer exposure source will raise the glass-blank or mask

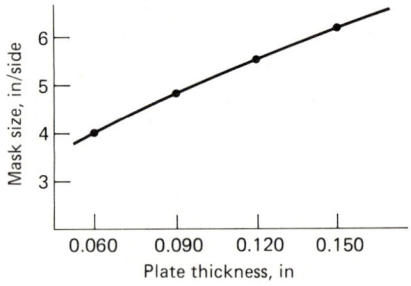

FIG. 2-13 Mask size versus plate thickness.

TABLE 2-8 *General glass-flatness specifications*

Classification	Runout, μm
Superflat	2.5
Master	5.0
Submaster	7.0
Print	10.0
Emulsion	≥10

temperature between 1 and 7°C. The thicker the glass plate, the more resistant it will be to the process temperature.

Flatness classification is given in terms of the amount of runout in micrometers over a specified plate size. Runout is the amount of deviation from a given plane or point on the mask. Flatness is usually expressed as "total flatness deviation." Flatness specifications are defined differently according to manufacturers and are listed in Table 2-8. The sizes used for these specifications are 4-in square with a 3.50-in^2 quality area in the center or a 5-in square plate with a 4.25-in^2 quality area.

Mask flatness is checked with a variety of equipment types including grating-incidence interferometers, laser interferometers, capacitive gauges, air gauges, and other optical interference devices. Laser interferometers are widely used for their resolution capability and accuracy. Laser interferometers have resolution and accuracy down to below 0.3 μm, with precision of 0.6 μm. Laser interferometry can provide full flatness profiles in an off-contact mode and glass positioning at 20°. Off-contact measurements are needed to prevent distortions that would cause erroneous readings. An operator checking glass flatness is shown in Fig. 2-14.

A typical laser-based interferometer is used to measure plates up to $4\frac{3}{16}$ by $5\frac{1}{2}$ in. As the laser beam is obliquely injected, it strikes the surface, and the deflection pattern is shown as a contour map. The screen has a line interval of 1 μm. The plate is kept in an inclined position, off-contact, and held by its own weight.

The specifications for this unit are tabulated below.

Unit of measurement	1 fringe = 1 μm
Sample support	Three carbide points, noncontact with the test surface
Measurable surface	$4\frac{3}{16}$ in × $5\frac{1}{2}$ in
Measurable objects	5 in square glass
Screen magnification	1:1
Light source	Helium-neon laser at 5 mW, 50/60 Hz, and wavelength of 6328 Å
Power source	AC 115 V = 10%
Dimensions	500 (w) × 377 (h) × 415 (d) mm
Weight	20 kg

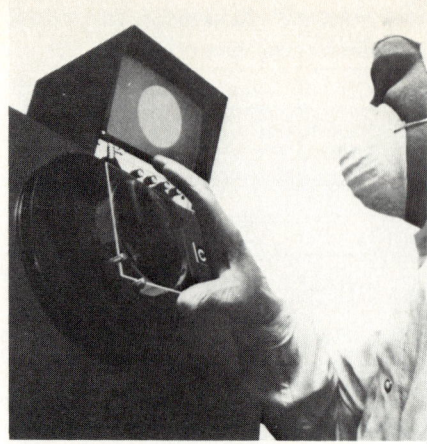

FIG. 2-14 Operator checking glass flatness.

The area of importance in measuring flatness of a blank or mask is the quality area, or the area consumed by the wafer. The approximate quality area for a given plate size is given in Table 2-9. The quality area is critical to maintaining high device yields, and dies outside the quality area are not generally counted or are only partial patterns.

The laser interferometer sometimes presents reading interpretation problems. A variety of optical fringe patterns from several different blanks can be caused from various sources. There is also a wide diversity in fringe-pattern shapes. An unskilled operator can easily misinterpret the amount of nonflatness or simply miscount the fringes.

Another device used to measure flatness is the capacitive gauge. This instrument compares the capacitance values between the internal struc-

TABLE 2-9 *Quality area of a blank for nominal plate size*

Nominal size, in	Approximate quality area, in	in^2
2 × 2	1.5	1.8
2.5 × 2.5	2.0	3.1
3.0 × 3.0	2.5	4.9
3.5 × 3.5	3.0	7.1
4.0 × 4.0	3.5	9.6
4.5 × 4.5	3.7	10.6
5.0 × 5.0	4.3	14.5
6.0 × 6.0	5.0	19.6

ture and the external surface. A probe is used to touch the blank at several different points. A single probe tester offers the advantage of keeping the plate stationary and taking several readings simultaneously. The capacitance signals are converted to a digital display of flatness. Single-probe testers yield a resolution of about 0.20 to 0.30 μm with an accuracy of 1 μm and precision of approximately 1.0 μm. The multiprobe testers have a typical accuracy of 1.0 μm, resolution of 0.03 μm, and precision of 0.6 μm. The main advantages of capacitance gauges are high resolution and rapid digital flatness readout. The potential disadvantages are substrate movement in the single-probe system and lack of full contour display to evaluate the substrate visually.

Air gauges are another way of determining mask flatness. These work on the principle of monitoring escaped gas between two surfaces and converting the reading to a flatness value. Nitrogen is pressurized between the glass surface and a special nozzle. The sensitivity of the air gauge is such that the reading essentially depicts the shape of the layer of pressurized gas pressed against the mask blank. The resolution of this device is about 0.5 μm and accuracy is between 0.5 and 1.0 μm. The precision is typically about 3.0 μm.

Warpage

There are several factors that lead to or cause nonflatness in a glass blank. Warpage is a deviation of a mask surface that results in a concave or convex shape that equals the mask diameter. Warpage can be caused by stresses in the glass that were not properly relieved or by having the mask placed under unequal pressure for a protracted period. High temperature can also cause warp in a mask blank. Warpage is closely correlated to substrate thickness, and mask blanks that are too thin are easily warped.

Plastic Flow

More subtle factors that affect microlithography are internal changes in the material itself. Plastic deformation is one example of such a change. Mask blanks in process are subjected to various temperatures, followed by much cooler rinses or air drying. The temperature itself can cause internal changes in the glass structure. Nonuniformities in glass composition, for example, will give rise to nonuniform stresses, warpage, or plastic deformation. These process-induced distortions are generally small, causing only 0.1- to 0.3-μm changes, but larger dimensional shifts will occur *if* proper process controls are not used. For example, taking a plate out of a hot cleaning solution and immersing or rinsing it in cold water will cause as much as 2 to 3 μm of distortion or nonflatness. While much of this will correct itself in time (hysteresis), plates imaged within an hour of such a thermal shock will suffer from the effects of the treatment. All plates that have been through a high-temperature operation should be allowed to equilibrate for several hours (2 to 3 hr).

Vacuum-Chuck Distortion

Nonflatness in masks can be caused by pressing masks under vacuum against various types of vacuum chucks that will stress and bend the glass. Chucks have many different types of configurations, including concentric grooves, exhaust ports, and other machined areas that cause nonuniform mask pressure. Generally, the smaller the size of the groove or open area in a chuck, the more uniform the pressure. Pinhole ports are thus the best for minimizing this contact-printing problem.

In contact printing, there is also the variation in vacuum itself that adds a variable to the process. The higher the vacuum, the greater the potential damage to the glass mask. However, increasing vacuum also increases resolution microimaging. The use of a high vacuum will press the mask and substrate being printed closer together, serving to flatten out any warp or bow in these two substrates. The main danger of a high vacuum is entrapment of particles between the two surfaces. This will not only cause possible surface damage but also create a separation that can distort the imaging. Extremely good cleaning including a nitrogen blow-dry should prevent contact-printing defects of this sort.

Gravitational Sag

The force of gravity on a mask blank is sufficient to cause a sag that will in turn distort the patterning of images. Gravitational sag has a predictable pattern and varies according to the type of fixture used. The five plots in Fig. 2-15 indicate the relationship between the type of fixturing used to hold the mask blank and the surface contour that results. This information is based on computer calculations and computer plots that started by assuming a perfectly flat and parallel plate. The variables that are included in this test, run at Corning Glass Works in Corning, New York, are as follows*: substrate size (length, width, and thickness), support mode (number of support pins, location of support pins relative to the substrate length and width, and the plane of support relative to the horizontal), and glass composition (as composition relates

---

* Corning Glass Works, *Corning Technical Bulletin on Gravitational Sag.*

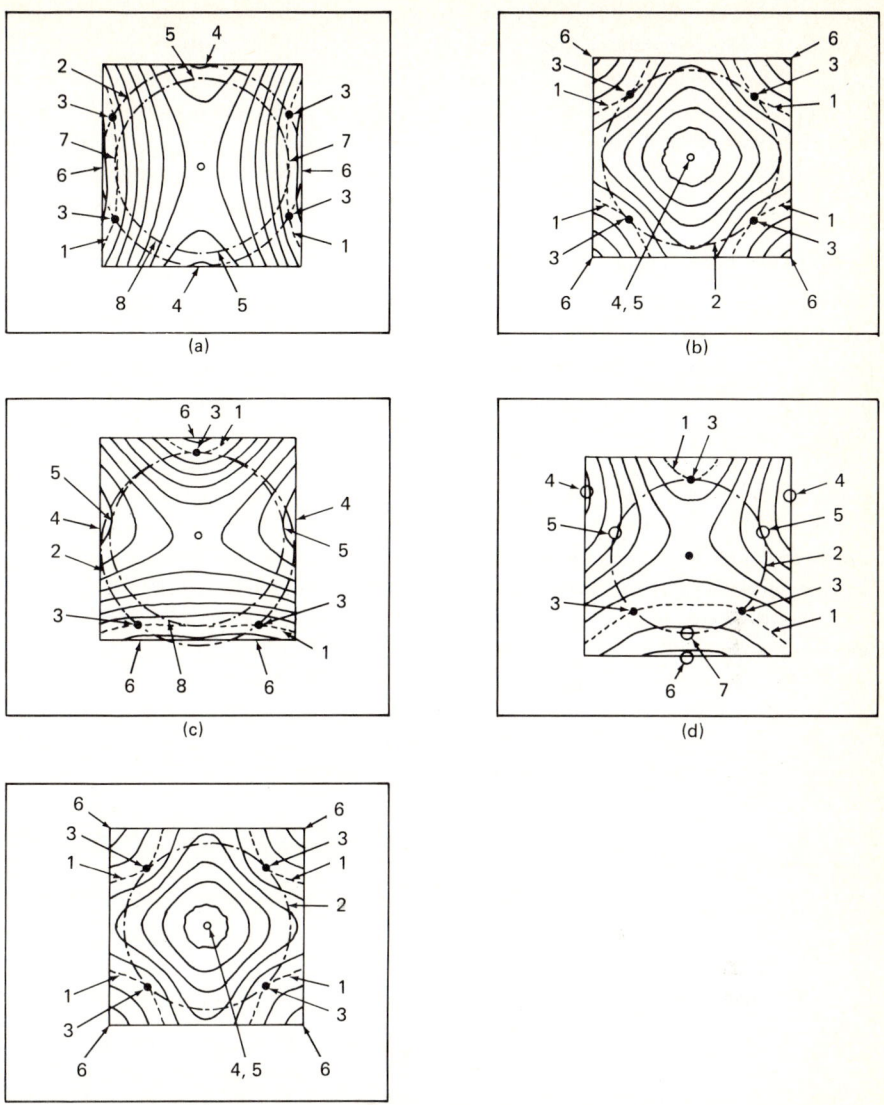

FIG. 2-15 Gravitational sag versus support points. Key to points indicated on each contour plot: 1. Contour line of zero deflection. 2. Support pin circle. 3. Support pin. 4. Point of maximum negative deflection on substrates. 5. Point of maximum negative deflection within flatness quality circle. 6. Point of maximum positive deflection on substrate. 7. Point of maximum positive deflection within flatness quality circle. 8. Flatness quality circle.

to the glass density, modulus of elasticity, and Poisson's ratio). The five contour plots shown in Fig. 2-15 indicate the deflections due to gravitational sag. It is generally assumed that these contours will be approximately the same for plates of sizes other than those tested. Also, it is possible to convert the contour deflections shown to new contours that would be created by changing the conditions using appropriate multiplying factors. These data were generated for Corning Glass 7059.

With current microlithography trends requiring flatter photomask substrates, consideration of gravitational effects on relatively thin sections of glass must be made. The comments and data noted below do not necessarily cover all combinations of variables found in the industry today. This information is based on computer calculations and computer plots that started by assuming a perfectly flat and parallel glass plate. The variables that are considered are photomask substrate *size, support mode,* and *glass composition.* Five contour plots and their corresponding deflections due to sag are given in Fig. 2-15. The contour plots are similar for other sizes of plates. In addition, conversion of the given contour deflections can be made for different conditions by using appropriate multiplying factors, discussed previously.

Gravitational sag is inversely proportional to the square of the glass thickness. Moving the fixturing points causes considerable change in the type of nonflatness of the surface. Moving the fixturing points, for example, from the edge of the plate to the center will reduce the amount of gravitational sag since the length of the unsupported glass span is reduced.

A good horizontal support fixture for a glass plate is a continuous vacuum chuck. This type of vacuum fixture uses a grooved channel around the edge of the mask generally on its top or working side. Many new types of vacuum fixtures have been developed to reduce the problem of applying improper pressure to mask blanks. A key parameter in all areas of concern for mask flatness is glass thickness. In short, the thicker the glass, the greater the possibility of maintaining overall flatness.

Seldom does the contour map of a given blank give a symmetrical pattern. The majority of blanks are nonsymmetrically flat, and flatness measurements should be made at two or three different plate orientations. Several plots of the glass surface will present a complete picture of contour. All glass-blank measurements must be made at room (ambient) temperatures ($21 \pm 1°C$) and only by operators wearing gloves. Glass plates should be thermally stabilized for 2 to 3 hr before the flatness is determined. Finally, flatness measurements should be made against a control standard obtained from the National Bureau of Standards in Washington, D.C.

PLATE SIZE VERSUS THICKNESS

One key point to remember is determining mask-flatness deformation as a function of heat absorbed during exposure is the amount of clear area versus chrome area. As the exposing energy passes from the lamp through the mask, the heat absorption is a function of the mask pattern. The clear-field masks absorb the most heat, of course, and dark-field masks reflect back most of the energy that would otherwise be absorbed. Thus, flatness measurements will vary considerably as the patterned area changes.

Since the size of masks keeps changing, an ideal standard thickness is used for a series of sizes (Table 2-10). The tolerance on thickness will vary according to the manufacturer. On an 0.060-in-thick plate, tolerance is about ±0.004 in, and on a 0.090-in plate, tolerance is about the same.

TABLE 2-10 *Mask size versus typical thickness*

Mask size, in	Plate thickness, in
2.5 × 2.5	0.060
3.0 × 3.0	0.060–0.090
3.5 × 3.5	0.060–0.090
4.0 × 4.0	0.060–0.090
4.5 × 4.5	0.090
5.0 × 5.0	0.090–0.120
6.0 × 6.0	0.090–0.120

EDGE BEVELING

Most of the plate types shown and discussed here are sold with beveled edges. The beveling prevents glass from flaking off the otherwise sharp corners, adding serious defect potential to the process. The bevel dimensions do vary, but typically are on the order of the dimensions given in the SEMI* specifications for hard-surface masks. Since the corners of the plates are potentially the largest source of defects and handling error, they are removed in the beveling process. In fact, most of the area outside the circular area taken up by the wafer could be removed if necessary.

* SEMI is the acronym for the Semiconductor Equipment and Materials Institute.

3
COATINGS FOR MASK BLANKS

INTRODUCTION

Mask blanks are coated with a wide variety of materials that are used as image-transfer mediums. The coating material is selected on the basis of its suitability for the specific mask application. A very broad categorical division can be made for all blank coatings: they can be hard-surface or soft-surface materials. In either case, the function is the same. Figure 3-1 is a cross-sectional diagram of the mask coating placed on the blank, *after* it has been imaged. The coating on the mask blank serves to hold back incident radiation. This incoming energy can be in the form of photons, x-rays, electrons, ions, or other energy forms.

Research on mask-blank coatings continues to explore the possible use of lower-cost and higher-resolution materials. The immediate avenue to obtaining higher resolution is to reduce the layer thicknesses of existing coatings. Unfortunately, as chrome and other materials are applied in layers less than 100 Å thick, pinhole incidence rises dramatically. The most desirable film would be one that had low reflectivity and high durability, was deposited in layers 300 to 800 Å thick with no

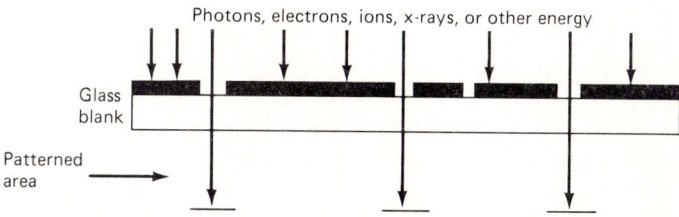

FIG. 3-1 Principle of selective energy masking with an imaged glass blank.

pinholes, and could be easily imaged and etched with high-resolution resists.

MASK-BLANK COATING TYPES

Many different materials have been used to coat mask blanks and serve as the masking medium. A current listing of major types now in production use includes the following:

Major types
1. Photoemulsion (silver halide based)
2. Diazo resin coatings
3. Photosensitive resists (diazo positive)
4. Chromium, white and black (Cr)
5. Chromium/chromium oxide (Cr_2O_x)
6. Iron oxide (Fe_2O_3)
7. Silicon (Si)

Other types used in limited quantities
8. Germanium/silicon (Ge/Si)
9. Germanium-glass
10. Germanium oxide (GeO)
11. Cadmium sulfide (CdS)
12. Zinc selenide (ZnSe)
13. Copper oxide (CuO)

Emulsion Mask Characteristics

Emulsion mask coatings are still the most widely used for noncritical working plates where geometries above 3 μm are common. Silver halide–based emulsions were the first production material to be used as the transfer medium in IC device fabrication. The advantages of this type of photoemulsion are numerous.

Advantages of Emulsion Masks

Low Cost Emulsions can be uniformly applied to glass substrates in high-volume production at relatively low cost. The price of silver is a factor in the cost of an emulsion blank, but simple silver-recovery systems have been made commercially available since the price of silver went above $5/oz. In the future, silver costs will undoubtedly continue to show a rising trend, and this may limit the market penetration of emulsions. Already a large percent of the total mask market has shifted from emulsion to hard chromium.

High Photosensitivity Silver halide emulsions are fast-exposing at standard light wavelengths, another important production requirement. Typical exposure times are several seconds. This functional property has turned out to be extremely important in reticle manufacturing, where thousands of individual exposures are needed to generate a complex IC pattern. Pattern-generation time is expensive, especially when one considers the price of the capital equipment against its throughput. The relative high speed of emulsion masks at least permits a process-compatible fit between exposure time, resolution, and commercial pattern-flashing equipment.

Good Image Resolution and Contrast Even though emulsions are quite thick as applied to the glass blanks, their resolution and contrast properties are quite good. Once again, their suitability as a material for VLSI image-pattern transfer rests on this critical functional property. Resolution in mask-making has continually increased, and this change is responsible for the shift toward higher-resolution chromium films for more advanced IC chip designs.

The limitation of emulsion resolution is determined by the mean grain size and distribution, shown in Fig. 3-2 for a standard silver halide emulsion (*a*) and for Agfa Gevaert Millimask HD. The grain size of the standard emulsions is typically about 0.05 μm with a spread of 0.0014. The improvements made in silver halide chemistry have pushed the resolution of these emulsions down into the 2-μm region. In addition to smaller grain sizes (0.035) and reduced distribution (0.0063), resolution is determined by light propagation in the emulsion, depicted in Fig. 3-3. In Chap. 4 on imaging we will discuss the chemistry and mechanics involved in generating images in silver halide emulsions. The major point about resolution is that emulsions, which swell and shrink during the image-formation process, are limited to production-process resolution of about 3 μm. In use as reticle masters, resolution down to below 2 μm has been achieved. The use of special image-enhancement techniques (developers, process cleverness) also aids in pushing resolution further downward.

Reversal Processing Reversal processing can have a very positive influence on mask and device yield. Figure 3-4 shows the result of a dust particle falling onto the surface of both positive- and negative-imaging emulsion (Agfa Millimask) layers. The flexibility of being able to use normal (negative) and reversal (positive) emulsions permits the manufacturer to preselect mask polarities to fit positive and negative resists for different mask levels. This, in turn, means they can use dark-field masks with positive resists and clear-field masks with negative resists.

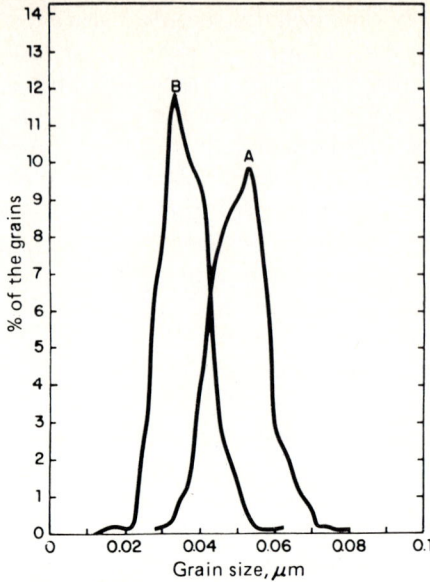

FIG. 3-2 Silver halide crystal grain size and distribution in a gelatin emulsion: (A) standard emulsion, and (B) Agfa Gevaert Millimask HD. [*Ref. 3.*]

Emulsion	Mean grain size, μm	Spread, μm
A	0.050	0.0074
B	0.035	0.0063

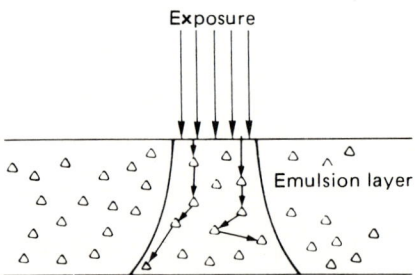

FIG. 3-3 Light propagation in an emulsion layer.

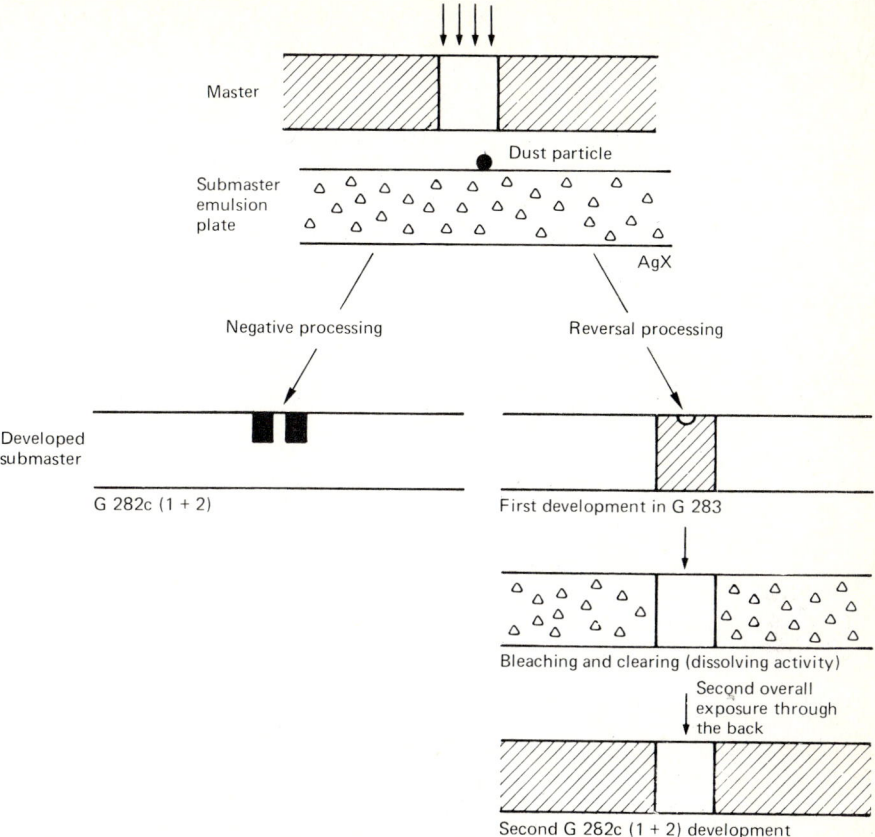

FIG. 3-4 Reversal processing and defect obstruction. [*Ref. 3.*]

The preselection "insulates" the resist from the negative effects of particle contamination.

Enhanced Image-Edge Effects Increased image density can be achieved by the influence of adjacency effects or scattered light rays that bounce against the substrate and reflect at angles that end up striking sidewall areas up to 1 μm above the substrate. This adjacency exposure ends up adding density to the top portion of an imaged microstructure, as shown in Fig. 3-5. Note the change in the image profile. This same effect of sidewall image sharpening can be achieved with Agfa Millimask emulsion plates by proper selection of a developer and special process parameters outlined in Agfa's literature.

The combined advantages of advanced emulsion coatings and software-controlled processing (imaging steps) provide a very useful medium

74 INTEGRATED CIRCUIT MASK TECHNOLOGY

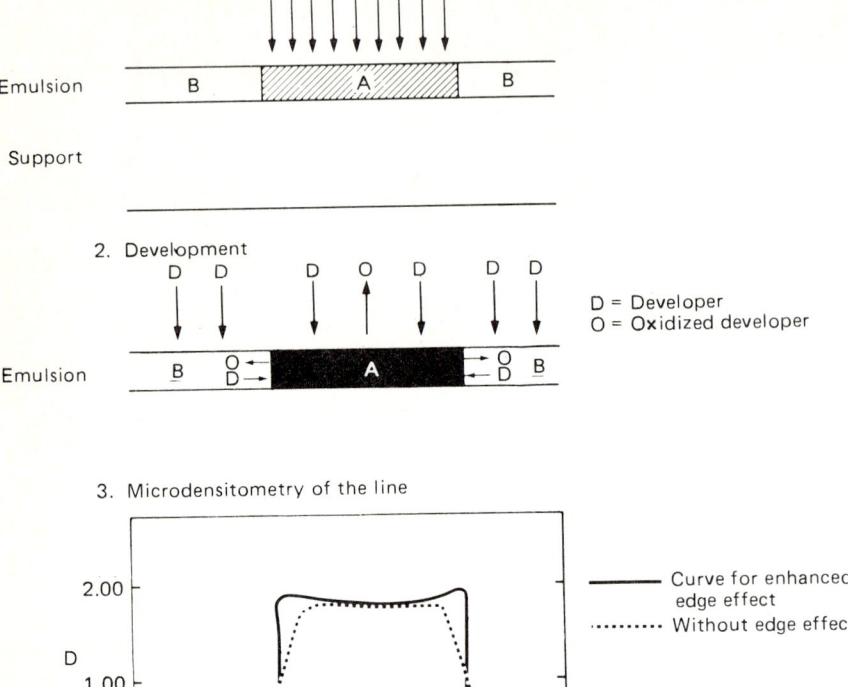

FIG. 3-5 Enhanced edge effect in Agfa Millimask emulsion. [*Ref. 3.*]

for VLSI reticle manufacturing. In lower-density IC designs, emulsions play a workhorse role when geometries from 3 μm and larger are encountered. The softness of the emulsion has an advantage in being able to absorb particle contaminants (dirt, glass flakes) without affecting the integrity of the coating. The mass of the coating gives it the ability to contain noncritical defects. Sharp epitaxial crystal spikes are another process problem, since they puncture holes in thin chromium-mask layers. The soft gelatinous emulsion absorbs the spikes, extending the number of useful contact prints that can be made from a single mask.

Weak Points of Emulsions

The advantages of emulsions in masking limit their market penetration. The soft, exposed gelatin surface absorbs developer solution and swells nonuniformly with the nonexposed areas, resulting in a relief image and a very "tender" and scratch-sensitive coating. The defect levels are relativley high in emulsions, due to the gel nature of the liquid emulsion and inability to completely filter with submicron absolute filters. Gels in the emulsion will disturb the resolution of a pattern element, potentially causing a defect. The soft emulsion, with its related sensitivity to handling, requires a special drying process, a step difficult to fully automate. Defect densities in the range of 0.3 to 1.4 defect/cm^2 are to be expected.

The softness of the emulsion layer works also to its disadvantage in contact printing. The vacuum pressure of the two surfaces rapidly degrades the quality of the imaged emulsion. Thus, while the cost of the blank is low initially, its final cost rises due to shorter life when compared to hard-surface materials.

Diazo Resin Coatings

Diazo chemistry figures in many different photosensitive films for semiconductor use. In mask-blank coating, diazo-based resin films are available as a substitute for silver halide emulsions. This is not to imply any functional superiority, but simply that these two materials stand alone in the more general category of "soft" mask material types.

One immediate difference between the silver halide and the diazo emulsion is filterability. Diazo resin coatings are filterable to the same level (0.2 µm) as photoresists. This means that masks made with the diazo emulsion will have fewer defects per square centimeter than silver halide emulsions, all other things being equal. In fact, actual data show diazo emulsion masks to provide fewer than 0.60 defect/cm^2. This figure reflects the product specification from the mask-blank manufacturer. The actual reading on several plates tested in a separate study showed fewer than 0.01 defect/cm^2.

Diazo resin emulsions offer solvent systems that dry rapidly, an important benefit in high-volume production. Rapid drying is important in keeping defects low. The most particle-sensitive stage of the plates' "life" is when the spin coating takes place and the substrate is then transferred to the soft-bake step. A tacky surface will capture particulates and retain them so that nitrogen blow-drying will not help. Thus, it is important to keep the drying time after spin coating the emulsion to a minimum.

The option to "coat your own" emulsion adds another important benefit to mask-making. Silver halide masks are coated in large sheets, then cut and broken into final size blanks. The resulting edges along scribe lines will give off flakes and chips of glass that redeposit onto the emulsion surface before or while the edges are beveled. While the edge beveling is designed to prevent this sort of problem, the damage is often done *before* the plate can be beveled. This problem is avoided when final plates are cut and beveled, and then, after complete cleaning, the diazo emulsion is applied by spin coating. This option does not exist for silver halides.

The cost of diazo coatings is relatively low despite its higher purity and lower defect level compared to silver halides. The same disadvantages apply to diazo emulsions, unfortunately, as were cited for silver halides. Diazos are soft, degrade rapidly in contact printing, and are usable for far fewer contact prints than can be obtained from a hard-surface mask.

Finally, diazo emulsions do not adhere well to glass, and adhesion problems may prevent good imaging yields in production. There are methods to help solve this problem, however. The resolution is better than for silver halides, but the image contrast is lower.

Resists as Mask Coatings

Photosensitive and electron-sensitive materials have been experimented with for use as masking mediums on glass. Resists offer several advantages for this application but have limitations that will most likely restrict their use to special market segment applications. Resists can be considered as soft-surface materials, even though they can be "toughened" through dips in strong oxidizing acids and exposure to a plasma-gas environment or heat and high-energy treatment. The most commonly used resist type for this application is a positive optical resist based on a diazo-naphthaquinone sensitizer and a novolak resin system.

Positive resists can be easily spin coated onto clean, dry glass blanks and imaged as they would normally be on a silicon wafer. The cost is low, and adhesion and optical properties are good, especially for deep-uv- and mid-uv-imaging applications since these resists have high absorbance in these regions. In fact, at 436 nm, where some of the positive resists have strong absorbance peaks, resist images would be good for use in optical stepping equipment.

One area that needs further experimentation in order for resist images to serve as mask materials is image transfer. The successful mask-blank coating will provide sufficient image contrast after the light passes through the mask so as to promote good modulation-transfer-function (MTF) values. The resist image would probably need to be dyed to build in a higher level of inherent optical contrast to better separate the light when the wafers are exposed through it. If a very high-contrast resist is used on the wafer being exposed, then a signal with an MTF as low as 35 percent may be sufficient. Typically, positive optical resists used to mask wafer oxides and other layers require a 60 percent MTF in the exposure energy pattern coming from the mask. Newer resists employed in bilevel and trilevel schemes can be used with lower MTF values.

Since the absorption spectra of a resist will largely determine its suitability as a mask-imaging or mask-patterning medium, we have listed the spectra of some current resists in Fig. 3-6. Note that the absorption peaks vary considerably. This opens up the possibility of using different resists at different wavelengths. Thus, one resist could be patterned onto a quartz blank and used directly as a mask in deep-uv exposure equipment. Other resists with high absorbance peaks in mid- and longer-wavelength uv could be similarly processed and used as projection masters in wafer-scanning and wafer-stepping exposure equipment. The ideal profile of a resist for this application has a sharply defined absorption peak that is coincident with the spectral output of the exposure aligner.

The other properties needed in this application are low defect levels and mechanical durability. We have mentioned treatments to improve durability that would provide nylon-brush and air- or water-spray resistance. The weak point in the area of durability for positive resists lies in their brittleness. Most positive resists are quite brittle and shatter readily when touched by a sharp-edged object such as the edge of wafer tweezers.

In terms of defect levels, positive resists fare about as well as the diazo emulsions mentioned previously in this chapter. Very high-level filtration and rapid softbaking is a key factor in preserving defect levels to less than $0.01/cm^2$. Future testing with positive resists that have had small dye additions might provide a low-cost, high-quality mask-imaging coating for production use. The strong point for resists is very high-resolution capabiliy, and if the other limitations can be partially or completely overcome, this would solve cost and defect problems associated with current materials such as chromium and iron oxide. The number of new positive-optical-resist chemistries now commercially available would encourage the would-be experimenter to pursue this approach.

Iron Oxide Coatings

Iron oxide has been developed as a see-through mask-coating material that has a hard surface. Its only common functional property with the positive optical resists just discussed is high transparency in the visible region of the spectrum, making alignment much simpler. Iron oxide

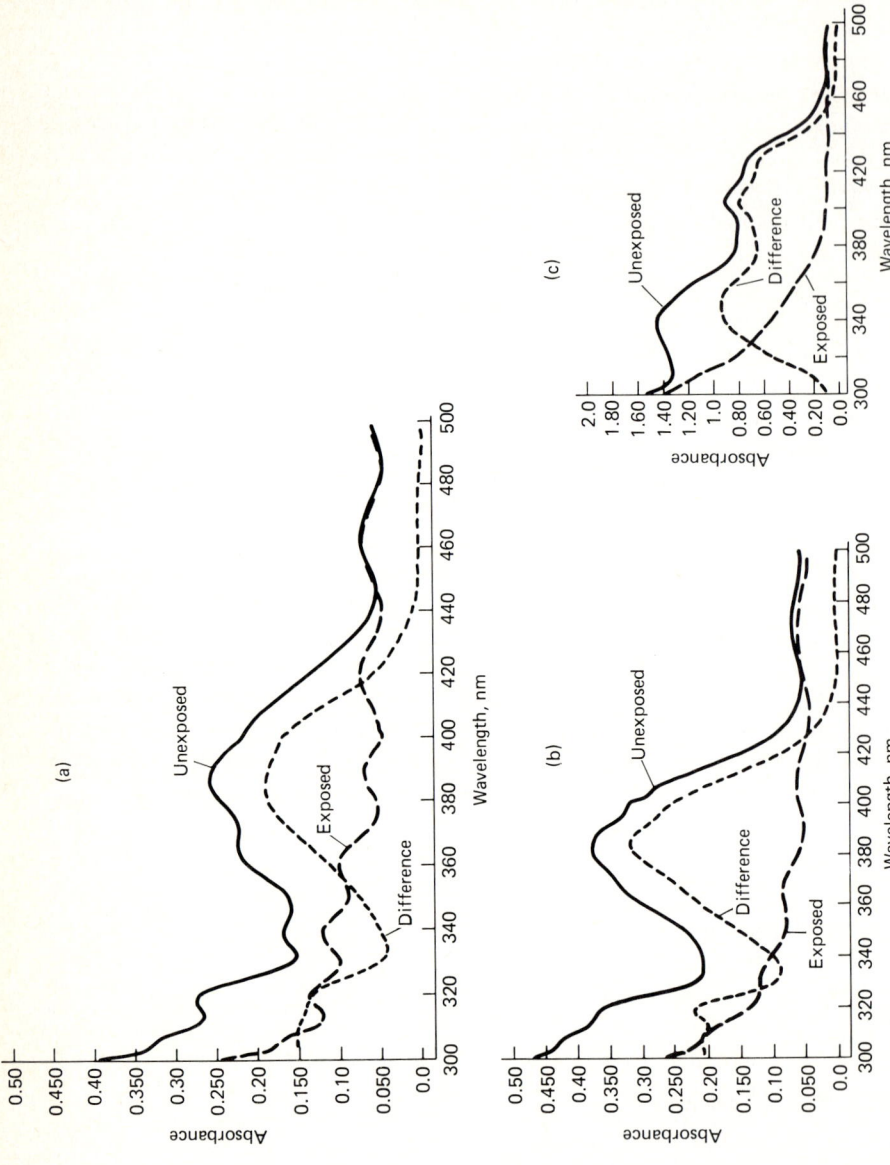

FIG. 3-6 Absorption spectra of some typical positive optical resists: (a) Microposit 2400 series photoresist, (b) Microposit 1300 series photoresist, (c) Microposit 111 series photoresist.

has many beneficial properties and few disadvantages as a mask-coating and mask-imaging material. The production use of this material for several years testifies to its suitability in this application. The combination of high density in the uv regions where it must stop exposing wavelengths is an ideal optical fit.

Iron oxide has very low reflectivity. This property solves the problems of unwanted resist exposure created by reflective mask materials such as chromium. Iron oxide also provides very simple processing with wide operating latitude. As a film, it is very durable and relatively hard, giving it good scratch resistance. The patterning of iron oxide with positive resist is easy for several reasons: the iron oxide surface is ideal for good resist adhesion; the resist need not be postbaked prior to etching, thus allowing the use of a wet process whereby plates go directly from the developer to the etchant; this process in turn, makes resist removal simple.

The hardness of iron oxide gives it a relatively good lifetime in production as well as mechanical resistance to handling with tweezers, scratches, and other normal process difficulties. Further, iron oxide is transparent to red and yellow light, and its optical density in the uv area, where stopping power is essential, is high. The contrast of signals put through iron oxide masks is good, primarily because of the good optical density shown in Fig. 3-7.

Another optical property that is important in mask use is transmittance in the red and infrared portions of the spectrum. These data for a Mettler Poliar iron oxide plate are shown in Fig. 3-8. The high values for infrared transmittance are important in maintaining good mask stability. The heat generated by the infrared wavelengths can cause considerable runout on VLSI masks. In some exposure aligners, special filters are incorporated to capture and reflect these wavelengths out of

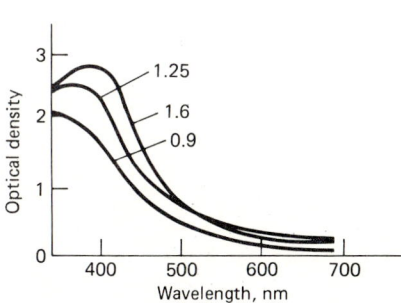

FIG. 3-7 Optical density of Mettler Poliar iron oxide. *(Mettler.)*

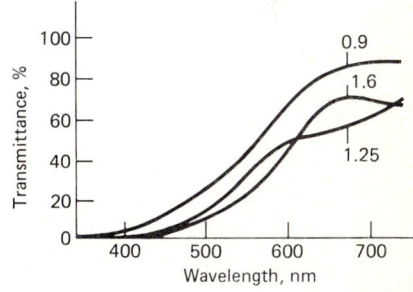

FIG. 3-8 Transmittance versus wavelength for Mettler Poliar iron oxide blanks. *(Mettler.)*

the optical path. Chromium will reflect some of these wavelengths but is much more prone to heating up.

The percent of reflected light is low with iron oxide. Figure 3-9 shows reflectance percent versus wavelength. At the wavelengths used for optical stepping (436 nm, 405 nm), the amount of reflected light is about 35 percent. This is extremely low in comparison with chromium and will certainly reduce the possibility of unwanted exposures caused by reflections during contact and proximity printing.

The functional properties of any given iron oxide layer will vary according to the method of deposition. Iron oxide can be applied by sputtering and by chemical-vapor deposition (CVD). When this material is deposited in a typical vacuum, there is the same level of buried particulates as occurs with any other vacuum applied material, such as chromium. These particulates come about from the mechanical abrasion of moving fixtures in the coating environment. The vacuum cycling of chamber components also gives rise to particle contamination during deposition.

In CVD, there are no rotating fixtures, and the direction taken by the material being deposited is not always from top to bottom or line of sight. Special precautions are taken to prevent contaminants from getting onto the substrate. The difference in defect density between vacuum-deposited materials and CVD-applied films is considerable. The typical figure for vacuum deposition is between 0.6 and 0.1 defect/cm^2.

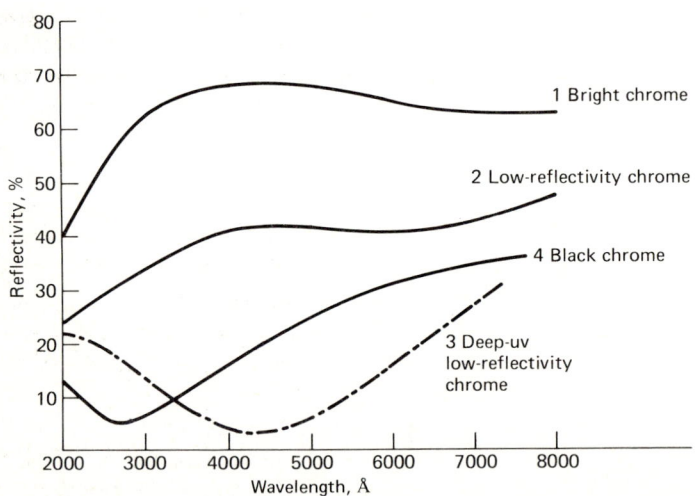

FIG. 3-9 **Reflectivity of several types of chrome films plotted against wavelength.** *(Balzers.)*

The defect levels in chemical-vapor deposition are much lower, on the order of 0.01 and 0.03 defect/cm^2.

Iron oxide has good resistance to most commonly used solutions and can be corrected for image defects more easily than chromium. In certain cleaning solutions there is a small amount of attack on the iron oxide. One solution used in production for iron oxide cleaning is Shipley Remover 1112A.

Overall, iron oxide possesses many desirable features for mask-making and is the second most popular material for hard-surface masking.

Chromium

Shiny chrome is the most popular hard-surface coating for glass blanks in VLSI mask-making applications. Chromium has proved successful as a high-resolution medium when used with positive optical resists. The one main difficulty with chromium is a high reflectivity, solved by using antireflection layers such as a second layer of chromium oxide. We will treat antireflective chromium separately.

The density of chromium is very high over a wide range of wavelengths. Densities are about 2 or greater between 3000 and 8000 Å with chrome-layer thicknesses as thin as 800 Å.

The adhesion of the chrome to the glass is aided when a chrome oxide forms at the glass interface. The chrome sensitivity to alkali ions coming out of regular soda-lime glass causes breakdown or etch of the chrome, leaving a void in the edge of a line and causing mouse-nipping.

Low-Reflectivity Chromium

The reflectivity of shiny chrome causes ghost images on the edges of resist patterns. The use of low-reflectivity or antireflective chrome solves this pattern-edge-exposure problem without taking away any of the other good functional properties of chrome films. There are several commerical types of antireflective chrome available from Japanese, European, and U.S. manufacturers.

Antireflective chrome is also called "black" chrome due to the very dark appearance of the composite film structure. Low-reflectivity chromium is produced by applying a thin layer of chrome oxide directly over the normal chromium layer. The preferred production technique is to keep the freshly coated chromium plate in the deposition environment and apply the chrome oxide immediately afterward. This minimizes the chance of particle contamination. The chromium is deposited to a thickness of 900 to 1100 Å or enough to achieve the required optical density. The chrome oxide layer is applied to achieve a reflectivity of less than 6 percent at the wavelengths where the resist is sensitive or has functional absorption. Functional absorption can be defined as those absorbing wavelengths that bring about an increase in the dissolution of the radiated areas in the developer. Straight optical absorption of a given resist system does not necessarily result in a corresponding change in the resist solubility behavior.

One of the primary functional requirements of the chrome oxide is that it etches uniformly in the same etching solutions as used for chrome, without undercutting the resist or adversely affecting the critical-dimension control parameters. The control to use in evaluating the chrome oxide layer is the standard chrome layer. The sharpness of the etched pattern edges of chrome oxide and chrome layers must be equivalent to the acuity of straight chrome patterns. The lower reflectivity of the chrome oxide chromium-compound layer typically results in an improvement in critical-dimension control compared to high-reflectivity chrome.

The reflectivity of various chrome coatings versus wavelength is given in Fig. 3-10. Note that bright-chrome reflectivity rises from about 40 percent at 2000 Å (where resists are not typically sensitive) to approximately 65 percent at 3000 Å wavelengths. The reflectance stabilizes at 300 nm and remains about the same across the range of wavelengths out to 800 nm. The second material shown is a chrome with some

FIG. 3-10 Programmable mask-cleaning equipment module.

reduction in reflectivity, brought about by either a change in the composition of the chrome (small amount of additive) or in the use of a separate antireflection coating. Reflection is still above 40 percent at the wavelengths where resist is sensitive. At this reflectance level, there would still be the problem of ghost-image generation.

Black chrome keeps a reflectance level below 20 percent in the wavelength range between 200 and 436 nm, the area where exposure equipment is used and resists are sensitive. Above 436 nm, black chrome reflectivity increases to about 35 percent, but in regions of no consequence. Low-reflectivity chrome films can be "toned" to provide both gold and black tones, and cleaning resistance is generally comparable to the iron oxide mask coatings, which is good provided cleaning solutions do not contain chemical agents that etch or react with the oxide.

GLASS-BLANK CLEANING PRIOR TO DEPOSITION OF THE MASKING LAYER

All glass blanks must be thoroughly cleaned prior to being placed in the vacuum-deposition, sputtering, or CVD environment. Cleaning is needed to remove chips of glass, dust particles, or other surface contaminants. A glass-cleaning procedure can vary considerably depending on the level of contamination suspected, how plates have been stored, the cleanness of the process area, and other variables. One technique that can be used to remove almost all forms of contamination is shown in Table 3-1.

Special cleaning equipment for ultrasonic, immersion, and spray treatment of glass blanks is used to implement various cleaning procedures in a production environment. These equipment systems are programmable to provide automatic cycling through the various solutions. All the solutions can be microfiltered to keep contamination at a minimum level. Figure 3-10 shows a typical piece of equipment used for plate cleaning. Highly aspirated spray, rotating plate holders, and ultrasonic energy are all examples of cleaning mechanisms employed to remove stubborn contaminants on blank surfaces.

High-resolution emulsions should be cleaned in ultrasonic processing systems with chemically pure, transistor- or VSLI-grade Freon TMC or similar solutions. All wetting and rinsing water should be deionized, and all solutions filtered to at least 0.45-μm pore-size absolute filters.

Glass-blank cleaning prior to deposition should also include an ionized air blow-off step to remove both dust and static electricity. A beta-ray static eliminator is one example of a device used to perform this function. Any technique that will generate high voltage makes the air conductive and thereby dissipates the static charges on the surface of the glass.

TABLE 3-1 *Glass-cleaning procedure prior to deposition (Hoya)*

Step	Procedure	Time	Temperature

1	Chromic acid immersion
	  Potassium bichromate, 400 g
	  Sulfuric acid (concd)—2000 mL
	  DI water—4000 mL
		100 min	50°C

2	DI water rinse	60 sec	Ambient
3	Second DI water rinse	60 sec	Ambient
4	Ammonium hydroxide neutralization	1 min	Ambient

5	Peroxide/hydroxide treatment
	  H_2O_2 (15%), 800 mL
	  Ammonium hydroxide, 800 mL
	  DI water, 4000 mL
	  (Mix directly before using)
		20 min	80°C

6	DI water rinse	15 min	Ambient
7	Ultrasonic methanol clean	5 min	Ambient
8	Store plates in methanol to keep clean and free from oxygen		
9	Before deposition, spin dry	20 sec, 4000 rpm	Ambient

GLASS-BLANK DEPOSITION TECHNIQUES

There are several methods used to apply mask coatings to glass blanks. These techniques include sputtering, chemical-vapor deposition, and vacuum deposition. A simple way to treat these techniques is to divide the vacuum from the nonvacuum technologies as follows:

Vacuum deposition method	Nonvacuum method
Sputtering Electron-beam evaporation Induction evaporation Flash evaporation Filament evaporation	Chemical-vapor deposition

Chemical-Vapor Deposition

Chemical-vapor deposition (CVD) is a very popular technique for applying thin uniform dielectric films onto both mask blanks and silicon wafers. Silicon dioxide and iron oxide are applied with this technique. The principal mechanism of CVD is one of decomposing or thermally reacting gas combinations or compounds that in a reaction chamber will form very stable films on the substrate placed in the chamber. CVD equipment can be configured several ways and requires a relatively high level of control to maintain proper film structure and reproducible layer thickness. All systems provide good control of the raw-material gases that are bled into the reaction chamber. These gas mixtures are kept under close parametric control. The operating parameters will vary according to the type of system used.

CVD reactors can be vertically, horizontally, or cylindrically oriented, as shown in Fig. 3-11. The vertical reactors have the glass blanks placed onto susceptors at the base of the reaction chamber, and the gas mixtures come up through the susceptor area as indicated in the figure. In the horizontal reactor type, there are two ways of providing the coated film. The older technique involves bleeding gas in one end of the chamber, across the glass blanks, and then out the opposite end. A variation on this method, developed to provide more uniform layer thicknesses, is a gas-blanketed downflow system.

The gas-blanketed approach has the gas coming down from the top (vertically) of the chamber. In production, the blanks would be conveyed through a nitrogen curtain and into the reaction chamber. As they move through the chamber, under precisely controlled conditions of gas flow, pressure, and temperature, the dielectric oxide layer is applied. Finally, the blanks are conveyed back out of the chamber through another nitrogen curtain that keeps the reaction gases contained and insulates the inside of the chamber from a contaminating outside environment.

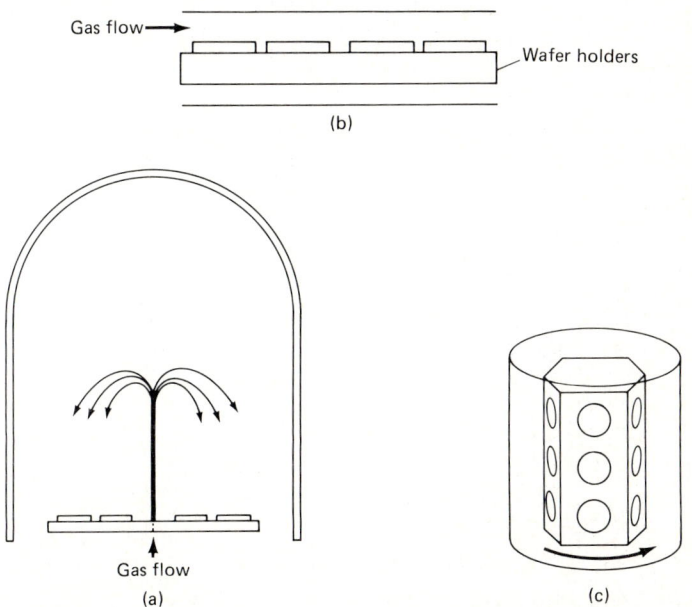

FIG. 3-11 CVD reactor types: (*a*) vertical, (*b*) horizontal, and (*c*) cylindrical. [*Ref. 8.*]

In the reaction chambers, the walls are a factor in the result obtained. "Cold-wall" reactors are ones in which reactions are slow to take place on the walls as opposed to the reactions occurring on the susceptors where the substrates are placed. The substrates are heated to temperatures much higher than the walls in a cold-wall system, thereby giving rise to the name of this reactor type. Cold-wall chemical-vapor deposition is achieved by two different forms of heating. In one case, an rf coil provides heat to a carbon susceptor, and glass blanks on the susceptor are heated to the prescribed temperature by conduction. The other method of heating in the cold-wall CVD reactor is by ultraviolet (uv) lamps that irradiate the wafers. In both rf and uv heating approaches, the wafers are heated fairly rapidly, followed by heating of the balance of the reaction chamber and its walls. CVD takes place at a much more rapid rate in the susceptor area than on the walls.

The heating principle for hot-wall CVD systems is thermal resistance, similar to the operation of a diffusion furnace. In hot-wall systems the thermal mass is much higher than in cold-wall systems, requiring longer times to heat and cool substrates. Also, the hot-wall system typically does not have the high rate of gas flow that the cold-wall system does. The higher rate of material deposition on reactor walls in hot-wall systems means more frequent cleaning is necessary in order to prevent flakes from dropping off and onto the substrates.

All CVD reactions have by-products. These are removed or exhausted by the pressure created by the flow of gas products in the chamber. The adhesion of the iron oxide to the substrate (glass blank) is aided by the energy of the deposited material forming on the glass. The uniformity of layers applied with CVD techniques is good, approximating that of sputtering. The fresh iron oxide coming out of a CVD reactor already possesses the excellent optical properties needed in masking: good transmission in the red and green wavelengths and high absorption in the blue and uv regions.

Freshly deposited iron oxide is tested immediately for reflective interference. The formula for determining interference minima is

$$2ne + z = \lambda k$$

where e = layer thickness
k = any number
n = refractive index
λ = wavelength
z = phase variation at air-oxide and oxide-glass interface

Thus, any optical thickness that is a multiple of $\lambda/2$ will provide maximum transmittance and minimum interference. Iron oxide coatings are generally to a thickness of 2500 Å, where they provide high-resolution images and good optical properties. In monitoring the quality of the final film, it is necessary to check for possible side-wall contaminants that might have co-deposited with the film. These types of contaminants can lead to poor resist adhesion, which in turn can cause rough edges in the iron oxide images. Close quality control of the entire CVD process, including good equipment maintenance, is important.

Some masks are used that employ a silicon coating. Silicon is hard, giving it good durability and long mask life. The CVD reaction to produce polycrystalline (short-range crystal) structure is

$$SiH_4 + heat \xrightarrow[H_2]{825-1100°C} Si + 2H_2$$
$$\text{(carrier)}$$

This same reaction will also take place with nitrogen as the carrier gas, run at around 650°C. The conditions for silicon formation are the absence of crystalline structure on the substrate and a deposition temperature below that required for single-crystal growth. Also, this material deposits best with very high deposition rates. The regulation of gas flow rate and reaction-chamber temperature will determine the final crystal structure. In summary, the major variables determining the quality of material deposition are

1. Type of gases
2. Gas(es) concentration
3. Flow rate of gases
4. Reactor design
5. Process temperature and control

Vacuum Deposition

There are many types of vacuum-deposition equipment, each with its own set of specific parameters, advantages, and disadvantages. There are some common denominators for all these systems, including

1. An enclosed area in which a vacuum can be provided
2. Software and hardware to manage the system parameters, including vacuum level, valve condition, and deposition layer thickness
3. Vacuum pump(s) to evacuate as much of the vacuum environment as possible
4. Material-deposition hardware

Vacuum chambers originally were glass bell-jar types, as shown in Fig. 3-11b. More recent systems are constructed with stainless steel, allowing for much more variety in size and shape. The pumps that evacuate the area under the bell-jar or vacuum-chamber enclosure are indicated in the figure, including a roughing pump for removing most of the air and an oil-diffusion pump for final vacuum "pull."

Sputtering, one of the most popular methods for applying chromium layers, works on the principle of electric discharge between two electrodes. The process occurs at a pressure of a few millitorrs; the low pressure causes the cathode to give up atoms which then coat the anode. When the vacuum chamber has been properly evacuated, inert-gas ions enter the chamber. These readily ionize when an electric field is introduced. The high-energy ionized atoms then bombard the target, a piece of chromium. If chromium atoms are to be dislodged, the energy bonding the individual chromium atoms together must be less than the incident energy of the bombarding ions. As the chromium atoms are sputtered off, they go to the opposite electrical end of the system.

Sputtering is done with rf and dc voltages and provides good adhesion of deposited material since the chrome or other particles reach the substrate with high energy values. Other advantages of sputtering include simple fixturing of the substrate, high rates of material deposition, and high coating-layer homogeneity. Sputtering provides about 10 times the adhesion of evaporation techniques in which the resist material reaches the substrate with very low energy values. One technique to provide even greater bonding of the coated film is bias sputtering, where the substrate is etched during the deposition process to provide maximum surface cleanliness. Ion bombardment before the deposition process accomplishes the same result. This technique is reported to provide better adhesion than its counterpart in vacuum evaporation, the glow discharge.

Some of the disadvantages or shortcomings of sputtering are substrate heating, causing possible distortions to the glass blank; higher level of operator training needed than for evaporation methods; high-energy-particle damage to the substrate; and more complex equipment. Triode, tetrode, and other sputtering-discharge methods are applied at low pressures. The advantage of this is the high-purity materials obtained at high efficiencies. Triode and tetrode sputtering are more expensive and more complex than simpler anode/cathode (rf/dc) configurations.

The reflectivity of sputtered chrome is about 60 to 65 percent, compared to vacuum-evaporated films, which have only about 50 percent reflectivity. The higher reflectivity is generally indicative of a denser film layer. Iron oxide is also applied by sputtering.

Evaporation

Vacuum evaporation is another deposition technique commonly used to apply chromium and other films used in mask fabrication. Chromium is vacuum-evaporated by heating at pressures of 10^{-5} to 10^{-6} torr. The melting temperature of chromium is 1900°C, and it has a sublimation temperature of 2200°C (only 1500 to 1600°C at 10^{-3} to approximately 10^{-2} torr). At these high temperatures, chromium is reduced to a vapor and coats the substrate.

The cooling chromium creates extremely high surface tension between itself and the underlying glass blank. A 1000-Å-thick layer will typically result in a tension force of 10,000 kg/cm^2.

Unlike sputtering, chrome evaporated at the glass surface bonds with relatively low energy. Since the bonding energy of the chrome to the glass is a function of arrival energy, evaporative chrome adhesion is relatively low. The evidence for this low adhesion may surface when the coated blank is cleaned and the chrome lifts off. One deposition technique used to overcome this liability is heating the glass substrate, thereby raising the surface energy of glass molecules and causing a stronger glass-chromium bond. A standard technique to help provide uniform chrome layers is substrate rotation during the deposition process.

Evaporation approaches include the following:

1. Crucible
2. Filament
3. Flash
4. Induction
5. Electron-beam

Crucible Evaporation

The old crucible method of evaporation made very efficient use of chromium, but was quite slow. The pressure of volume-production cost-efficient use of capital equipment requires good substrate throughput.

Filament Evaporation

Filament evaporation is relatively simple, as diagrammed in Fig. 3-12. The principle of operation is one of placing high-purity chromium wire above a filament and providing current to the filament. As the temperature increases in the filament, the chromium will first melt and flow

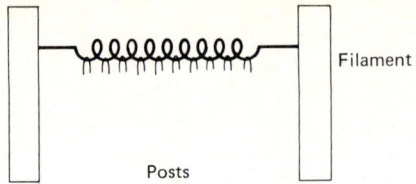

FIG. 3-12 Principle of filament evaporation. [*Ref. 8.*]

onto the filament. Once the filament is covered with chrome, the voltage is increased, and the evaporation of chrome takes place. Filament evaporation, as you can see, is relatively straightforward, but contamination may arise from the filament or other sources.

Flash Evaporation

Flash evaporation, like the filament-evaporation method, employs a thermal-resistance heating technique as well. However, flash evaporation operates by routing the chrome, which enters as a powder, pellet, or spool-fed wire, onto a ceramic bar that is then heated to "flash off" to chrome. Figure 3-13 shows a diagram of a typical flash-evaporation setup. The main advantages of flash methods are good throughput and reduced contamination as compared to filament evaporation. The ceramic material used to flash the chrome is an inherently cleaner material than filament materials. Also, unlike filament methods, composite materials can be evaporated.

Induction Evaporation

Induction evaporation employs a radio-frequency source to heat the chromium in the crucible, indicated in Fig. 3-14. The configuration shown will allow evaporation to occur in certain areas only.

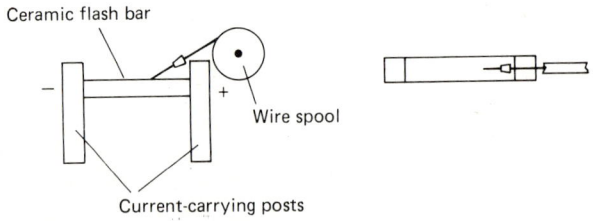

FIG. 3-13 Principle of flash evaporation. [*Ref. 8.*]

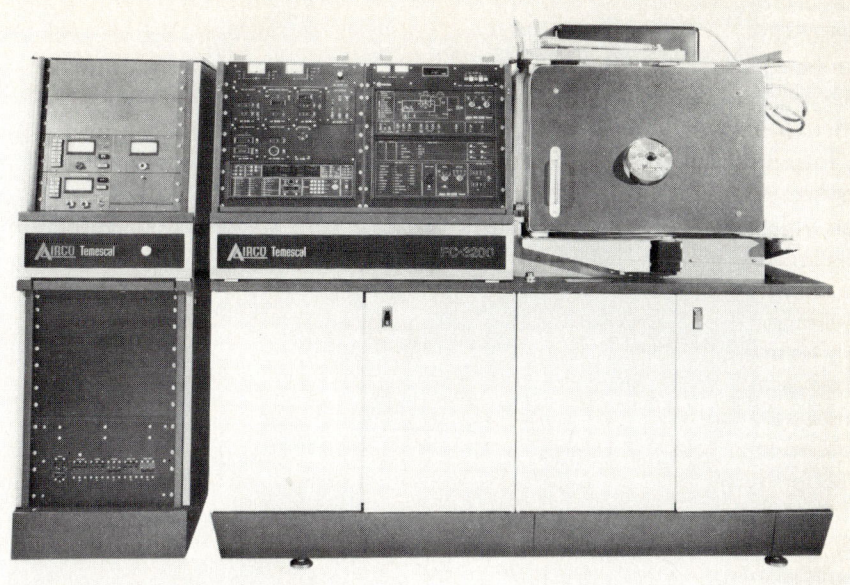

FIG. 3-14 Electron-beam evaporator.

General Vacuum Deposition Criteria

All the vacuum metallization methods discussed must provide very high-quality films to be useful in producing VLSI-grade substrates. All the substrates that enter the vacuum environment need to be rigorously cleaned to avoid contaminating both the vacuum system and the layer being deposited. All deposited films must be extemely uniform (± 50 Å) to help provide good critical-dimension control in mask-imaging operations. The adhesion of the deposited layer must be sufficiently strong to survive cleaning, resist imaging, etching, and yet another cleaning operation. Further, the mask will be repeatedly cleaned as it collects dust and other contaminants from use in exposure equipment. Adhesion must also be uniform, since changes in adhesion can cause unpredictable and random changes in pattern widths in etching. A good quality-control procedure will ensure that all the above factors are provided on an ongoing basis in production.

REFERENCES

1. Mettler Optic AG: *Data Sheet on Poliar Ironoxide Photoplates*, Greifensee, Switzerland, 1979.
2. BMI Technical Data on Processing of Glass Blanks.

3. Agfa-Gevaert: *Data Sheet on Millimask HD System,* Mortsel, Belgium, 1978.
4. Stelter, M. K., and K. H. Paterson: "Evaluation of Photomask Materials and Their Effect on Yield," *SPIEJ* **80** p. 47, 1976.
5. Uchiya, Fumitoshi: private communication, Hoya Corporation, Tokyo.
6. Triacca, Joe: private communication, Photronics Labs, Brookfield, Conn.
7. Harada, S., and F. Uchiya: *IC Photomask Blanks Meet Stringent Requirements,* Hoya Electronics Co., Ltd., Tokyo.
8. Fairchild Corporation: *Semiconductor and Integrated Circuit Fabrication Techniques,* Reston, Reston, Va., 1979, chap. 12, p. 111 and chap. 13, p. 120.

4
Substrate Imaging

INTRODUCTION

Imaging coated mask and reticle substrates is the most critical step in the mask-fabrication sequence. Much that has been done prior to the imaging step was to prepare for the rigors of high-resolution image formation. The imaging process takes advantage of the high-quality glass and its flatness features. The uniformity of the layer to be imaged and the layer to be etched are held to tight tolerances so that the imaging step will result in uniformly sized patterns across the entire active field. Since the imaging processes actually form the mask and reticle patterns, albeit with the help of a uniform substrate and coated layer, much attention is given to this step. The imaging capability, with respect to resolution and line-geometry control, really drives mask technology. Substrate, metallization, and etching technology tend to fall into line when imaging capabilities are extended to a new level.

There are many different pathways to be taken between the digitized pattern files and the wafer. Figure 4-1 shows the variety of different process options available to arrive at a mask or a means of patterning the wafer. The trends in mask imaging have generally been toward a shorter process between the pattern data in the digitizer and the wafer-imaging operation. Earlier process sequences would begin with the pattern generator to produce a light-field emulsion reticle, typically at $10\times$. This reticle was then contact-printed to yield a dark-field emulsion reticle. The third generation was a contact print of the intermediate emulsion $10\times$ reticle to a hard-surface blank. The fourth-generation step was to take the hard-surface reticle and step-and-repeat it into $1\times$ emulsion master masks. In the fifth-generation step, these were contact-printed emulsion masters that were contact-printed with sixth-generation

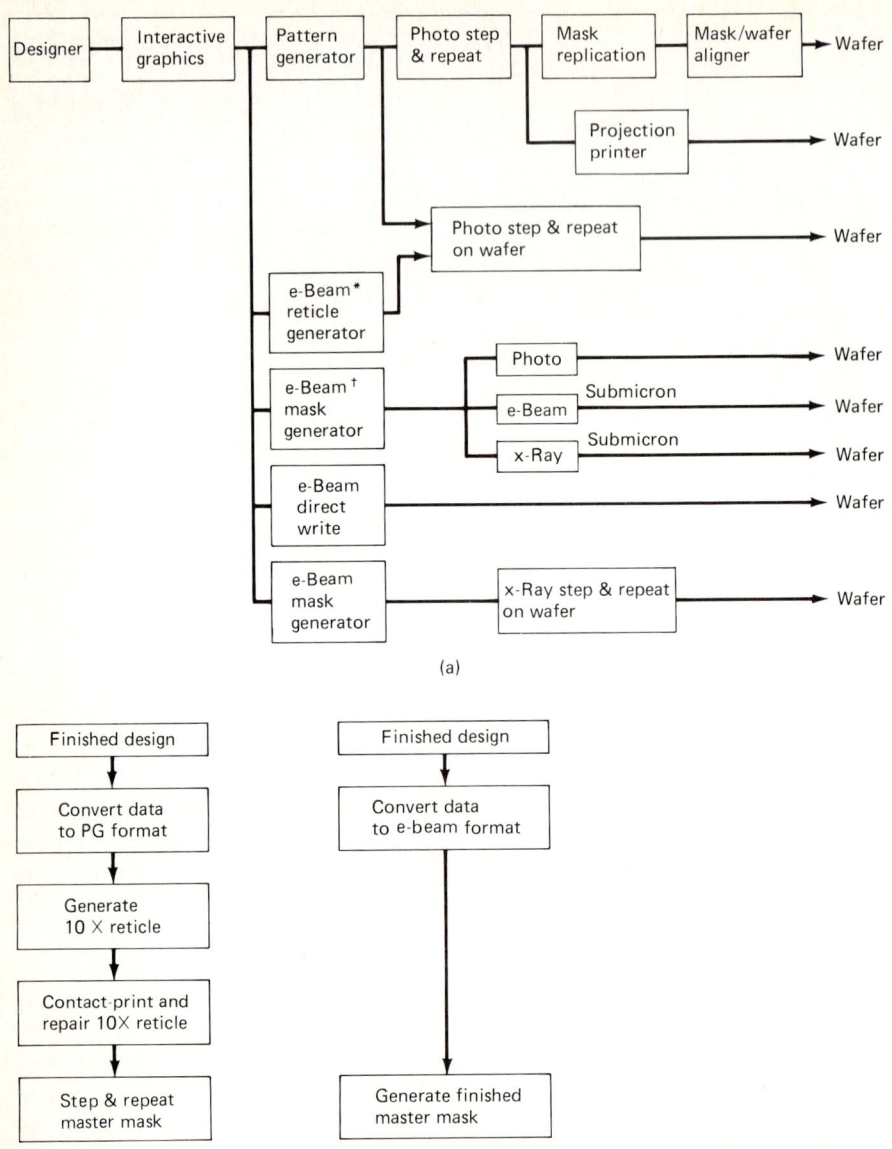

FIG. 4-1 (a) Process steps for various mask-making approaches. (b) Optical versus e-beam processing for master-mask production. * At 2:1 for geometries between 1 and 2.5 μm. † 1:1 for geometries >2.5 μm.

hard-surface working plates. Overall, a considerable amount of processing and loss of resolution is due to so many intermediate steps.

In this chapter we will discuss electron-beam-imaging and optical-imaging techniques used at various levels in the mask-fabrication process. Exposure equipment and resist-imaging parameters are discussed in detail. Emphasis is placed on managing various process steps to achieve a high level of pattern-geometry control. The developing process is discussed including solvent developers for electron-beam resists and aqueous developers for positive optical resists. Optical parameters including MTF, depth of focus, and reflectance are reviewed in terms of their impact in the image-patterning and transfer processes. The evolution of a more complex imaging process toward simpler and more direct conversion of VLSI design data to finished masks and reticles is also covered.

IMAGING

Resist and emulsion imaging tends to stand out among the various mask-fabrication steps, perhaps because of its degree of difficulty and the yield leverage it exerts. This step begins with the mask blank that has been coated with either an emulsion layer or a chromium layer and subsequently prepared (cleaned, deionized) for imaging. In the case of emulsion materials, imaging simply involves exposing the light-sensitive layer and then developing it to create a partial relief structure. Where light strikes a silver halide emulsion and developing takes place, silver salts are converted to metallic silver and form an opaque area that serves nicely as an optical mask.

Hard-surface mask imaging involves application of a resist layer to the chromium, or other hard-surface material, followed by the image-forming steps of exposure and development. Imaging is a critical step since much can go wrong, and a fair degree of process control is therefore used to keep the image-formation parameters within process specification.

Mask pattern data are taken from magnetic tape and sent into one of many possible processes to generate a finished reticle or 1× master. Examples of the types of masks imaged are shown in the following series of photographs.

Figure 4-2 shows a multiple-image 1× master mask that is used in several types of wafer aligner, including contact, soft-contact, proximity, and projection. Note the number of die sites reserved for testing the alignment, focus, and resolution of the pattern and equipment. These test dice are placed at strategic locations and will identify such problems as nonuniform light intensity, warped wafers, or poor light collimation.

96 INTEGRATED CIRCUIT MASK TECHNOLOGY

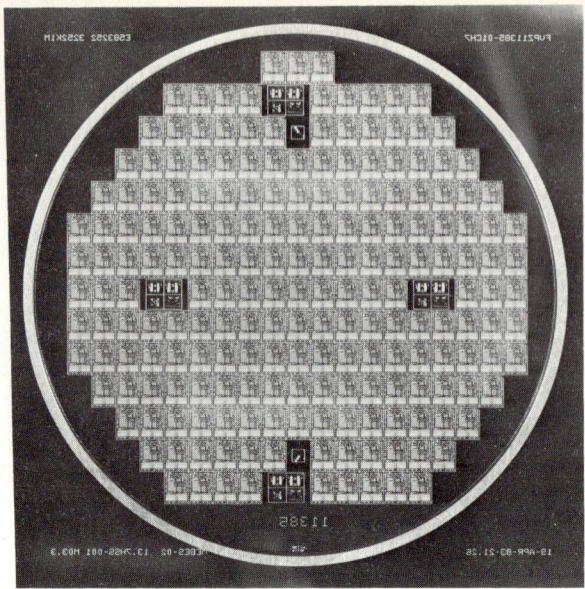

FIG. 4-2 A pellicized multiple-image 1× master (5×5). *(RCA, Solid State Division.)*

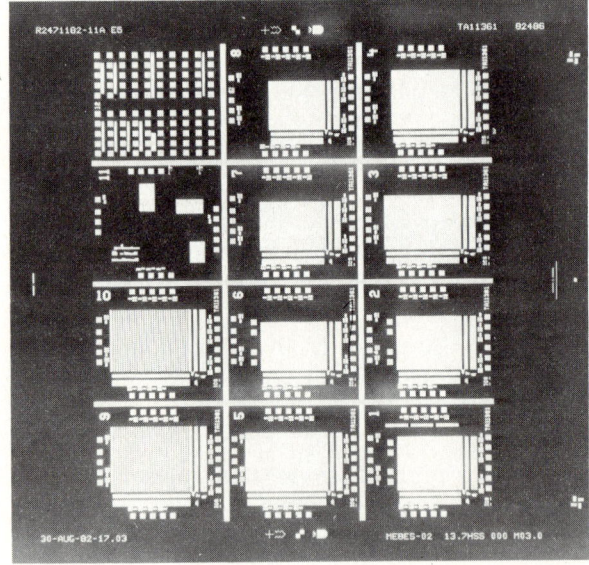

FIG. 4-3 A 10× multiple-image reticle. *(RCA, Solid State Division.)*

The master mask, shown in Fig. 4-2, is a pellicized multiple-image 1× master (5×5). Note the ring surrounding the active area where the membrane is supported. Pellicles protect the image from contamination and thereby reduce the amount of cleaning needed in a mask's production life.

Figure 4-3 is a 10× multiple-image reticle used on a wafer stepper. This particular reticle covers a 384-mil-square area and is typical of the type of mask needed to support the large increase in direct-step-on-wafer units.

The mask photo in Fig. 4-4 portrays a multiple-image 2× reticle that would be placed in a Canon step-and-repeat camera. This pattern represents a charge-coupled pattern device (CCD). The pattern shown will be repeatedly imaged onto production wafers with the step-and-repeat camera. Thus, the term "reticle" refers to a pattern on glass used as a tool or master pattern for yet another imaging step.

Figure 4-5 is a single-image 10× reticle used in a wide-field step-and-repeat machine. The use of more than just one image on a reticle fills up the imaging lens and limits movement of the stage during

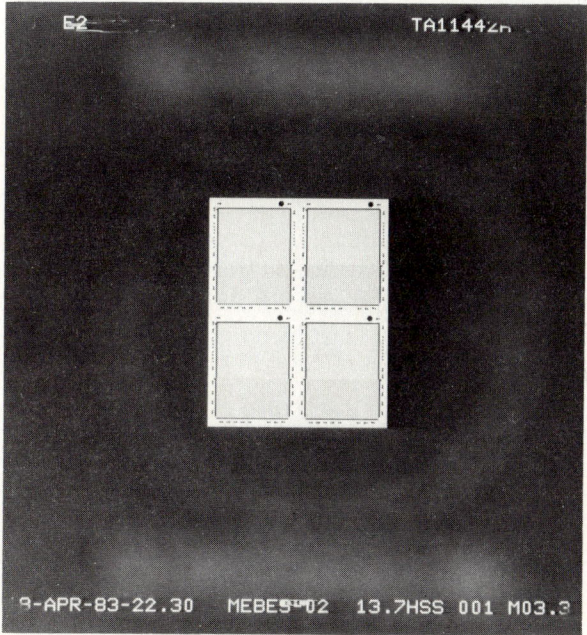

FIG. 4-4 A multiple-image 2× reticle for use in a Canon step-and-repeat aligner, TRE aligner, or similar exposure system. *(RCA, Solid State Division.)*

98 INTEGRATED CIRCUIT MASK TECHNOLOGY

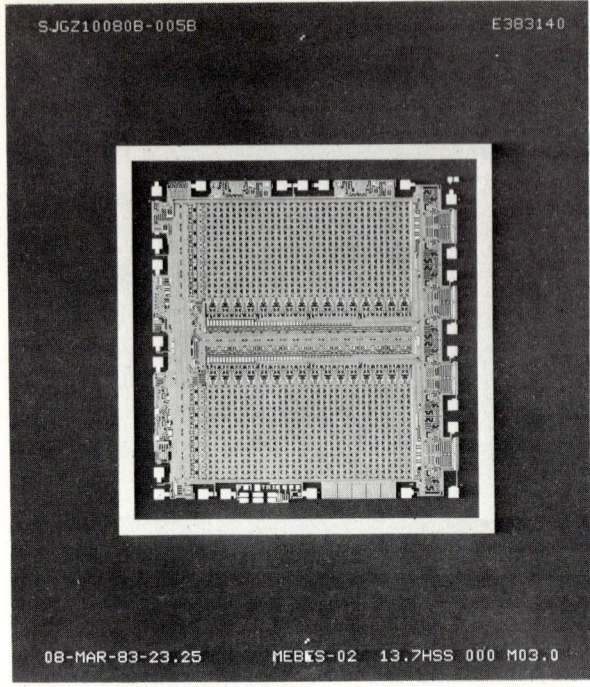

FIG. 4-5 A single-image 10× reticle (5 × 5) for a wide-field step-and-repeat camera. *(RCA, Solid State Division.)*

imaging. The presence of several images at 10× in the reticle allows the operator to select and pellicize a "perfect" pattern.

A multiple-image 1× CCD reticle is shown in Fig. 4-6. This is a CCD reticle to be used in an Ultratech 1X step-and-repeat camera. These photos represent a few of the various types of mask and reticle patterns employed in VLSI device production. The particular examples shown are black chrome masks, although many masks and reticles are imaged with bright chromium as the mask medium.

Photoresists and emulsions are both exposed in optical-flash equipment where a series of software-driven movements propels the blank to all of the thousands of exposure locations needed to create the IC image.

ELECTRON-BEAM IMAGING

Electron-beam exposure of resists for mask imaging has been established as a viable method for VLSI device mask production. The parallel

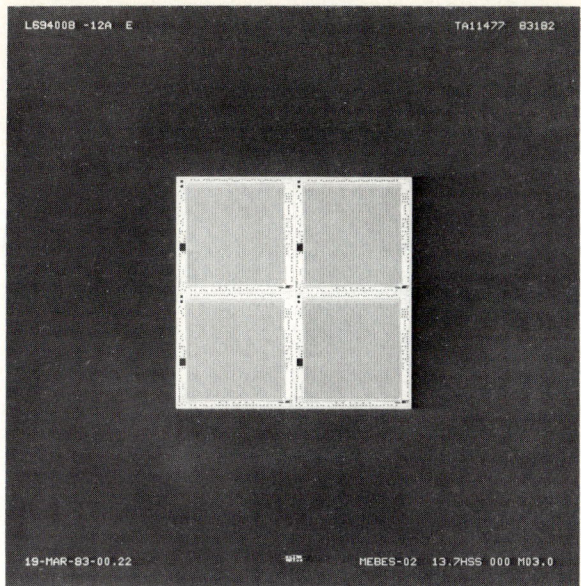

FIG. 4-6 A multiple-image 1× CCD reticle for a Canon step-and-repeat camera. *(RCA, Solid State Division.)*

development of resists sensitive to electron-beam energy and exposure equipment to deliver the energy doses needed has resulted in systems and processes for volume production. The mask industry has needed a high-resolution imaging tool that provides rapid turnaround on new mask-pattern designs, and the electron-beam approach has provided the means to do this.

The development of electron-beam writing tools for microlithography stems from their inherent resolution potential and capability. Also, electron-beam-imaging systems can be software driven to write any sequence and configuration of pattern elements needed to create a given set of masks. The smaller dimensions required for mask-making brought the need for closer layer-to-layer registration tolerances. Larger chips created time pressure on the optical equipment used to pattern 4× and 10× reticles, so electron-beam writing was used to generate reticles with better turnaround. The new, complex designs for these large chips also went through a series of timely design and mask-set evaluations before being reduced to production. The electron-beam writing approach allowed for quick test design, saving precious time in the commercialization of a new semiconductor device.

A popular way to increase profitability of a given IC design is to shrink the overall dimensions, a process called "scaling." The reduction of all the dimensions sometimes causes lithography problems on one or two areas of the device, perhaps at only one mask level. This lack of good scaling behavior is corrected by changing only part of the design, a debugging process made easier by electron-beam (e-beam) generation of test masks. Rapid tooling for scaled down designs is a major e-beam-imaging application.

In summary, the benefits of e-beam technology for mask fabrication and eventual device writing are

1. Rapid turnaround on new designs and scaled designs.
2. Unlimited device size (larger chips)
3. Reduced defects (vacuum-processed)
4. Software capabilities (changing pattern and feature sizes easily)
5. Compensation for distortions
6. Beam writing directly onto surface
7. Submicron resolution
8. Good critical-dimension control
9. Good overlay and registration accuracy

Rapid Turnaround

The turn-around capability is illustrated in Fig. 4-7. Note the time requirements for masks processed through the optical shop compared to the rapid and direct route to test for an e-beam-generated reticle or mask. The designs that are extremely complex, requiring over 2 million individual "flashes" or exposures on an optical pattern generator, require over 90 hr of running time on most optical equipment; comparable processing on an e-beam machine can finish these in 1 to 2 hr. These complex devices, called "megaflash" chips, are widely used for memory applications. In a more conventional cycle, a design must pass through all the steps of the process for testing (see Fig. 4-7b). Several months may be spent confirming the production readiness of the design. Megaflash devices are quickly debugged, and mask sets are generated by using e-beam writing.

Optical versus Electron-Beam Processes

The comparison of processes used in optical and e-beam mask fabrication shows the elimination of the need for a $10\times$ reticle in the case of electron-beam. By removing the $10\times$ reticle and subsequent contact-

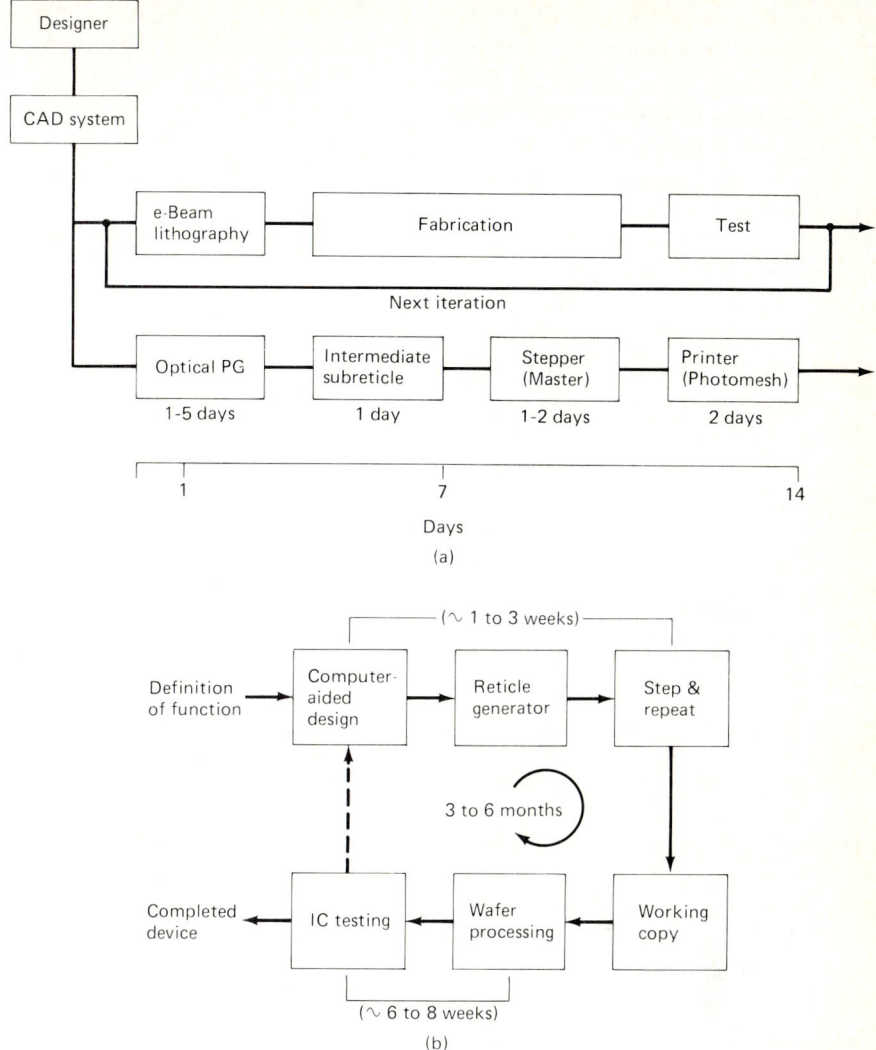

FIG. 4-7 (a) Development cycle of IC design from CAD through chip testing. (b) Comparison of e-beam and optical masks for optimizing design for quick turnaround. *(Varian, Extrion Division.)*

print step, e-beam processing bypasses two defect-collecting operations. In optical processes, a pattern-generated reticle must be inspected and repaired. The $10\times$ reticle should be almost perfect so that masks stepped at $1\times$ are free of defects. The reticle can have, at $10\times$, some small incursions on lines as well as defects that, when reduced 10 times, essentially disappear. This is one of the inherent advantages of working at 10 times the final circuit size. Shorter runs on complex device designs are a major advantage and strong role for electron-beam-imaging systems. Despite many resolution and throughput improvements made in optical pattern generators and image-repeater systems, the overall time required to generate test masks cannot compete with the time factors for e-beam-generated masks. Figure 4-7*b* shows the rapid cycle possible with e-beam masks.

Finally, optical systems are prey to dust and optical-distortion limits as well as field-size limitations. These inherent problems limit the output and resolution quality of an optical shop in producing completely defect-free reticles for large-area memories. The result for mask makers is a hybrid of optical- and electron-beam-imaging tools, each being used in the application and area of greatest advantage.

Raster versus Vector Scan

Two primary types of beam scanning are used with electron-beam-imaging systems, raster and vector scan. These are compared in principle in Fig. 4-8.

In raster scan, the patterns are made by running the beam in a back-and-forth, ploughed-field manner. The electron energy is allowed to expose or "blank" only where the pattern is to be made, by use of a shutter device in the system. The raster scan thus passes over every possible address area on a mask substrate. The simplicity of running a beam in "off-on" modes over a given area gives it a relatively good writing rate capability, despite the fact that it covers a larger number of spots or data points on the substrate. The EBES system is based on this principle. One problem with raster-scan writing is "butting error," where a discontinuity occurs as the beam crosses a writing-field boundary.

Vector scan has a less restricted beam-movement strategy wherein the beam moves only to areas where pattern data are required. The beam exposes resist in these areas and then is directed to the next area for feature exposure. In the writing mode, a vector-scan machine uses several exposure methods to fill in the pattern area, including a raster scan and a variable spot-size and shape exposure. It can also be programmed to outline the area to be patterned, and then use wide-area exposures to fill in the area. The approach uses fewer addresses, and improvements in blanking schemes with variable spot sizes and variable-shaped beam patterns have given greater throughput with this method. Vector scan shares with raster scan the problem of butting error. Vector-scan machines are supplied by several companies, as are raster-scan units, as listed in Table 4-1.

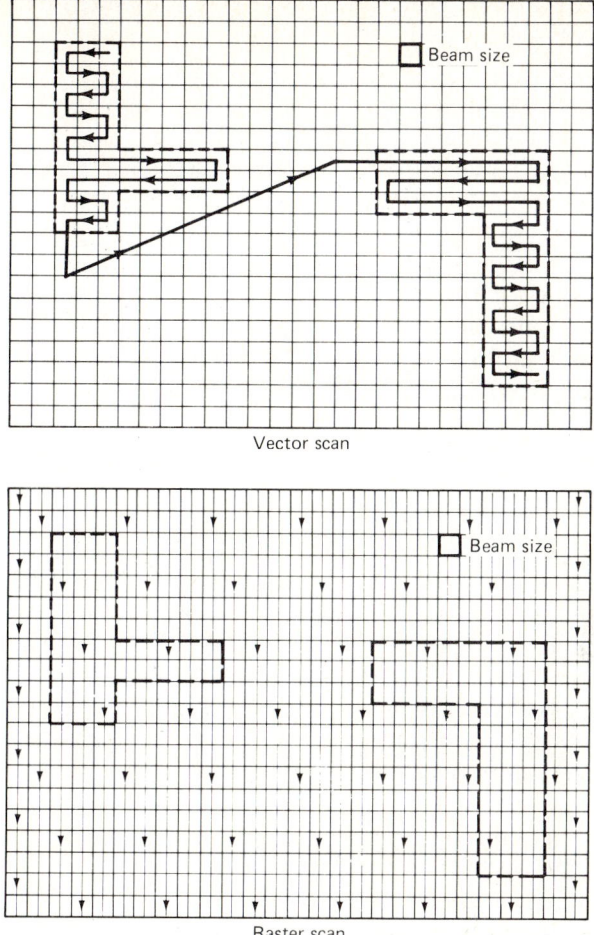

FIG. 4-8 Raster and vector-scan writing with an electron beam.

This list is expanding constantly, and the variety of stage-motion options as well as writing strategies gives the mask manufacturer considerable choice in matching a system to fit an application.

The production use of these systems has caused a drop in the cost of reticles. For example, a $10\times$ reticle costing approximately \$800 in 1977 would now cost about \$2. The improvement in e-beam machines is responsible for much of the cost reduction. Electron-beam-generated masks show similar cost reductions. A 3-in array that had a cost of \$250 in 1977 would now cost less than \$50 if it is produced with a shaped-

TABLE 4-1 Electron-beam vector- and raster-scan equipment suppliers

Manufacturer	Stage motion	Writing strategy	Class
Cambridge	Step and repeat	Vector and round gaussian	Laboratory
EBM	Step and repeat	Vector and multibeam	Laboratory
ETEC	Continuous	Raster and round gaussian	Manufacturing
GCA	Step and repeat	Vector and variable shaped	Manufacturing
Hewlett-Packard	Step and repeat	Raster and round gaussian	Manufacturing
Hughes	Step and repeat	Vector and variable shaped	Laboratory
IBM	Step and repeat	Vector and variable shaped	Manufacturing
JEOL	Step and repeat	Vector and variable shaped	Laboratory and manufacturing
Microbit	Step and repeat	Vector and fly's eye, single beam	—
Philips	Step and repeat	Vector and round gaussian	Manufacturing
Thompson CSF	Continuous	Vector and variable shaped	Laboratory
Texas Instruments	Step and repeat	Vector and round uniform	Manufacturing
Toshiba	Continuous	Raster and round gaussian	Manufacturing
Varian	Continuous	Raster and round gaussian	Manufacturing
Veeco	Step and repeat	Vector and fly's eye, single beam	—
Western Electric	Continuous	Raster and round gaussian	Manufacturing

beam writing system. The advancements made in computer language also reduce the cost and time required for producing a given reticle or mask. This time is referred to as pattern-conversion time.

ELECTRON-BEAM SYSTEM CAPABILITIES

The commercially available systems for e-beam writing feature a variety of options, but certain "core" capabilities are regarded as standard. The list of these features includes

1. 1-μm geometries
2. 40-Mhz data rate
3. $\frac{1}{64}$-nm stage-postion resolution
4. Deflection-distortion correction
5. Computer-linked diagnostics center
6. Solid-state pattern memory (4 to 8 Mbytes)
7. LaB_6 single-crystal cathode
8. 1-mm deflection field

Throughput

These features are typical for the most popular systems in production throughout the world, using raster-scan writing methods. The throughput is largely a function of address size, which in turn is determined by the minimum feature size. For example, a 0.5-µm spot size used on a mask with 2 to 3 µm geometries and 35 percent image area will require about 3 hr of run time to produce a 4-in, 1× mask. A 10× reticle using the same pattern will require about 1.3 hr at 2.5 MHz. Higher data rates will reduce this time considerably. Writing at 40 MHz with an air-to-air autoload and four-position cure chamber, a 10-mask set can be completely written in under 4 hr! This assumes a 30-min cure time for the negative resist. Better e-beam resists with reduced cure times will shorten the overall process time if the write time goes below 30 min. When writing at 20 MHz, the same 10-mask set would require just under 8 hr. Since these machines are run on 7-hr shifts, two shifts per day and overtime if needed, payback on a $2 to 3 million machine can be rapid if the unit is kept running, producing volumes of near-perfect 10× reticles. The most important factor in justifying a major capital outlay of this magnitude is productivity. For the same amount of capital several optical steppers can be purchased and kept equally productive with perhaps wider process flexibility (wafer and mask imaging).

Key features important to producing high-quality reticles and masks are automatic substrate handling rapid writing rates (40 MHz), a bright electron source, wide-stage travel (6 to 7 in), and large pattern memory. Rapid conversion of pattern data is important. A 30-min production time for a master mask (to produce a 200×, 200-mil chip) is not unusual. This time figure includes overhead time for loading, blank handling, and the actual write time. Provided a system runs 80 to 90 percent of the time (uptime) and a trained specialist is available for service, it is difficult to compete with e-beam writing for master mask and reticle production, even with the best optical mask-making equipment. Service allocation of 8 to 10 percent will help ensure a high uptime in production, and every 15 shifts a dedicated "service shift" should be used to quality-check the machine. Quality checks help preserve low defect levels and keep mask quality at or above all mask and reticle specifications. Typical defect levels on e-beam machines should be less than 2 defective chips per square inch.

Some of the other capabilities for a commercial e-beam writing system are 40 cm²/min coverage rate with 1-µm resolution, automatic blank handling, minimum resolution of 0.25 µm, edge roughness of ±0.05 µm, 6 × 6 substrate handling or larger, correction for in-plane and out-of-plane distortion, proximity compensation by varying the exposure dose, overlay position tolerance of ±0.10 μm, minimum beam size of 0.10 μm, and large scan field (5 to 6 mm) with distortion correction. These features are expected for an advanced system, several of which are in use.

Electron Optics versus Light Optics

Comparing electron optics to light optics may be an "apples-and-oranges" situation, but these systems do compete in the marketplace. The wavelength of an electron-optics system is less than 1 Å, compared to 4360 Å for optical systems. Some mask-making equipment uses 3650 Å light, and recent exposure at mid and deep uv brings the shortest optical wavelength down to about 2000 Å. In this area of comparison, electron sources have a strong resolution-potential advantage. In mask-making, the use of monochromatic energy is important in minimizing standing-wave patterns, since calculating for odd-quarter multiples in an optical thickness and providing a cancellation or offset situation are easier to accomplish for a single wavelength. While there is some natural cancellation of wavelengths with polychromatic light (electrons are monochromatic), it can be difficult to predict and control, since substrates vary. Overall, electron and light optics present equivalent problems with monochromaticity in mask-making.

Uniformity of exposure energy is always a primary concern and the dose profile for a typical electron-beam is shown in Fig. 4-9.

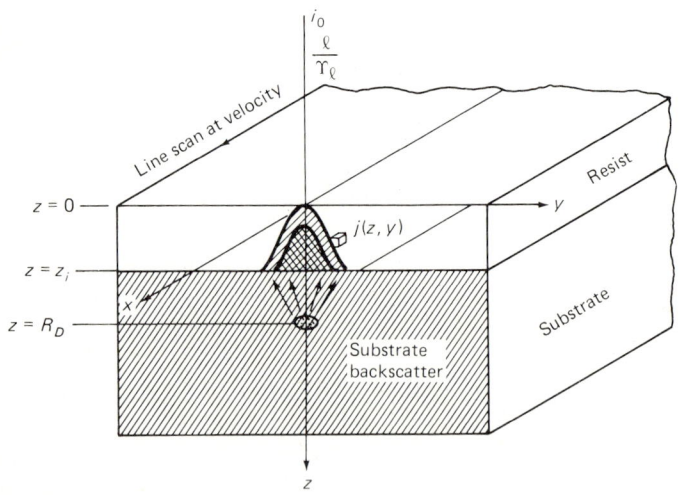

FIG. 4-9 Electron-dose profile.

Energy uniformity for electrons is about 3 percent over a 6-inch area, compared to 4 to 5 percent for the same area with light optics. Energy uniformity of both types of systems has improved as refinements in the equipment and sources are incorporated into commercial systems. Depth of focus gives an advantage to the e-beam system with between 30- and 100-μm focus depth, compared to light optics at 1 to 3 μm. These figures are based on an *f*-number rating of approximately 100 for electron optics and approximately 3 for light optics. Resolution for mask-making is less than 1 μm for electron optics and for light optics with recently developed shorter-wavelength lenses. Finally, measuring the speed of flashing, electron optics is greater than or equal to 20×10^6/sec compared to ≤ 100/sec for light optics. Overall the e-beam system unquestionably rises above the optical system in total resolution potential. This at least gives it a niche in those applications where extreme resolution, combined with the other key attributes of very low defects and rapid throughput of $10\times$ reticles, allows it to surpass optical alternatives. An electron-optical column is shown in Fig. 4-10.

Electron Sources

Several electron sources are used in the industry. The most common types are shown in Table 4-2, together with their primary attributes. The lanthanum hexaboride source is popular because it provides a good combination of high brightness and long life without extremely high vacuum conditions. Brighter sources are being researched in hopes of shortening the exposure times needed and also providing still higher resolution.

Facilities Requirements

Electron-beam processing requires several minor changes in process equipment compared to optical-mask shops, but these are not significant changes. The area required, for example, is about 5000 ft², the same area needed for the optical process. The level of cleanness is also specified at the same level, as Class 500 or better. The dry-nitrogen

TABLE 4-2   Electron sources

Source	Relative brightness	Life	Remarks
Tungsten hairpin	1	Short	Longer life desirable
Thoriated tungsten	1–1.3	Long	Requires very good vacuum
Lanthanum hexaboride	10	Long	Requires very good vacuum
Field emission	500	Very long	Requires ultrahigh vacuum

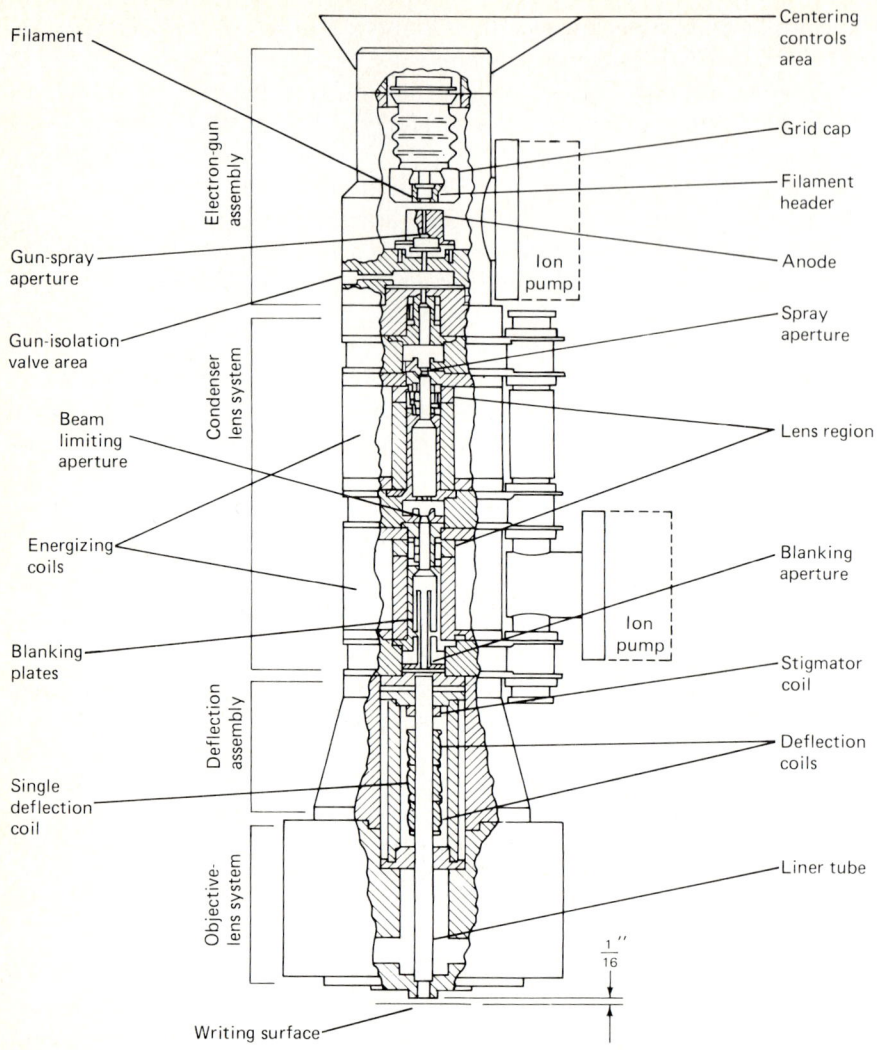

FIG. 4-10 Electron-optical column. *(ETEC.)*

supply is often specified as LN$_2$ Dewar, and both optical- and electron-beam mask-making areas use the same type. Deionized (DI) water at a level of approximately 6 gal/min at ≥12 MΩ is recommended. The suggested air supply is at 160 psig, at 20 ft^3/min, and at least 1-μm absolute filtration; its dew point must be less than 40°F.

Temperature control in optical and electron mask-making areas should be ±1°F, and the comfortable room temperature for operators is 68 to 70°F. The most critical temperature is that immediately surrounding the imaging equipment. This temperature should be controlled to ±0.2°F, and the humidity should be controlled at 45 ± 5 percent RH. This can be most easily accomplished by placing the exposure equipment and support hardware in a separate room with limited operator access to keep particle levels low and room air temperature relatively constant. The other area where temperature is important to control to a fraction of a degree is in resist developing.

A good deal of time is spent in the repair and inspection of 10× reticles and 1× master masks. The suggested list of equipment for these operations would include

1. Chrome-deposition system
2. Laser repair (opaque and clear defects)
3. Inspection system tied to laser repair
4. Nikon Lampas pattern analyzer
5. Leitz orthoplanar microscope
6. Low-power microscopes
7. Class 50 clean hoods and benches to house smaller equipment

The remaining equipment would be for resist processing and should include

1. Spin coater
2. Soft-bake and hard-bake ovens
3. Developer systems (2) with software control
4. Plasma de-scum
5. Wet chrome etcher
6. Dry chrome etcher
7. Wet bench for resist removal and substrate cleaning
8. Yellow room lights and several (12) Class 100 clean-air modules
9. Optical microscopes (Leitz orthoplanar)
10. Temperature-control system for resist developer

A typical facilities layout is shown in Fig. 4-11.

WRITING STRATEGIES

Several writing strategies are employed in e-beam imaging. The EBES writing strategy, originating at Bell Laboratories in Murray Hill, New

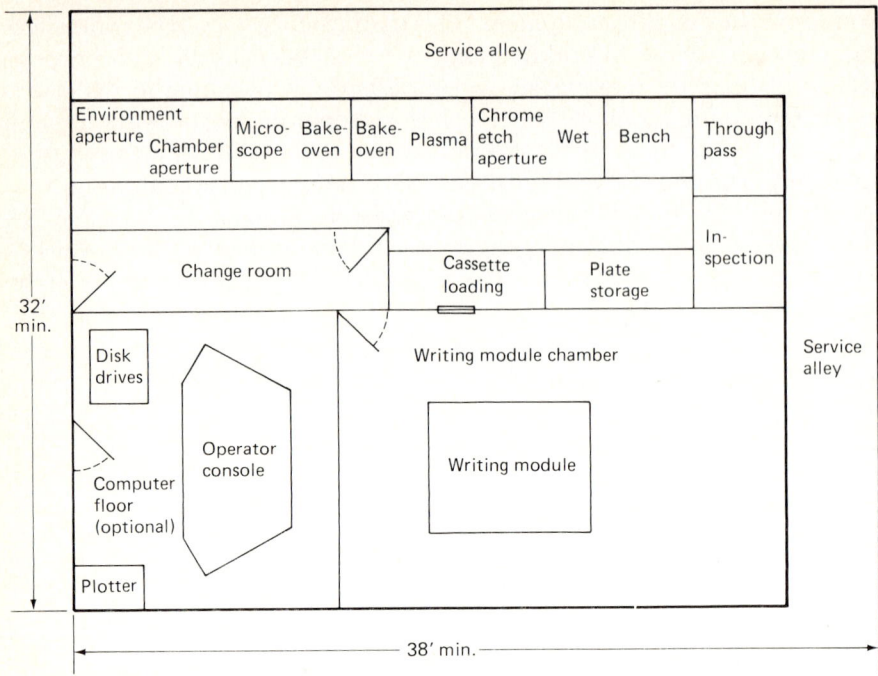

FIG. 4-11 Typical layout for e-beam facilities. *(Varian.)*

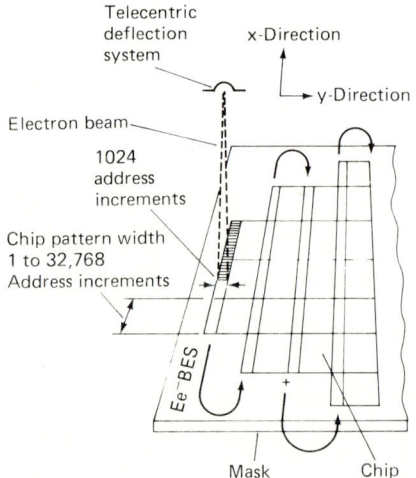

FIG. 4-12 EBES writing procedure. *(Bell Laboratories.)*

Jersey, is shown in Fig. 4-12. The EBES system has small-field electron optics combined with compound (electrical and mechanical) scanning exposure for reticles and masks. The EBES system is also used in direct-write applications for wafers. In the imaging sequence, the electron-beam is electronically deflected about 0.3 mm. Unlike vector-scan systems, where the stage is stationary, the stage in the EBES system is moved. Typically, the electron-beam is deflected in the y axis, and the stage moves forward in the x plane. Coordination of the x-y movements is accomplished with the reading of data from a pattern memory by the pattern data computer. The pattern composition process is outlined in Fig. 4-13.

The stage is kept moving in a forward direction. Resist exposure is governed by a potential applied to the electrostatic blanking plates mounted just above the deflection area. Blanking cuts off the flow of electrons to the resist. The accuracy of the various beam and stage movements is controlled by a laser interferometer that feeds information to the beam-deflection channels. Stage-position accuracy is less than the positioning accuracy of the beam ($\pm \frac{1}{64}$ µm), so this correction and positioning system is needed. The fail-safe mechanism, which keeps stage-positioning errors from being recorded in the resist, is simple: electron energy that creates the pattern will *not* pass to the beam-blanking plates until the stage-position-error and the compensating

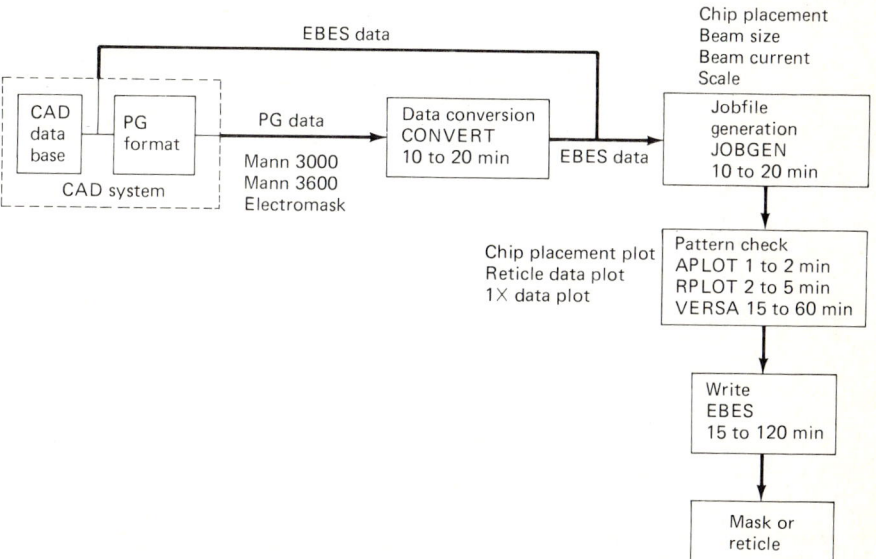

FIG. 4-13 EBES pattern composition process. *(Bell Laboratories.)*

beam-deflection steps are completed. This guarantees writing accuracy, and the beam is kept to a tolerance of 0.3 mm from its undeflected position.

The resist images are constructed by abutting the series of written "beam stripes." Before the pattern is created, the computer processes all writing information, thereby directing the system. Unlike reticles and masks in an optical fabrication process, there are no reference or fiducial marks to check the accuracy of the imaging. However, a fiducial mark is placed on the stage for this purpose, and beam drift caused by one of several variables (vibration, temperature shift, electronic noise, etc.) is corrected while the beam is "on the fly."

The electron optics of the EBES system is shown in Fig. 4-14. This system is similar to the electron optics to be shown later for the MEBES electron-beam sytem. The similarity to the optics used in a conventional scanning electron microscope is noted in the use of three lenses in the optical column. The first condenser lens is used essentially to collect the wide pattern of electrons coming from the gun and to image the newly reduced pattern of electrons onto the limiting aperture. This aperture controls the angle of acceptance of electrons as well as the spot current.

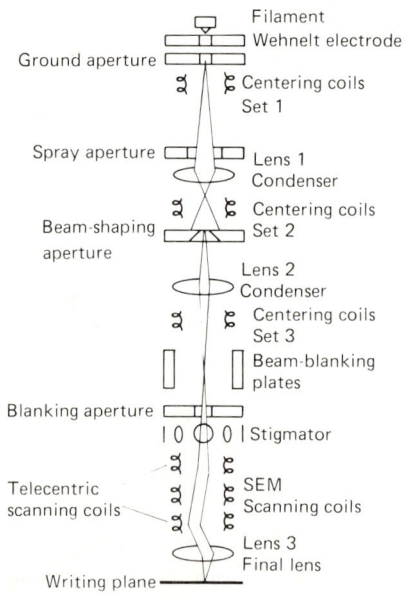

FIG. 4-14 EBES electron optics: longitudinal section of the e-beam column. *(Bell Laboratories.)*

This movement of the limiting aperture up or down the electron optical column will vary the beam diameter by changing the electron acceptance angle. The beam energy or gun emission is controlled by an active electron-gun bias feedback system.

The second condenser lens shown in the optical column adjusts the second crossover point of the beam so that its center (minimum) occurs at the very center of the blanking plates. This keeps the movement of the beam at a minimum when blanking occurs. Finer adjustments of the beam are made by the use of the magnetic coils shown in the figure. These compensate for the fact that mechanical controls cannot be provided that come close to the inherent positioning accuracy of the beam ($\frac{1}{64}$ μm). The optical elements in the column are also subject to drift, just as they are in a photo-optical system.

The third lens shown is telecentric, ensuring a 90° angle of incidence of electrons on the resist surface despite deflections in the beam amplitude. Writing and other functions with the EBES system are all computer-controlled except that the writing may also be manually controlled. A pattern data computer determines the signals that go to the beam-blanking plates. The point where the beam begins writing (xy coordinates) is established in the pattern data and then sent to the servomechanism that controls stage movement. The stage is then positioned and the beam blanked "on" for resist exposure. The computer ensures that deflections are all kept in sequence to provide a high-resolution-pattern image in the electron resist. After one mask level is complete, the beam is reregistered by checking it against the fiducial mark on the stage.

Electron-beam systems have, as a major requirement, the writing of high-resolution patterns for VLSI masks employing high-density designs. The writing rate is directly related to the current density, beam spot size, and resist sensitivity. The address size and beam diameter are typically kept the same. The current density available can vary, but it is generally around 10 Å/cm^2. Since the exposure current is proportional to the spot size, a $\frac{1}{2}$-μm spot will have 4 times the current of $\frac{1}{4}$-μm beam spot size. This is where resolution trades off with throughput or total write time. At 10× magnification in reticle production, larger spot sizes and greater writing speeds are possible than when producing 1× masters. The e-beam-imaging tool is therefore more ideally suited for 10× reticle production.

The final piece of the write-time formula is the resist sensitivity. Resists for electron exposure generally have a threshold or minimum charge (exposure) requirement to completely cross-link or solubilize the material in its developer. Thus, the writing rate is inversely proportional to the square of the address size. The formula for calculating exposure time is

$$\text{Exposure time} = \frac{A}{T_w} + O$$

where A = area to be written
T_w = writing rate, in cm²/min
O = overhead

and
$$T_w \propto \frac{1}{(\text{beam diameter})^2}$$

Overhead is composed of several elements, including substrate-handling time, "slewing" time when the stage moves without any resist writing, data-process or core-loading time, and reregistration time. In some cases, the writing time will exceed overhead by a considerable amount, especially when very high-resolution patterning is required and address sizes of 0.25 μm are used. In 1× mask-making applications, exposure time or writing time will typically exceed overhead. Improvements from the EBES I to EBES II to Ec-BES-40A-2 show progressions in the form of increased writing rates (1.25, 2.5, and 5.0 cm²/min for a 0.5-μm address, respectively), larger substrate-handling sizes, data rate increases from 10 to 40 MHz, automatic-handling features, and of course, shorter writing times. EBES I and EBES II were Bell Laboratories' designs, while the third type (Ec-BES-40A-2) contains design advancements made on EBES II technology (licensed from Western Electric) by Varian's Extrion Division. A photograph of the Varian system and a diagram of its key parts are shown in Fig. 4-15 *a* and *b*, respectively.

RETICLES

One key feature for process flexibility is substrate interchangeability. In the process of writing patterns, a defect or other problem can arise. The automatic-handling feature allows the problem mask to be withdrawn and a new mask from the same level to be substituted. This permits essentially uninterrupted writing. In reticle production, where a large part of the machine time is dedicated to data processing, this can be an important feature. Reticles continue to be a major application for EBES and other e-beam writing systems. Reticles are now the main application for all e-beam writing systems since the flash time on optical pattern generators has exceeded practical limits because of the complex VLSI patterns and memory chip sizes. Also, the wafer production process has incorporated an increasingly larger number of wafer steppers. Many of the steppers operate at 10×, reducing the reticle image to 1× at the wafer. This has resulted in a strong demand for 10×

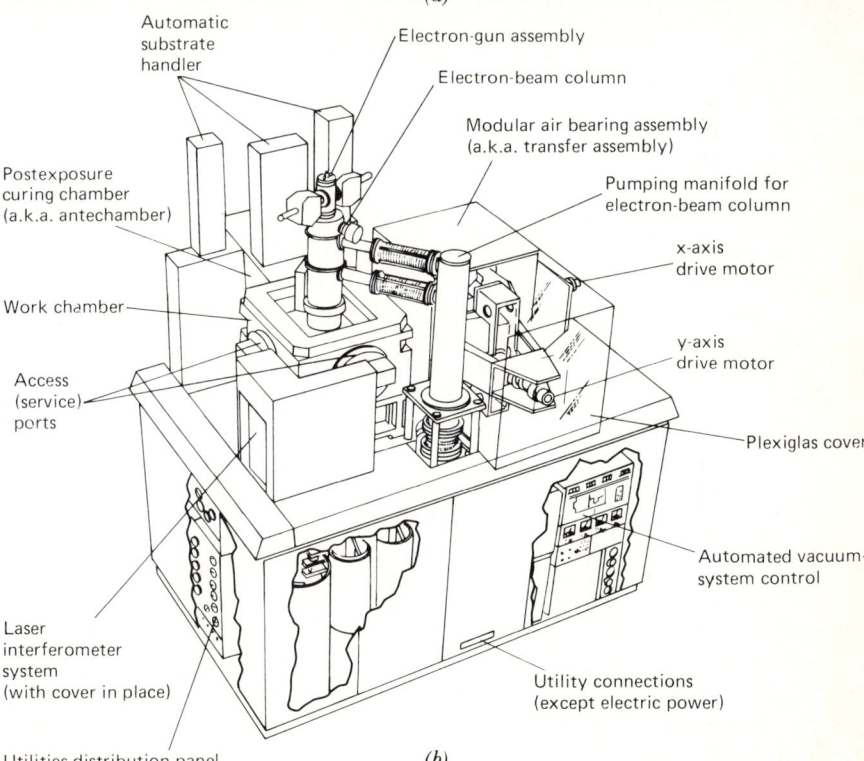

FIG. 4-15 Varian e-beam system (Ec-BES-40A-2): (*a*) The entire system; (*b*) diagram of key parts. (*Varian.*)

reticles. The additional handling of reticles also shortens their life span, adding more demand for reticle production.

The crossover point from optical pattern generation to e-beam writing is around 1×10^6 flashes. Patterns requiring a larger number of flashes are more economically produced with e-beam systems. The beam diameter may cause some edge roughening since a series of overlapping circles (beam-shaped) must be very closely spaced to even out the natural scalloping effect. At $10\times$, this edge effect is small but noticeable in a finished reticle. After reducing the pattern to $1\times$ on the wafer or on a master mask, it is nearly undetectable and essentially "washes out" during subsequent photoprocessing where resist undercut, etching, and similar processes have a smoothing effect.

Reticles of high resolution are routinely produced in about 45 min with 1-μm spot sizes. Pattern geometries of 2 μm at $10\times$ are 20 μm at the writing surface, and a 1-μm spot size at the $10\times$ level is 10 μm at the writing surface. This gives plenty of latitude for small edge errors or other minor pattern defects in the writing process. The 45-min reticle at a 1-μm spot size would run close to 18 hr on an optical pattern generator.

MEBES

The ETEC MEBES e-beam system is also a version originating from the Bell Laboratories EBES e-beam design, again with modification. The writing scheme is similar, where the writing scheme is divided into stripes as shown in Fig. 4-16a, b, and c. The example shown uses a 512-address wide-stripe pattern, and a single chip of an IC level is shown in Fig. 4-16a. Figure 4-16b shows the x dimension of the chip pattern fully written. After the first stripe has been written on all the chip locations, the beam moves back to the originating point and begins writing the second stripe, shown in Fig. 4-16c.

Data Format

The format for MEBES pattern data is polygons that are fractured into trapezoids. Figure 4-17 shows the MEBES trapezoid along with a geometry that has been divided into trapezoids. Note that the tops and bottoms of the trapezoid shapes are parallel to the x axis. Described in seven 16-bit words which identify x, y, Δx_1, Δx_2, L, and H, they are fed into a file belonging to that particular mask set. In the job file is stored information relating to other macromask parameters, including scaling information, test-element locations, die placement, and so on.

Data are produced and stored in magnetic-tape form on most VLSI

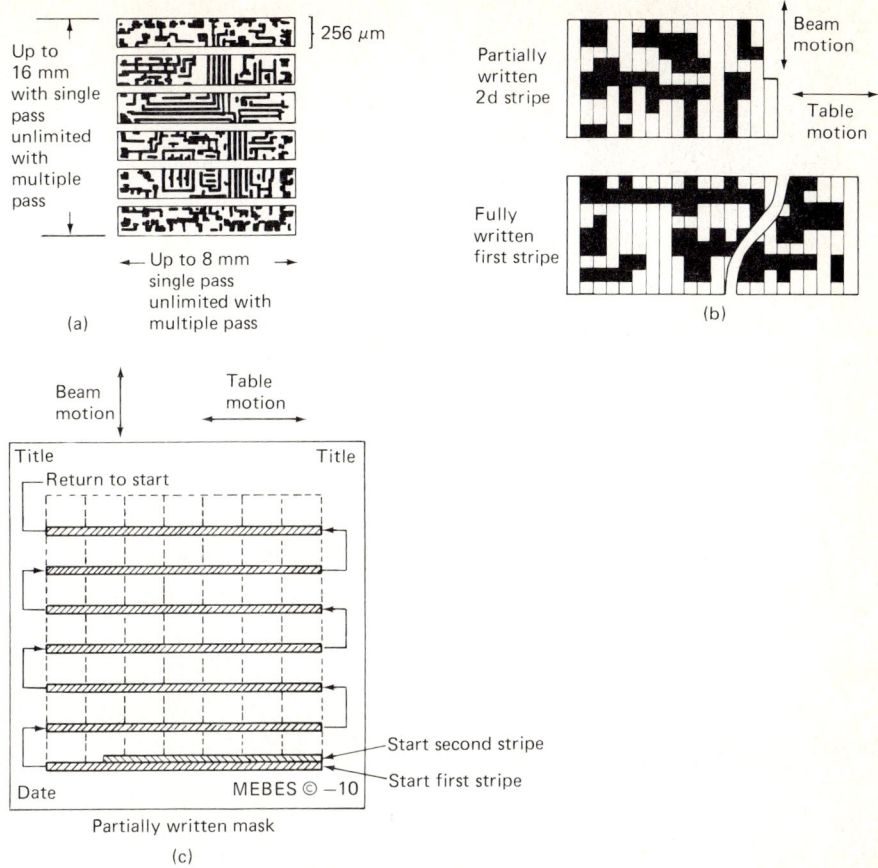

FIG. 4-16 (*a*) IC pattern broken into stripes; all numbers assume 0.5-μm adders. (*b*) Detail of a single stripe. (*c*) Partly written mask with stripe locations.

patterns for masks. The conversion of data is facilitated by special software programs. For example, a mask shop using only optical pattern generators and image repeaters needs to send outside to have extra mask sets made. The outside vendor uses only the electron-beam for mask generation and must then run the pattern-generator data through a software conversion program to convert it into EBES format for acceptance by the EBES computer. Many CAD companies provide software formats for pattern-data conversion.

VECTOR-SCAN WRITING IN PRODUCTION

While much of the production use of e-beam writing systems is accomplished with raster-scan methods, an equally active but perhaps smaller

118 INTEGRATED CIRCUIT MASK TECHNOLOGY

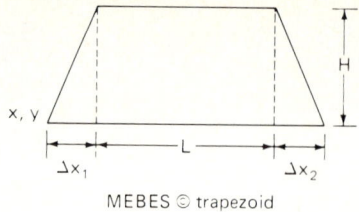

MEBES trapezoid

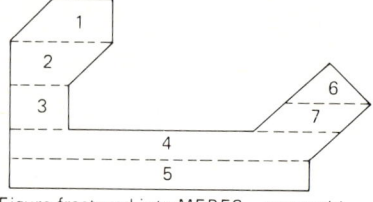

Figure fractured into MEBES trapezoid

FIG. 4-17 MEBES trapezoid definition and IC geometry broken into trapezoids. *(Bell Laboratories.)*

level of activity exists in vector-scan electron-beam systems. Vector-scan e-beam machines, specifically the Vector-Scan I (VS-I) system described by IBM, are useful for $10\times$ reticle and $1\times$ master-mask production. The VS-I system uses a laser interferometer servosystem along with the standard registration marks on scan-field corners, a feature that aids in high-level registration for $1\times$ writing of very large chips requiring stitching at field boundaries. Very large chips are easily written with this approach. The application of chrome-mask fabrication for VS-I is a natural one since the current density of the machine is high enough to permit the use of AZ-1350 positive resist. This is a real advantage considering the very good chrome-etching properties of AZ-1350, already a worldwide standard masking material on chrome.

The VS-I scans a field made up of 16,384 spots in both x and y directions. Field size is variable between 5 mm and a fraction of a millimeter and is controlled by an attenuator. The adjustment of attenuation will permit easy scaling, in either direction, for a given pattern. The major fundamental difference (and advantage) of the vector-scan system compared to raster-scan writing is that only the pattern area to be created is addressed or "vectored to." The data are broken down by VS-I into shapes, as they were for EBES pattern data. The shapes used for VS-I are triangles, rectangles, and parallelograms. Serial exposure results in a filled-in shape; the beam finishes one geometric shape and then vectors to the next, scans the geometric area and fills it in, and again vectors on to the next shape; hence the name vector scan. The time saved by this approach is understood easily in terms of the percent area consumed by a pattern in a given VLSI design. For example, the average field-effect transition (FET) memory chip has only about 20 percent pattern area at all mask levels. Raster-scan methods write over 100 percent of the area, and vector-scan systems write the 20 percent pattern area plus some overhead time in vectoring from one shape to the next.

The other advantage of the vector-scan system is simplicity of the pattern data. In the raster-scan system, remember that each line segment of a scan required a separate software definition. In vector scanning, only five words are used to define the variety of pattern shapes: x, y (position for shape origin); Δx, Δy (for size and shape); and a control word for the type of shape and exposure clock. This approach shortens data transfer times in the system computer by simpler definition of shapes, especially where pattern values are redundant and need not be respecified and processed in the computer but simply are assigned a single value and rapidly written. High stepping rates result, along with a significant compaction of the data in designs employing repetitive elements such as large memories. In any given memory chip, a cell may be repeated identically thousands of times. In vector-scan machines, the shape is processed once by the computer and assigned a value; this description occurs just this initial time, and all subsequent uses of this shape in the memory require only a vector-distance command. The arrayed shape continues to be reproduced without consuming expensive computer time. This powerful feature means that several million shapes can be written with the vectored beam using a description in the computer of less than 12 words. Obviously, the VS-I is well suited for fabricating sizable memory arrays.

The substrates used with VS-I are standard plates coated with antireflective chrome, "gold" chrome, or "black" chrome. These low-reflectance layers are standard materials highly suited for hard-surface masks employing high-density patterns. The problem of charging and secondary electron scatter is minimized by proper grounding of the plates. The 1350 resist is then coated to the desired thickness and processed as it would be for any mask-making application. Specific processes are cited later in this chapter. The sensitivity of AZ-1350 to electron energy varies between 1×10^5 and 5×10^5, depending on softbake and developer conditions. The ability to "plug in" an optical resist with an e-beam writing system simplifies all subsequent processing. Most e-beam resists requires more process control than AZ-1350 in developing (control of developer temperature, concentration, agitation). The dry-etch resistance of AZ-1350 is also very good, and plasma descumming is typically not required as it is with most e-beam resists.

The VS-I is used in 10× reticle production, where its ability to stitch together several scan fields is utilized. One of the limitations of the VS-I system is in patterning 1-μm and smaller dimensions. The electron-scattering effects show, in Fig. 4-18, that the images in the middle of the pattern group are not the same as lines at the edge of the grouping. This example used glass as the substrate and a $\frac{1}{2}$-μm-thick layer of resist exposed to 20-kV electrons. Apparently there is still too much bulk thickness in the 5000-Å resist layer, and excessive scattering distorts the image shapes. The possibility of using thinner resist layers is promising as a way to reduce the electron-scattering effects. Coatings as thin as 1000 Å have been successfully spin coated onto chrome, and the chrome is then wet-etched with very low defect (pinhole) densities. Incidentally, defects are always very low when using e-beam imaging.

Commercial vector-scan equipment is supplied by several manufacturers. A widely used system, called the Microfabricator and supplied by Cambridge Instruments, is shown in Fig. 4-19. The e-beam-diameter

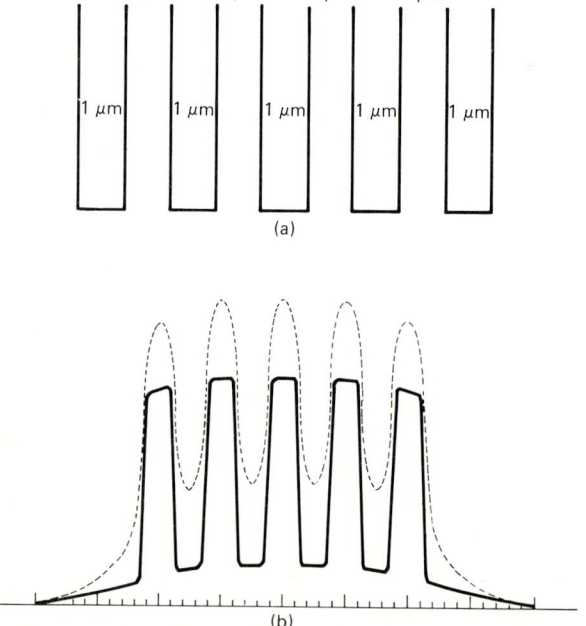

FIG. 4-18 Secondary electron-scattering effects on microimages: (*a*) ideal from pattern data, and (*b*) image as written.

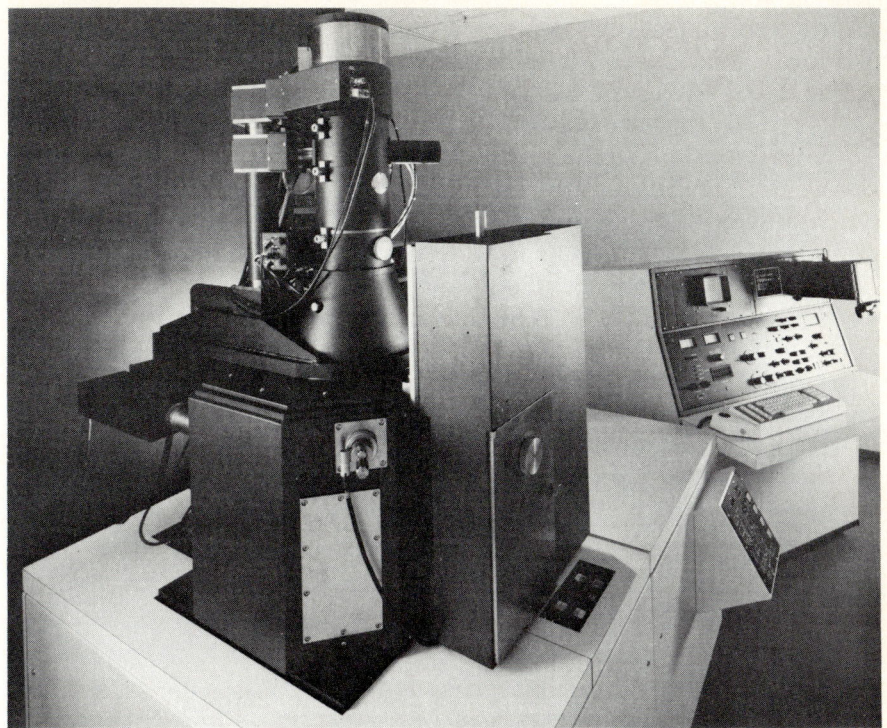

FIG. 4-19 Microfabricator e-beam system. *(Cambridge Instruments.)*

range available from the system is 0.05 to 1.0 μm. The electron energy, supplied by LaB_6 rods, is generated in beam currents from 10^{-12} to 10^{-6} A. Tungsten hairpin sources are also used. One important feature of this system is thermoelectric temperature control of the work chamber and airlock to greater than 0.1°C. This provides an excellent thermally stable environment for large glass substrates, and greatly reduces the need and incumbent cost to control the entire room to such exact levels. The viewing system is also versatile, giving the operator three microscopes for viewing: one for live array write viewing, one for program and information display, and one for pattern-information viewing and checking prior to writing. The electronic packs shown in the photograph provide data-entry capability via magnetic tape, disk memory for pattern storage and execution programs, and the computer interface to the electron-beam system.

In operation, the system uses the same writing principle as described previously for the VS-I, where the beam is deflected onto feature sites in the precalculated field locations. The beam is then blanked until this section is complete; it then vectors on to the next field and commences writing again. Overall, vector scanning continues to be a powerful writing strategy for electron-beam imaging of reticles and masks.

VARIABLE-SHAPED-BEAM WRITING

Variations of the vector-scan e-beam writing system include variable-beam shaping and an inverted optical column, both of which are contained in the Cameca (Thompson CSF Division) fast electron-beam pattern generator (FEPG). This system is shown in Fig. 4-20 in schematic form, with the inverted optical column on the left and the principle of operation on the right. In operation the crossover of the tungsten hairpin filament gun is magnified and imaged on the aperture labeled A1. This aperture has a minimum of one right angle. The A1 aperture is imaged at scale one on aperture A2. A rectangle is formed by the combination of images from both apertures. Location D1 is a deflector

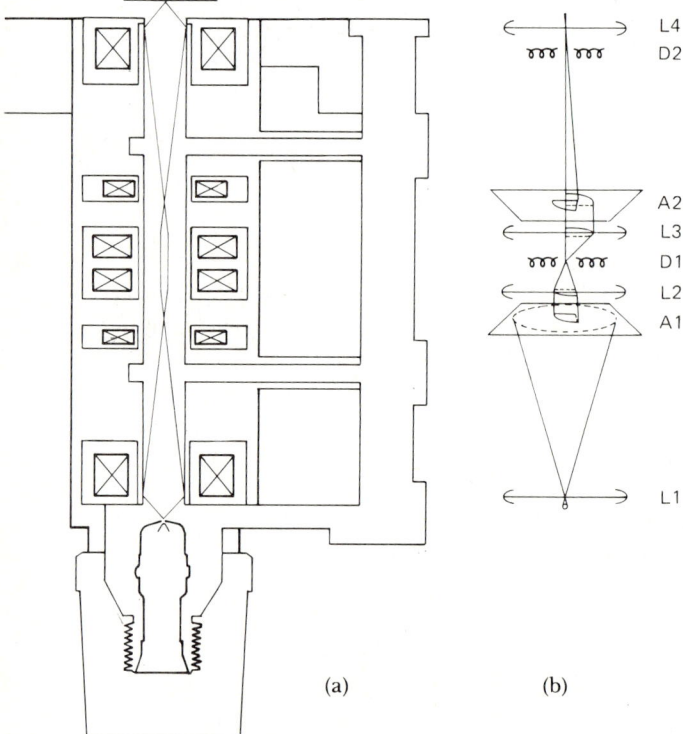

FIG. 4-20 (*a*) Inverted optical column of the Cameca fast e-beam pattern generator. (*b*) Operating principle of the optical column. (*Thompson CSF Division.*)

that will alter the dimensions of this rectangular electron-beam image. The lens at location L4 provides image demagnification and focuses directly onto the mask, reticle, or wafer surface. When the beam position needs to be changed, deflector D2 moves the beam to the desired location in coordination with stage movements.

A key feature provided by the inverted optical column is rapid access of substrates for efficient loading and unloading. Productivity must be high if electron-beam-system payback is to be realized as quickly as competitive optical-image-generation equipment. High reticle and mask throughput is aided by production-oriented features such as the one described. Another throughput benefit is provided by using the variable-shaped beam. This capability helps to reduce the total writing time and, in conjunction with advancements in writing strategies, to provide good reticle or mask production. A further production need is minimal plant space usage. The system just described consumes only about 1 m² of floor area. The combination of high resolution (1 μm) and good throughput (6 min for a 50 percent area written mask, 3-in size) is needed for VLSI reticle and mask production. Finally, resists with medium-level e-beam sensitivity ($5 \times 10^{-6}/cm^2$) can be used.

CONTACT PRINTING

Contact printing is still unsurpassed in providing the best reproduction of a mask or reticle pattern in a resist layer. The intimate contact generated at standard vacuum levels (25in Hg) allows the image to be transferred with 1:1 reproduction fidelity and practically zero lateral scattering. Resist sidewall angles are perpendicular, and the edges are extremely sharp, as shown in the contact-printed image of a 1-μm resist layer in Fig. 4-21. Despite the problems of dust and particle entrapment on mask surfaces that then degrade the image quality of the substrate

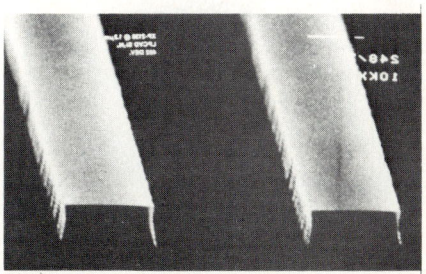

FIG. 4-21 Contact-printed resist image. (Shipley XP 2138 imaged on Canon PLA 120.) *(Shipley.)*

during exposure at high vacuum, contact printing is widely used. The mass production or reproduction of 1× master masks and 1× intermediate masks (reverse polarity) can only be performed by this printing technique with the cost efficiencies required by process economies. Contact printing is fast, provides excellent image reproduction, and can be implemented with minimum operator training and relatively low capital outlay. Contact printers are available from several manufacturers, and the quality of the equipment for VLSI mask duplication is quite good. A standard contact printer used in the microelectronics industry is shown in Fig. 4-22. This unit, model 85310, is manufactured by the Oriel Corporation in Stamford, Connecticut. The system will accept 8 × 8-in plates and uses a 1000-W mercury-xenon arc lamp for short exposure times. A very efficient ellipsoidal mirror collects and concentrates the light energy to minimize loss of light. The system is semiautomatic and will handle both chrome plates and emulsion-coated substrates. The master masks to be copied are loaded into the vacuum and placed on three support pins with the resist or emulsion side up. A master vacuum switch then locks the two plates together, the second copy plate being loaded also on three pins located on the door frame

FIG. 4-22 **Contact printer.** *(Oriel Corporation, Stamford, Conn.)*

that swings against the unit. Various plate sizes are accommodated by using interchangeable plate inserts.

Exposure Parameters

Exposure of high-resolution (HR) emulsions is facilitated by the insertion of a 546-nm green attenuating filter. The normal output of the light source, a 1000-W mercury-xenon lamp, is strong in the 350- and 450-nm regions, and the optical system provides exposure uniformity over the entire image area of ±5 percent. Exposure uniformity is one of the most important aspects of the contact-printing process, since 1:1 reproduction of the master mask (or as close to 1:1 as the system can get) is the objective. "Hot" spots in any area of the optical system that are imaged at the mask plane will change pattern geometries and possibly cause a rejected mask. Figure 4-23 shows the plot of a test pattern copied from a chrome master onto (*a*) a bright chrome plate and (*b*) a black chrome plate.

The first major difference noted is sizing differences between spaces and lines. The images in the copied bright chrome are enlarged relative to the original reflections from the underlying surface. The positive resist picks up these reflections and, after normal development, dissolves away at the chrome interface where the reflected light caused exposure. On the black chrome plate, low reflectivity kept the window sizing much smaller but still slightly enlarged due to the exposure, which is typically 5 to 10 percent greater than the energy needed to barely clear the resist to the chrome interface. The line geometries, on the other hand, come out undersized relative to the mask. The bright chrome plate registered sizing up to 0.6 μm *smaller* than the original. Note the figures at the ends of the plotted lines showing exposure time in seconds and developing time, also in seconds. Control of the printed resist or emulsion images is easily adjusted with good control by small changes in exposure time as shown in the line plots.

Keeping the window *and* line dimensions close to those of the mask is far easier with the use of any antireflective (AR) chrome, including AR black, gold, and overcoated (antireflection) chromium layers. Over the range of pattern dimensions from 1 to 6 μm, line and window sizes are held fairly constant, an indication of controlled resist or emulsion processing.

Most contact printers provide sensitive exposure control dials, fractioning the seconds into tenths or quarters. Since silver halide–emulsion photosensitivity is high and exposure times are on the order of 2 to 4 sec, control at this level is necessary in order to establish precise image sizing. Positive photoresists, at the 4000- to 8000-Å-thickness level, are

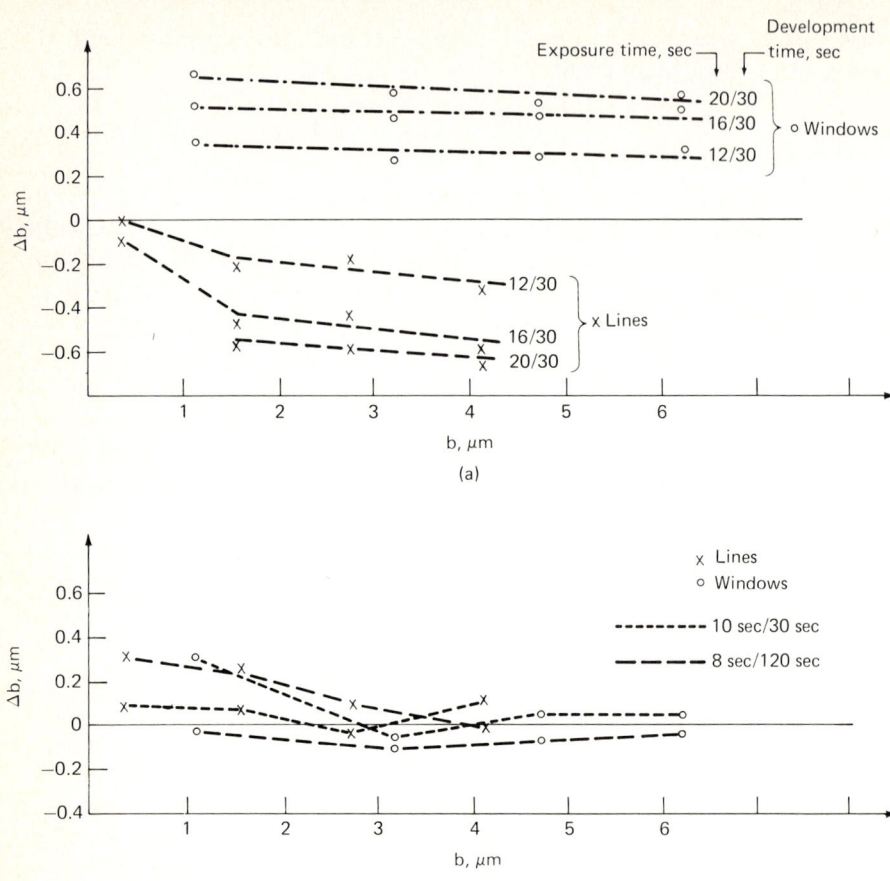

FIG. 4-23 Plot of image sizes contact-printed onto (*a*) shiny, and (*b*) black chrome surfaces. Key: b = width in μm of lines or windows; Δb = difference in μm between widths on copy and original.

considerably slower, and typical exposure times in a control printer run 2.5 to 5.0 sec. The shutter and timer controls on the Oriel Model 85310 are digitally controlled with a range of 0 to 999.9 sec in 0.1-sec intervals.

The exposure optics of the Oriel contact printer take the energy from the wraparound ellipsoidal reflector and optically integrate the light into a uniform beam. In the optical path a dichroic mirror is used to selectively filter off longer-wavelength infrared energy to keep the system cool. Long-wave visible wavelengths are also filtered out. Uniform output of the lamp is regulated by employing a captive lamp power supply, and wattage is thereby kept constant. Additional controls are used for the lamp power supply. The control of illumination is proportioned so that a 10 percent change in power (line voltage) will result in only 1 percent change in light output. The high-intensity light column then passes through the solenoid-actuated split-blade shutter, governed by the timer. During exposure both the master, or original, and the copy mask blank, held against the three pin supports, are vacuum bound. When the exposure sequence begins, the plates are held apart by differential pressure until the airspace is nearly evacuated. The advantage of this mechanism is elimination of air entrapment between the two plate surfaces that could cause nonuniform exposures due to differential contact pressure. When the pump-down is complete and the desired vacuum level is reached, the shutter opens and exposes the plate. At the end of this part of the automatic cycle, the vacuum is released, releasing the plates and allowing the next copy plate to be loaded. Contact pressure is adjustable, and during exposure the plates are held at uniform atmospheric pressure to minimize distortion and runout.

Negative resists are seldom used in the contact-printing process since positive resists provide a higher level of resolution and edge sharpness. However, applications arise where reverse polarity from what positive resists give is needed, and a single-step contact print with negative resist is the most direct means of obtaining the copy mask. Negative resists have sensitivity to oxygen and must be exposed in an inert-gas atmosphere to prevent surface cross-linking and subsequent scumming caused by the oxygen reaction. Almost all contact, proximity, and projection printers used in microelectronics anticipate this problem by providing an inert-gas purge. Nitrogen is the most common gas substituted for air in this case.

Hard- and Soft-Contact Printing

Hard-contact printing refers to the use of high-vacuum contact pressure, and it unquestionably provides the maximum level of image fidelity from the master to the copy plate. The consequence of hard-contact printing is maximum wear and degradation of the imaged chrome film or emulsion or any combination of imaged and to-be-imaged coatings. Geometry specifications may permit the use of soft-contact printing, where the vacuum pressure is reduced down to a level of approximately 1 to 5 inHg. The reduced vacuum pressure has several consequences. First, the reduction of pressure between the sensitive mask coatings reduces wear on image edges, allowing a greater number of contact prints to be made with the original mask before it is reprocessed (emulsion-stripped, chrome-etched, recoated, and imaged) or discarded.

The coat of increasing mask life is loss of some fidelity and, more important, loss of image resolution.

Device designs that have critical dimensions above 0.5 μm and line sizes above 4 to 5 μm are able to be soft-contact or proximity printed with reasonable yields. Smaller dimensions can also be controlled and printed with reduced pressure *if* the glass flatness is good. A highly repeatable soft-contact-printing process will permit reasonably high resolution until a warped or bowed substrate is used. The nonflatness in most glass plates is overcome by the high pressure of hard-contact printing. Assuming very flat (ultraflat grade) plates are used, production runs with longer mask life are possible. A quick flatness check before printing will permit screening of "out-of-spec" plates. Plates that are not caught by the pre-imaging check are often caught by the subsequent "red-light" viewing in the contact printer. The Oriel and some other printers provide a red safelight that is switched on prior to imaging for fringe viewing. Nonflatness can be seen, measured, photographed (panchromatic black and white film), and calculated. The ability to have live viewing of mask-to-mask surface-contact uniformity, by counting interference patterns on a production line, is a true fringe benefit.

Contact printing is regarded by many lithographers as a nearly medieval and certainly primitive imaging method. The evaluation of mask and wafer printing has been slowly moving away from contact printing as equipment has incorporated optical refinements needed to provide the required resolution. The position left for contact printing in the imaging spectrum is one of low-cost, high-volume reproduction of working-level masks. Recent trends point to a possible resurgence of contact printing.

PROCESSING PHOTORESISTS AND ELECTRON RESISTS

There are many types of resists, besides silver halide and other emulsions, used to fabricate VLSI IC masks and reticles. In this section we will discuss the processing aspects of photoresists and electron resists, with special emphasis on process control. This section begins with the properly coated substrate. Assuming that reticle and mask surfaces are properly cleaned and coated with a highly uniform layer of resist, the processing job is to image these presensitized plates to the specified process dimensions in volume and consistency throughout the expected life of the IC design.

The imaging process in mask fabrication is probably the most complex of any of the individual separate steps. Compared to etching, glass preparation, and other key processes, imaging presents the greatest number of singular variables with the highest level of interdependence.

The aspect of interdependence in the imaging process is dealt with by using a "divide-and-conquer" strategy; each imaging step is characterized first as a single unit, and then its relationships to each of the other steps are characterized. Finally, models that contain all of the behavioral aspects are created. Computer modeling of resist-process parameters is a relatively powerful tool to better predict and control production processes. In mask-making, the planar topography and imaging criteria are much less complicated than they are in wafer-fabrication imaging. We will therefore limit our analysis of resist processing to a hands-on, user-oriented discussion of process variables and practical control methods. The lower the level of complication in resist process control, the greater the likelihood of maintaining a consistent quality level. Most mask makers rely on techniques that have been proved to deliver uniform results, and are dependable, simplistic in nature, and easy to define.

The objective of any mask- or reticle-imaging process is providing consistent and accurate pattern replication. Resists seem to have a nature that sometimes runs at cross-purposes to this objective and are given to very wide excursions at all levels of processing. This degree of potential variability, left out of control, will literally bankrupt any process. The question is: What are some of the main evaluation and control methods needed to keep a production mask- or reticle-imaging process running smoothly? In high-volume production, a mask operation can process anywhere between 10,000 and 35,000 individual high-density plates per day. In this situation, more production time can be spent *checking* plates than is spent *producing* plates. In such an environment, control reigns supreme.

Exposure Control

The first step after resist coating and softbake is exposure. This is also the first step for an emulsion mask process. The greatest real concern in the exposure step is variability of the exposure energy. This will cause greater pattern shifts than small changes (or equivalent percent changes) in resist sensitivity, substrate reflectance, or other variables in the exposure process. A test used widely in wafer fabrication involves making a partial exposure into the resist layer. Figure 4-24 shows a cross section of the partial exposure and a development test used to spot exposure illumination or intensity variations. The exposure given to the resist is typically 15 percent of the normal dose. A positive optical resist might require approximately 25 mJ/cm^2 of exposure energy, and therefore the partial exposure requires setting the imaging equipment at 3.75 mJ/cm^2.

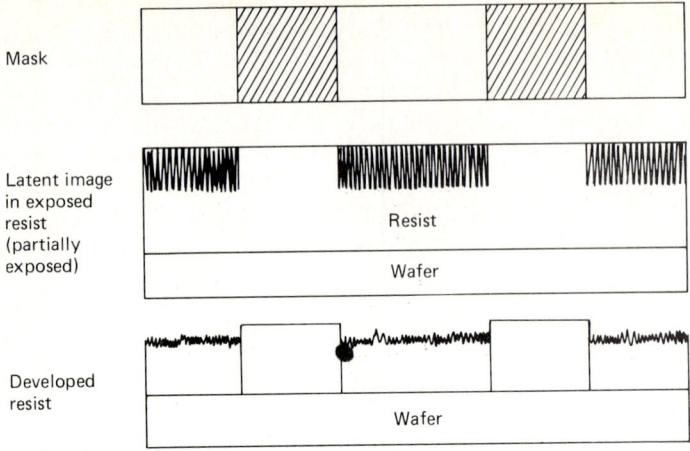

FIG. 4-24 Cross-sectional diagram of the partial exposure–development test for detecting nonuniform illumination.

In the figure the variation in light intensity registers a latent image in the resist at various depths. Following development through the standard cycle for a fully exposed plate, the image left behind registers topographical differences that correspond to the intensity profile. Standard visual observation of this plate will show interference fringes viewed at a 90° angle to the plate. The process operator will have already checked the plate flatness (before resist is applied) to rule out the possibility of fringing caused by nonflatness. At 1× magnification, blanket exposure in a contact printer provides the partial-exposure condition. In image repeaters, the beam is simply blanked for a series of steps across the active area, then developed normally. It is recommended that this test be run on at least two to three plates if the first plate indicates an intensity problem. This will require another few minutes of process time but will ensure accurate reporting of the problem. The plate position in the exposure is important, since the pattern left in the resist will generally not be radial but will show random intensity fluctuations. Referencing the area of the variation back to the lamp for fine adjustments, for example, a reflector-surface or lens-element adjustment, is necessary. The fringes are very precise thickness indicators, being an even half multiple of the illuminating wavelength.

The next variable to check in the exposure step is resist-sensitivity variation. This parameter is a function of resist soft-bake temperature, the surface reflectance, length of time the resist has been on the plate surface, batch of resist used, and plate temperature and humidity level

TABLE 4-3 Checking variables of resist sensitivity

Variable	Tests and methods
1. Soft-bake level	1a. Weight loss
	1b. Thickness
	1c. Developer attack in unexposed areas
2. Batch-to-batch variation	2a. Sensitivity, step wedge, and resolution target
	2b. Characteristic curve plot
3. Resist age on plates	3. Remove and repeat with fresh resist
4. Humidity and temperature changes	4. Maintain 45 ± 5% RH at 70°F

in the process area. Most of these separate variables can be checked as shown in Table 4-3.

In an attempt to increase production rates, there is a strong temptation to underexpose the resist, shortening the main imaging bottleneck. Underexposure in mask-making leads to uneven and incomplete clearing or developing of the resist, which in turn causes uneven and incomplete etching. Sometimes there are extremely thin films left that cannot be detected with optical microscopes. To quickly check for an underexposed condition, overexposure (with $2\times$ the normal energy) a portion of the resist-coated mask and note the developing rate. The positive resist, in a completely and properly exposed condition, will show immediate "red clouding" as dissolved resist swirls off from the exposed areas. The resist image, in a properly baked, exposed, and developed specimen, will form within the first 10 sec of immersion developing, and much faster (3 to 4 sec, typically) when spray- or puddle-developing at elevated temperatures (heated heads on in-line equipment) is used.

The more practical and easily performed on-line checks for exposure levels help keep a production line moving and give process operators a better feel for the interdependency of resist-process steps. Exposure-equipment variations are common and cannot be programmed out of the process, thereby creating the need for these types of tests.

Resist Developing

Second to exposure in terms of impact on pattern-geometry resolution and control is development. The developers used for positive optical resists all have an alkaline base and generally provide wide development-process latitude. The main categories of development are immersion, spray (aspirated and puddle dispense), and spin spray. Immersion developing is widely used since many parts can be processed at once and semiautomatic developing equipment can be used to hold close

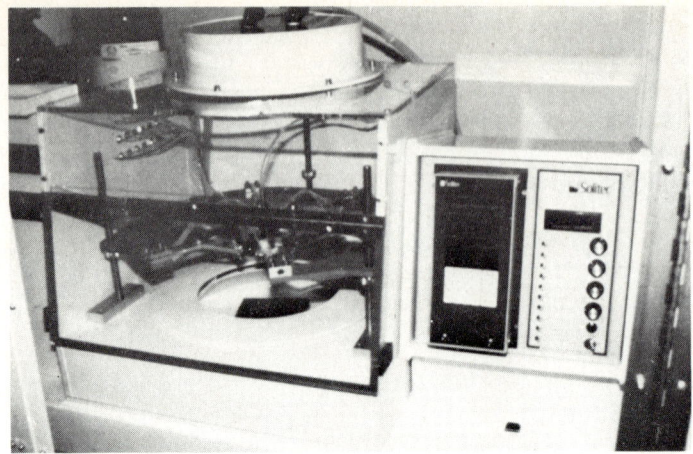

FIG. 4-25 Mask-developing unit. (*Solitec.*)

tolerances on the main variables. A typical plate-developing unit is shown in Fig. 4-25. Equipment of this type takes up a small amount of process area, is software controlled, and will keep developer solution temperature, time, and solution agitation constant within a few percent. The other major developer variable is concentration. If the developer is sprayed on while the plate is spinning (as it is in this unit) and not recirculated, all the resist will ever see is fresh developer. Some spray units recirculate the developer and bleed in small amounts of concentrate or made-up bath to keep the developer normality at a uniform level.

Developer solution may be dispensed onto the plate and left in a puddle while the developer begins acting in the exposed resist. This method, called "puddle developing," is used when metal ion-free (MIF) developers are the product of choice. Puddle developing for the specified number of seconds is followed by a spin and spin-rinse, and finally a spin-dry cycle.

Major developer types are metal-containing and metal-free developers. MIF and other low-sodium developers are designed to prevent sodium and other (potassium) metal ions from contaminating wafer surfaces, leading to possible electrical failures. In mask-making, the only reason for using an MIF developer would be for its compatibility with spray equipment. Many metal-containing developers leave behind metal salts that are formed when the developing solution is allowed to dry in the spray equipment. Clogged spray nozzles are difficult to clean and will leave chunks of dried developer on wafer surfaces, which will cause reject devices. Metal-free developers for positive optical resists use an organic source of alkalinity for the active ingredient that dissolves the base-soluble exposed areas. Metal-free developers do not form a "cake" residue when left to dry in spray or other in-line equipment.

Masks and reticles imaged with positive optical resist are typically developed in metal-containing developers. Near the end of development, the rinse step is overlapped on the developing cycle. This rinses the developer out of the spray lines and nozzle. The primary reason for using the metal-containing developers is for the wide operating latitude they offer. They have a much slower attack or dissolution rate on the unexposed resist, giving the system better overall differential solubility. Improved metal-free developers have reduced the solubility gap between the two types, but it remains sufficiently wide to make a strong case for continued use of metal-containing developers.

Imaging Sequence for a Positive Optical Resist

A basic imaging sequence is shown in Table 4-4. This process can be used for any mask or reticle using a hard-surface coating material, including various types of chrome (antireflective, bright, etc.) iron oxide, silicon, and others. The Microposit 1350 photoresist (Shipley Company)

TABLE 4-4 Process sequence for imaging positive optical resist on hard-surface masks

Process step	Equipment	Conditions
Resist Coating ↓	Headway spin coater	AZ-1350, 5000Å
Prebaking ↓	Oven	90°C, 30 min
Exposure ↓	Tamarack Model 142	55 mJ/cm^2
Development ↓	APT Model 914	AZ developer 1:1, 22°C, 40 sec
Rinse ↓	APT Model 914	Deionized water, 60 sec
Spin dry ↓	APT Model 914	2300 rpm, 25 sec
(Postbaking) ↓	(Oven)	(120°C, 30 min)
Etching ↓	Thermostatic vessel	19 ± 0.1°C (with stirring)
Resist Removal	Thermostatic vessel	concd H_2SO_4 80°C, 3 min
Etchant		
Ceric ammonium nitrate	Ce(NH$_4$)$_2$(NO$_3$)$_6$	165 g
Perchloric acid	HClO$_4$(70%)	42 mL
Adding deionized water		1000 mL

SOURCE: Data sheet courtesy of Hoya Corp., Tokyo.

is a striation-free grade used for mask-making. It differs functionally from the resist shown in the process sequence only in its ability to be striation-free. The resist film is a typical $\frac{1}{2}$-μm thickness used in mask-making, as is the 90°C bake for 30 min. Shorter bake times are not recommended as excess solvent may be left in the resist coating, leading to pinhole formation in the resist. Exposure on a Tamarack Model 142 printer requires 55 mJ/cm^2. A photograph of a Tamarack contact printer is shown in Fig. 4-26.

Developer Control

Immersion processing of exposed plates through the developer is usually a manual process and subject to the variability of any hand-operated process. Mechanized-immersion batch processing is perhaps one of the best methods of developing in terms of process control, throughput, and cost efficiency. Another, more highly controlled, means of developing is automatic spray processing, using equipment shown earlier in this chapter. Proper characterization of optimum developer normality, time, temperature, and concentration will be needed before large volumes of plates can be processed through an automatic system.

FIG. 4-26 Tamarack contact printer used in mask fabrication. *(Tamarack.)*

However, the time spent performing a complete imaging-system characterization will pay off in good process yields once the production cycle is started.

A high level of control over pattern-feature size in developing can be achieved by using developers of relatively low normality. This will extend the development time to several minutes instead of the 30 to 90 sec typically used to process 0.5-μm-thick positive-resist films. The effect of longer development time with lower developer normality is really limited to immersion developing since spray action accelerates the rate of development considerably. A mechanized-immersion developing process with $\pm 0.1°C$ bath temperature control and digital control of solution normality with a simple bath controller will yield more predictable pattern-geometry control and reliability than spray or puddle development.

One alternative to this method is to provide the same type of control on an in-line processor by retrofitting normality and high-level temperature control. Puddle or low-pressure spray nozzle application and precise digital timing of the cycle will result in a production process with high reliability, free of operator variability.

The advent of development rate monitors has increased the level of control possible in characterizing and running a resist process. The use of laser end point-type equipment will permit a resist system to be precisely characterized relative to softbake, exposure dose, and corresponding developer removal rate, and volume for a given set of well-controlled developer conditions. These systems are now commercially available and are highly recommended for any resist-imaging-process development effort.

Resist-developer control includes containment of the developer, in a way that insulates it from the process environment. One major problem is particulates in the developer, brought in from plate edges, air particles, resist flakes, and operator contamination. Particulates also form in the developer when its temperature is too low and it is frozen for a short period, or, when insoluble constituents form from improper manufacturing and/or filtration before use. Any of these particulates will find their way to the surface of a plate and cause a reject. Proper filtration with the equipment shown in Fig. 4-27 will protect against this possibility. This equipment serves as a solution to two major problems. First, particles are caught on an absolute filter membrane or in the nominal prefilter upstream. Second, the developer, being a solvent *or* an alkaline-type solution, is not exposed to the air. Positive-resist developers react with carbon dioxide $2OH^- + CO_2 \rightarrow CO_3^- + H_2O$ to form carbonate, thereby converting the active ingredient in the developer (NaOH or other alkaline species) to an inactive compound. Pressurized nitrogen

136 INTEGRATED CIRCUIT MASK TECHNOLOGY

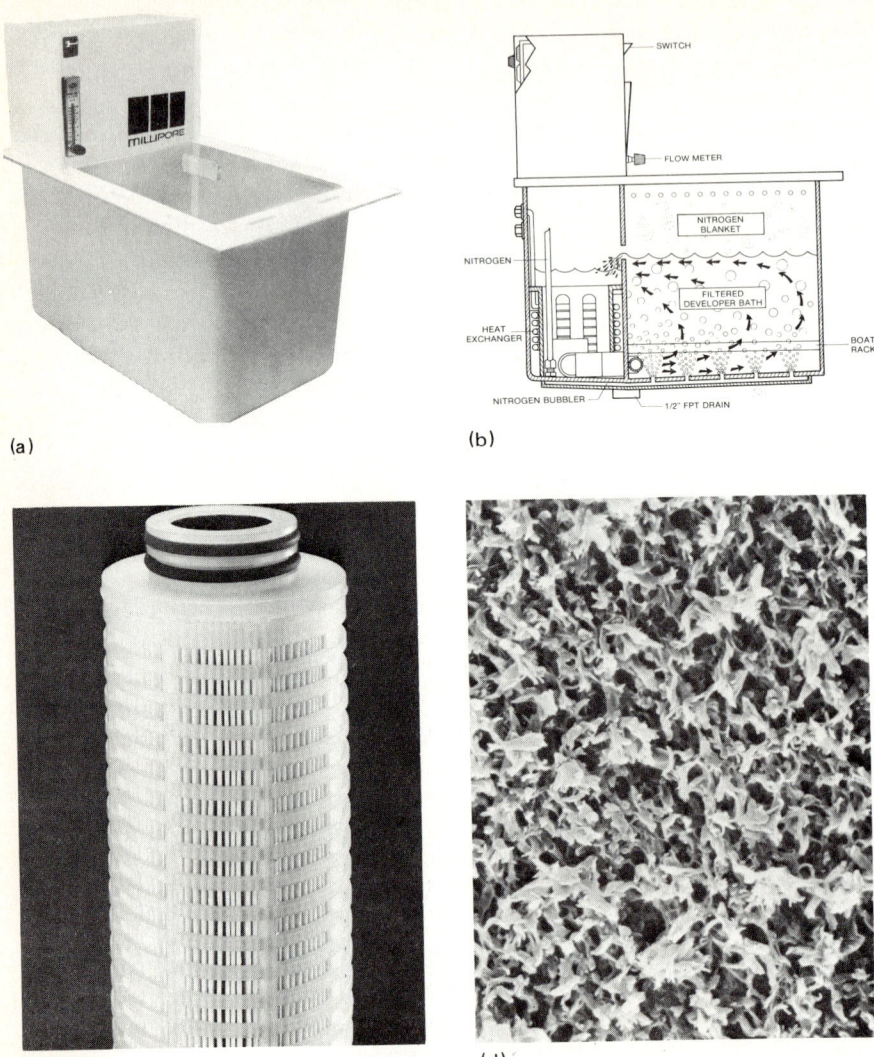

FIG. 4-27 Developer filtration equipment: (*a*) Millipore positive-developer Filterchem module, (*b*) cross section of Millipore positive-developer Filterchem module, (*c*) the Millipore filter used, and (*d*) a close-up of the filter. *(Millipore Corporation, Bedford, Mass.)*

keeps the developer clean and free from air, essential in controlling developer guidelines.

Developers for resists, especially positive resists, have the same need for batch-to-batch monitoring. Simple titration procedures are used to measure the precise level of the normality, and a functional test should also be part of incoming quality control on developers. Developer lots can be blended, as can resist batches, to even out functional and physical differences between various lots. If a facility can provide a large, clean nitrogen-blanketed holding tank or 5-gal stainless-steel pressure vessels for storage, blending can be done with little effort and good benefit to process control. Most processes hold the developer and resist parameters (sensitivity, normality) within 2 to 3 percent for the 1-μm line widths and 5 to 6 percent for 2- to 3-μm pattern dimensions. The same kind of control should be applied to process times and temperatures. The higher the level of control, the better the critical-dimension control. Adding up the total number of variations possible, in just the exposure and development steps in resist imaging, shows how important extreme control is in a process. Fortunately, new analytical tools and instrumentation, including good software, are becoming available for these kinds of control problems.

One example of the result of a control and characterization test to study the behavior of a developer is shown in Fig. 4-28. The increasing time, as expected, reduces the width of the resist line until a lessening of the developer dissolution rate creates a flat or more gently sloping part of the curve. This is the point where, ideally, a process should be set. Any excursions from a parameter on a nearly flat curve will have little or no effect on the pattern dimension. This is true of spin coatings, where spin time is set at a point where the curve begins to taper off. If production rate is not seriously reduced by placing imaging parameters on the flatter parts of the curves, then resist systems should be characterized and a process set up in this fashion.

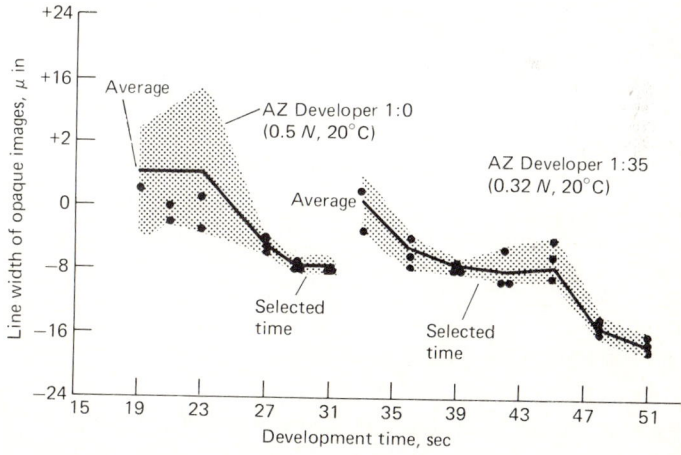

FIG. 4-28 Line width of resist pattern plotted against developer time.

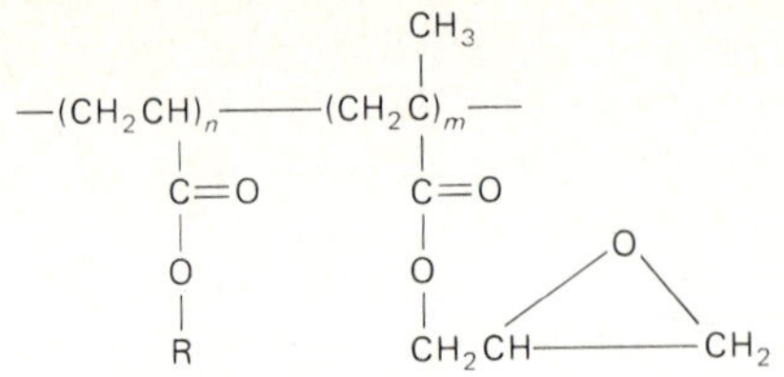

FIG. 4-29 Structural formula of poly(glycidyl methacrylate-co-ethyl acrylate), parent polymer of COP-type resist (R = alkyl or alkenyl).

Positive-resist developers, at reduced strength, have very flat points on the curve plotting line width against development time. In an attempt to keep production rates high, one parameter that is needed to control the dimension (normality) can be reduced, and another parameter that does not sacrifice this control but helps preserve production rates can be increased (developer temperature).

COP Negative Electron Resist

COP, based on a polymer of P(GMA-co-EA), is a widely used negative electron resist. Its sensitivity is in the range of 3×10^{-6} keV, and 1-μm geometries can be easily obtained with this material. The parent polymer structure for this resist is shown in Fig. 4-9. COP negative electron resist is developed in a 70:30 mixture of MEK (methyl ethyl ketone) and ethanol for 30 sec. This is followed by a rinse for 30 sec in a 25:75 mixture of MIBK (methyl isobutyl ketone) and 2-propanol. These two steps should have a 5-sec overlap. The third step is a second rinse in 2-propanol for 30 sec. The first and second rinse steps are also overlapped for 30 sec. The final step is a spin dry with heated nitrogen to prevent water condensation.

The dry-process resistance of COP is acceptable, and COP is now widely used in e-beam-imaging processes. There are several commercial suppliers of COP, including Mead Chemical Corporation in Rolla, Missouri.

PBS Positive Electron Resist

PBS is a positive electron resist with sensitivity of 8×10^{-7} C/cm² at 10 keV. PBS has resolution capability down to about 0.5 μm. The parent polymer structure for this resist is shown in Fig. 4-30. The developer formula for this resist is

PBS developer I (5-Methyl-2-hexanone + 2-pentanone) + $x\%$ H_2O

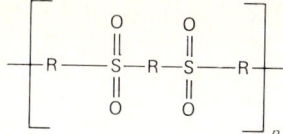

FIG. 4-30 Structural formula of parent polymer of PBS e-beam resist (R = pentene, butene, cyclopentene, or styrene).

Process the resist in this solution for 30 sec or more. In an ATF processor (liquid spray) developing is rapid, and careful control of developing time is needed. The temperature control should be 16 ± 0.5°C, and relative humidity should be 35 ± 5%. This resist will develop faster when the humidity is increased, and its sensitivity to both temperature and humidity is high.

Another developing process involves PBS developer II (5-methyl-2-hexanone, or MIAK). This is for use in a Solitec-type system as a pirating-type developer with a high rate. This is followed by a 5-sec overlap and then PBS rinse (MIAK:2-propanol made up in a 40:60 ratio) for 30 sec. This step is followed by a spin dry using ambient dry nitrogen.

Other Electron Resists

Table 4-5 (page 140) shows many of the electron resists available in both positive and negative polarities. The recent improvements in electron-resist latitude and dry-etch resistance make them very usable for high-density masks, where previous resists were difficult to control in production environments. Some of the most frequently used resists are tabulated below.

Positive		Negative	
Resist	Comment	Resist	Comments
PBS	Marginal dry process resistance	COP OEBR 100 SEL N B	All have reasonable process resistance, COP being lowest for dry-etch resistance.
PMMA (poly methyl methacrylate)	Good process resistance		

Backscatter in Resist Films

One of the aspects to check for in measuring and predicting resist behavior in electron-beam imaging is the movements of electrons

TABLE 4-5 Commonly used electron-beam resists and their properties

Resist trade name	Present manufacturer	Type	Polymer	Sensitivity C/cm²	Suggested minimum geometry
COP	Mead Chemical Corp.	Negative	P(GMA-co-EA)*	3×10^{-7} (10 keV)	1.0 µm
PBS	Mead Chemical Corp.	Positive	PBS†	8×10^{-7} (10 keV)	0.5 µm
Waycoat negative e-beam resist	Hunt Chemical Corp.	Negative	P(GMA-co-EA)	3×10^{-7} (10 keV)	1.0 µm
OEBR-100	Tokyo Ohka	Negative	PGMA‡	5×10^{-7} (20 keV)	1.0 µm
SEL-N	Somaru	Negative	Unknown	4×10^{-7} (27 keV)	0.5 µm
FMR-E 101	Fuji Chemical	Positive	PCA§	5×10^{-7} (20 keV)	0.5 µm

* P(GMA-co-EA) = poly (glycidyl methacrylate-co-ethyl acrylate).
† PBS = poly (butene-1-sulfone).
§ PCA = copolymer of α-cyano ethyl acrylate and α-amide ethyl acrylate.
‡ PGMA = poly (glycidyl methacrylate).

throughout the film, including both forward and backward (reflected) backscatter. Figure 4-31 shows some of the pathways taken by electrons as a beam is in the process of writing a pattern. Compensation for these effects and other process steps that impact geometries such as developing can be made adjusting the exposure level by one of the following methods:

1. Varying the dwell time (or scan speed of the beam) (easy for vector-scan systems, hard for raster-scan systems.)
2. Use a customized integrated exposure algorithm.
3. Pattern manipulation: changing both the size and location of patterns.

An example of a line-size adjustment is shown in Fig. 4-32. The dashed lines at the top indicate where a very small amount of the pattern is affected, indicating how precise this method can be.

Multilayer Resist Process

Multilayer resist processing is used primarily in wafer processes. There are occasional applications, however, in mask-making. One example is

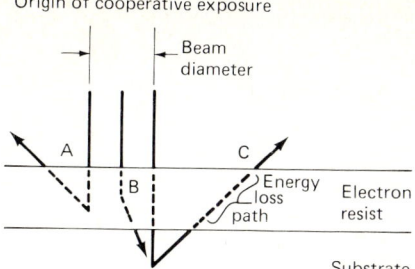

FIG. 4-31 Pathways for electrons in a substrate coated with resist. Key: Dashed line indicates energy-loss path in resist; A is backscatter in resist; B is forwardscatter in resist; C is backscatter in substrate.

when an extremely fine resolution pattern is required and a lift-off process is needed for an additive metal mask. In this case the blank would be coated first with a thick layer of the subcoat or nonimage material. This step is followed by the second or "top" coat (4000 Å) of the resist that will delineate the resist pattern. A process for a two-layer, multilevel imaging scheme that has worked in production is given as follows:

1. Spin coat PMMA (496,000 mol wt)
2. Bake at 180°C
3. Spin coat Kodak 809 resist
4. Bake at 82°C
5. Expose
6. Develop Kodak 809 resist

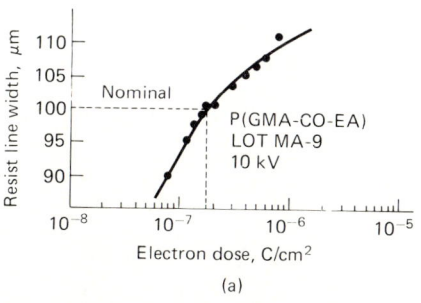
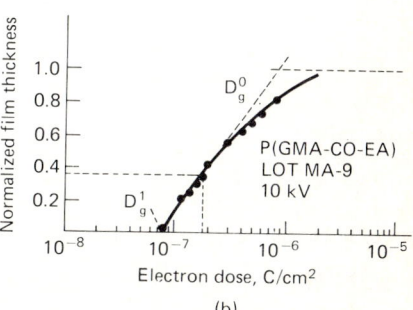

FIG. 4-32 Line-width adjustment in e-beam exposure.

7. Deep-uv flood PMMA for 2 min
8. Redevelop Kodak 809 resist in dilute MX-931
9. Develop PMMA in MIBK

This process was developed for wafer fabrication by Dr. Bartlett and coworkers at Hewlett-Packard,[1] and the results indicate the possibility of good submicron structures with optical lithography in production environments. This technology could be adapted to mask fabrication if the need exists for thicker coatings with submicron resolution. Thinner resist layers are being used as a means to finer resolution, and eventually pinhole incidence will be a preventive factor for mask makers, at which time they need not to turn to a two-layer process.

AZ-2400 as an Electron Resist

Some optical resists are excellent imaging materials in e-beam processes. One of the best-known examples of this adaptation is AZ-2400, an optical resist with e-beam sensitivity and process resistance that is suitable for mask fabrication. A process that is used for patterning chrome in an e-beam process with AZ-2400* is given in the following table. Publications have shown AZ-2400 to be an interesting material because of the following advantages in comparison to PMMA: higher sensitivity (1 to 4 times more sensitive than PMMA), ease of processing, and better resistance to plasma-etching conditions. The following information is available at present:

Process or Parameter	Condition
1. Sensitivity	2×10^{-5} C/cm², 20 kV
2. Thickness	0.6 μm is standard. Other thicknesses upon request.
3. Prebake	80°C for 1 hr. Already done on plates supplied by Shipley Company.
4. Developer	Shipley 2401, diluted: 1 part developer in 3.5 parts H_2O. Development time at room temperature is 1 to 4 min.
5. Postbake	Not necessary for usual chrome etchants.
6. Etching	Chemical or plasma etching possible.
7. Stripping	Shipley Remover 1112A, diluted: 1 part remover in 2 parts H_2O.

Electron-Beam Resist Troubleshooting

The main problem encountered in processing e-beam resists is troubleshooting the following areas: defects, image or pattern-size changes,

* AZ is a trademark of the American Hoechst Corporation.

swelling of the images, and edge roughness. Table 4-6 gives guidelines for troubleshooting these problems.

Electron-Beam Resist Selection

The primary determinants in choosing a resist for e-beam imaging are the type of hardware (e-beam machine) and the pattern resolution and critical-dimension control needed. Many e-beam writers will process optical resists that have been adapted for electron-beam imaging and that have relatively low sensitivity, while others require high-speed resists. The large number of different resists available for e-beam writing have various properties individually, but no single resist, positive or negative, has been developed that possesses all the key functional properties needed in e-beam writing.

Since the pattern-generated reticle, produced on a photo-optical system, can be dark-field or light-field depending on the type of emulsion used (reversal or negative), positive or negative resists can be selected for e-beam writing. Main resist properties to identify before selection are

1. Chemical stability and toxicity (should be nontoxic)
2. Shelf life (6 months minimum)
3. Polydispersivity (molecular weight distribution)
4. Coating uniformity (no striations)
5. Sensitivity
6. Developer latitude (important)
7. Image contrast (maximum aspect ratio)
8. Dry- and wet-etch resistance
9. Thermal stability

All resist components should be nontoxic (desirable) and must be noncarcinogenic. Chemical stability figures into the defect picture as a potential problem. Filtration before use will usually remove insoluble components, but *then* the functional properties may change, especially if some sensitizer or solids content is removed, which is probably what happens. Chemical stability is checked by various quality-control tests. Shelf life is related to chemical stability, except the aspect of toxicity is removed. Shelf life is simply the ability of the product to remain as a true solution in the process environment for a specified minimum period of time. Accelerated shelf-life tests are commonly run by placing the resist sample in an oven at 100 to 120°F for several hours and then

TABLE 4-6 Trouble-shooting Chart

Problem	Possible cause	Corrective action
Line-width fluctuation	Dose arrows	Check spot current and run exposure series for resist.
	Spot-size variation	Recalibrate spot size with some reproducible, preferably automated, method.
	Resist thickness problems	Check spin speed and compare color of problem resist with control plate.
	Sensitivity change	Run an exposure series for any new resist batch received.
	Developer change	Time developer steps. Look for variations in: dispense pressures, solvent flow rates, solvent lot, manufacturer, or concentration. Check for solvent or plumbing contaminants.
	Cure time inadequate	Adjust to approximately one-half of write time.
	Mask-temperature variation	Equilibrate mask with developer environment.
	Nozzle-temperature variation	Adjust to within ±0.5°C of known acceptable nozzle temperature.
	Relative-humidity variations	Check room hygrometer for possible humidity excursions of greater than 1 ±5% RH.
Edge roughness	Insufficient dose	Increase spot current and control within ±5%.
	Focus poor	Focus beam with some reproducible automated procedure.
	Mask plane and focal plane not coincident	Examine mask mounting system for possible problems.
	Insufficient cure time	Consult resist technology package accompanying resist.
	Recoated plates improperly cleaned	Check plate cleaning and coating procedures.
	Spray pressure too high	Check N_2 regulators and aspirate delivery pressure for variations. Check solvent dispense pressure on unaspirated system.
	Spray not uniform	Examine spray nozzles and solvent lines for contamination.

TABLE 4-6 Trouble-shooting Chart *(Continued)*

Problem	Possible cause	Corrective action
Swelling	Overdevelopment	Adjust develop time.
	Developer concentration too high	Consult developer supplier for possible solvent changes.
	Develop cycle too long	Time develop cycle.
	Rinse cycle too long	Time rinse step.
	Relative humidity too high	Monitor room RH.
	Water in developer	Determine developer content and history.
	Resist overexposed	Run exposure series.
Defects Chrome spots and pinholes	Water condensation	Dry N_2 purge needed, or humidity too high.
	Solvent contaminated	Examine solvents and plumbing for particulates.
	Resist too thin	Increase resist thickness.
	Dispense or aspirate pressure too high	Reduce pressure.
	Processing or exposure facility not Class 10,000 or better	Perform particle count in critical areas. All hoods and the exposure area should be Class 100 or better.
	Poor clean-room procedures	No comment.

running a battery of key property tests such as sensitivity, resolution, solids content, and others.

Molecular weight distribution has a direct effect on the functional properties and is always specified at a certain level each time a new lot of resist is ordered. Control of this parameter is extremely important in processes where very high resolution is required. Since some masks or reticles (written at $10\times$ for final geometries as large as 3 to 4 μm) are not in a highly critical resolution area, molecular weight specifications can be broader.

Coating uniformity is a standard industry requirement for all resists, and a test to measure a given resist behavior in this area should be part of incoming quality-control testing. Sensitivity is another standard functional property that should be checked on each new lot, both by the manufacturer and by the user. A double check is necessary, first to verify the results of the manufacturer and second to guard against possible damage to the material in transit.

Developer latitude is process characterization performed by the user and involves running a matrix or two on line size versus the key developer variables cited earlier in this chapter. Image contrast is, in a sense, a measure of the resist-system latitude. It indicates how fine the resolved images can be in the exposed (negative) or unexposed (positive) areas, whether they are with straight or slightly sloping sidewalls, how sharp the image edges are, and how thick the coating can be. The thicker the coating (up to 1 μm), the better the protection against pinholes, coating defects, overdeveloping, and sheer handling resistance. The higher the contrast, the greater the difference in solubility between exposed and unexposed areas. VLSI resolution requirements seek pattern sizes at 0.5 μm with a coating thickness of 1.0 μm.

Dry-etch resistance is a fundamental property since many production masks and reticles are etched in plasma and other dry-etching environments. Dry-etch resistance can be checked by taking high-magnification scanning electron micrographs of the resist surface, cross sections of exact thickness (also in a SEM), and isometric pictures of the microstructures on the substrate. After etching, take the same three different angles, checking for degradation of the surface, films or resist scum left around the substrate, a change (reduction) of the thickness indicating attack, and an overall reduction of image sharpness. Dry-etch parameters can be varied and different etch gases or ratios of the same gas tried to achieve better resist compatibility. Finally, resists can be hardened before etching with chemical, thermal, or photo-optical treatments to provide increased resistance to the etch. Common treatments are postbaking, postexposure baking, postdevelopment exposure (broadband exposure for wet-etch resistance and deep-uv flood exposure for thermal resistance), and chemical treatments to cross-link the surface for improved wet- and dry-etch resistance.

Thermal stability is primarily a function of the glass transition temperature of the resin system in the resist. In addition to a 10- to 30-min flood exposure to high-intensity deep-uv sources, resist images can be baked *above* their range of thermal instability. For example, a heat source that can carry the resist through its glass transition zone in a few seconds will keep the resist dimensionally stable. Conventional ovens that heat more slowly to reach a high temperature above resist glass transition spend too much time at all temperature levels, permitting considerable resist thermal flow and image distortion.

PATTERN GENERATION

Pattern generators are optical-flash exposure systems used to produce the pattern data for a mask or reticle from digital input. The optical pattern generator takes the material software result of the CAD digitized tapes and converts it to a series of exposures on either an emulsion or photoresist-coated chrome plate at $10\times$. Pattern generators have worked "longer hours" since VLSI patterns have become so complex that the number of flash exposures required by the system often exceeds several hundred thousand. The increase in run time has been dramatic as a result of these more complex masks, going from 2 to 4 hr for simpler pre-VLSI patterns to up to 40 hr for a multiple-die reticle on a chrome plate. Typical pattern-generation time on one level can exceed 30 to 40 hr per level, with over 600,000 flashes required to print all the pattern information. The large amount of time required has been the main reason for e-beam writing as a method for reticle generation.

The wafer stepper is a main factor in creating the need for a faster method than pattern generation in complex IC designs. In order to keep defects low, near-perfect arrays at $10\times$ times the final size are required. Making several arrays of the pattern on a single plate helps ensure that at leat one is good or has near-zero defect levels. An arrayed reticle takes several times the pattern generation time of earlier reticles. Despite these technology changes and the concomitant pressures placed on pattern generators, the e-beam writing alternative is very costly, and many manufacturers have stayed with conventional photo-optical pattern-generation techniques. The main arguments used to justify the e-beam equipment expenditure are low defects, high critical-dimension control, and excellent registration, all for state-of-the-art patterns. The defect issue is critical in cost justification since it is the main leveraging parameter in establishing process yields. The need for $1\times$ master plates, also defect-free, for use in the 1:1 scanning projection printers is equally strong. Electron-beam and photo-optical step-and-repeat mask-making equipment is used to fill these needs. The geometries on these masks at $1\times$ are in the 1-μm region with registration accuracies of 0.25 μm and smaller.

Pattern-Generator Capabilities

High-resolution pattern generators for imaging emulsion and chrome are widely used in reticle production, both arrayed and nonarrayed. Figure 4-33 shows a photograph of the GCA/Mann Type 3600 pattern generator. This system features interchangeable light sources for various light-sensitive materials and interchangeable lenses for patterning at different sizes and formats. Photoresist exposure requires one wavelength, while silver halide requires another. This unit has a laser-metered

148 INTEGRATED CIRCUIT MASK TECHNOLOGY

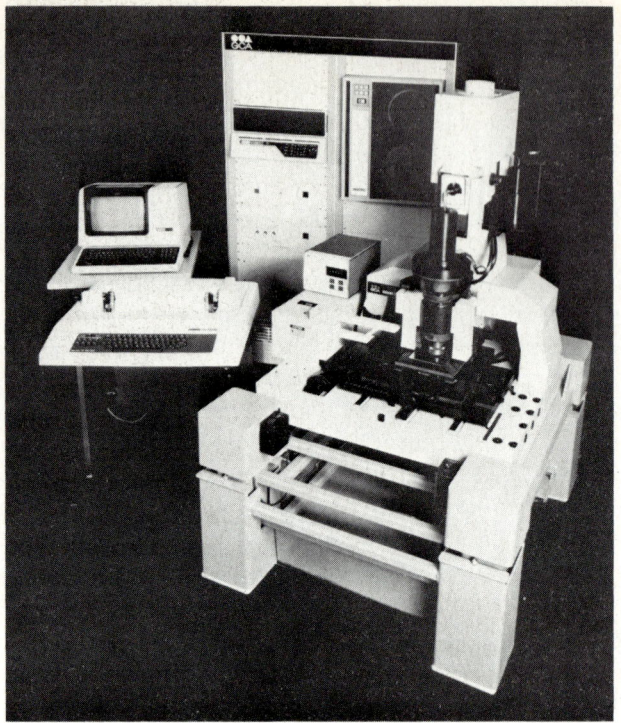

FIG. 4-33 GCA/Mann Type 3600 optical pattern generator. *(GCA Corp. Bedford, Mass.)*

xy stage and is placed in an environmental chamber to keep particulates and other clean-room contaminants at a minimum. The conversion from an emulsion-printing mode to a resist-printing mode can be made in several minutes, an important production feature since both materials are widely used. The system has its own computer for processing pattern data in both emulsion and photoresist exposure modes. The input via the keyboard can be used to vary exposure parameters such as intensity and time.

Highly linear stage movements are controlled by a laser interferometric metering system over a 6 × 6 in (150 × 150 mm) area. The input for the computer can be in metric or USCS units. The *xy* resolution is 1 μin and 0.1 μm. Image-placement stability and accuracy for VLSI mask or reticle patterns are very critical. The 3600 pattern generator has image-placement accuracy controlled by directly referencing the laser-interferometer system to the optical column.

Plate Stability

The optical flashing of the pattern generator can be very precisely controlled in terms of exposure dose, exposure position, and mechanical stability. However, the plate being imaged is a supercoated liquid structure that moves enough to upset the critical-dimension tolerances of VLSI patterns. For example, gravitational sag *alone* can cause a given mask level to be run out of specification *while* the pattern generator is running over the 20- to 40-hr imaging time. Plate flatness may even be poor when the unexposed plate is brought into the production area for exposure. The temperature of the plate, the imaging environment, and even the temperature maximum and minimum levels the plate has experienced up to 24 hr *before* reaching the pattern generator are important. Hysteresis effects, caused by the glass relieving itself in the clean-room (pattern-generator) area after experiencing very warm or cool ambients, should be measured and accommodated so that they do not influence the patterning process.

The stability of the glass or quartz substrate is first controlled by verifying the thermal history of the glass plate 24 hr before reaching the pattern generator. Next, the plate should be quickly checked for real-time flatness and then can be loaded assuming cleanliness and other data needed for processing are complete. Once in the sytem, the plate-holding environment can impact flatness. In the GCA/Mann 3600 system, vacuum plate holders provide a means of keeping the flatness at a level needed for high-resolution imaging. The variety of features possible in the imaging process, all software delivered, include device scaling, aperture incrementing, origin offset, mirror imaging, and rotation. In the next section we will review key functional properties of this system that determine its performance in a production line.

Staging

The 6 × 6 in (150 × 150 mm) stage travel area is governed by coarse- and fine-focus frictionless motions. An HP5501A laser transducer with closed-loop servocontrol manages the stage positioning and references it directly to the optical axis. Laser metering of the stage is a key to maintaining the close registration tolerances required in the reticle- or mask-pattern specifications.

The speed of the stage in both x and y axes is 50 mm/sec (2 in/sec). The least count of xy motion is $\lambda/16$ with data input of 1 μin in USCS mode and 0.1 μm in metric mode. Accuracy for full travel is ±0.6 μm in each axis, and positional precision is ±0.26 μm. Orthogonality of stage motion is ±1.0 arc second or better.

Control System

A teletype and digital controller system are part of the electronic control system of the 3600 and can be supplemented by adding a keyboard video terminal. At the teletype keyboard, the operator runs the pattern generator as magnetic-tape data are fed through the system. This control is extended to the area around the hardware by the laser measurement system, which will automatically adjust the instrument to compensate for changes in the ambient temperature. Other control aspects include a vibration base, fundamental to elimination of low- and high-frequency vibrations that can, if unchecked, alter the accuracy of the imaging. Part of the installation procedure for this type of equipment is checking to be sure the location is *not* directly over a main carrying beam, which will increase the amount of vibration many times.

Close temperature control is another needed factor in pattern generation. The glass elements in the lens system are all subject to the predictable movement based on their composition and coefficient of linear expansion. VLSI geometries are calling for image control in tenths of a micrometer, so temperature control in tenths of a degree are not unreasonable. A typical specification for temperature is ±0.1°C (±0.2°F) at 20°C (68°F) ambient. The air-quality needs of the pattern-generation process are those of a clean-room. The concept of enclosing the pattern generator in its own Class 50 clean-room-level chamber adds increased insulation from potential defect sources. The cost of this additional control is small when measured against the value of near-zero defect–level reticles.

Plate Handling

Plates for pattern generation need to be processed with minimal operator involvement for the sake of defect control. On the GCA/Mann 3600 system an automatic plate-changing system permits up to 20 plates to be run without operator interference. Plates are cycled via an integrated air-cushion transfer and vacuum holding system. The plates are moved in and out of cassettes in darkroom safelight conditions. Resist lighting for diazo positive materials is a yellow or gold fluorescent tube, while a red safelight is needed for silver-halide emulsions.

Special Kodak filter numbers are available if the user specifies the type and number of the emulsion. Silver halide coatings are produced to different wavelength sensitivities. Emulsion exposure is made with a $10\times$ e-line lens in the 3600 pattern generator. A xenon flash is the light source, with a maximum flash rate of 100 flashes per second.

Photoresist exposure is made with a $10\times$ g-line reduction lens and a 350-W mercury arc source. One-millisecond exposure increments are provided over a range from 0.1 to 4.0 sec using a high-speed shutter. In the GCA Type 3600F pattern generator, the exposure energy is integrated for a decrease of up to 50 percent of the original lamp intensity level. This is an extremely important feature for any pattern generator, photorepeater, or wafer exposure system. All mercury-lamp exposure systems have the problem of metal deposition on the quartz envelope surrounding the light source. As this material coats the sidewalls of the bulb structure, transmission is reduced, and without exposure integration, significant losses in exposure dose would result.

The uniformity of illumination is second in importance to having a constant intensity. Typical uniformity specifications on pattern generators run between ± 3 and ± 7 percent, depending on the manufacturer. The GCA Type 3600F calls out a uniformity of ± 5 percent. Exposure uniformity determines, in part, the size of the patterns reproduced in emulsion or photoresist and electron resist. Figure 4-34 shows the line

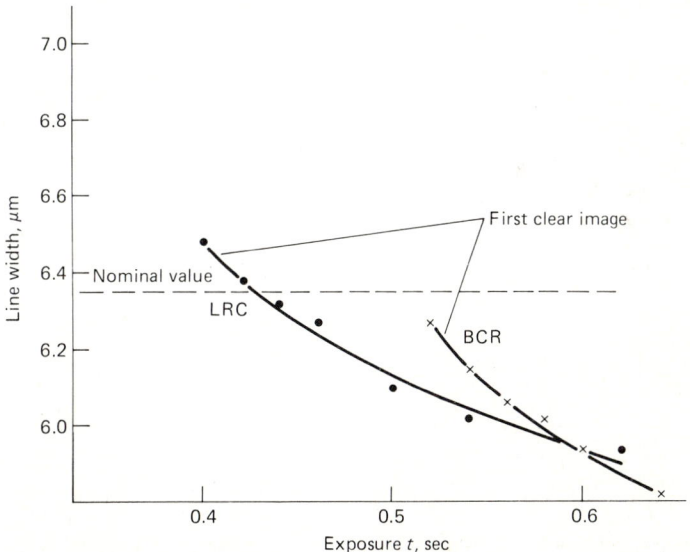

FIG. 4-34 Exposure versus line width for substrates of varying reflectivity. Key: BCR is chrome; LRC is low-reflectivity chrome.

152 INTEGRATED CIRCUIT MASK TECHNOLOGY

width in micrometers versus relative exposure, plotted for substrates of varying reflectivity. Note that even the changes in reflectivity of several percent will make significant changes in line width, especially for geometries in the 1-μm region. Exposure energy control is the most important aspect of mask-image transfer processes. Uniformity of illumination over the active area, including intensity control from the exposure source, is a major variable to control in the imaging process.

Exposure Energy versus Line Width

The variations in pattern sizes are most generally caused by energy-dose variations in exposure. Contrast of the image also plays a role in the line width since it also affects the amount of energy that reaches the resist or emulsion layers. Figure 4-35 shows a comparison of the effects of variations in the contrast of the exposure energy. The high-

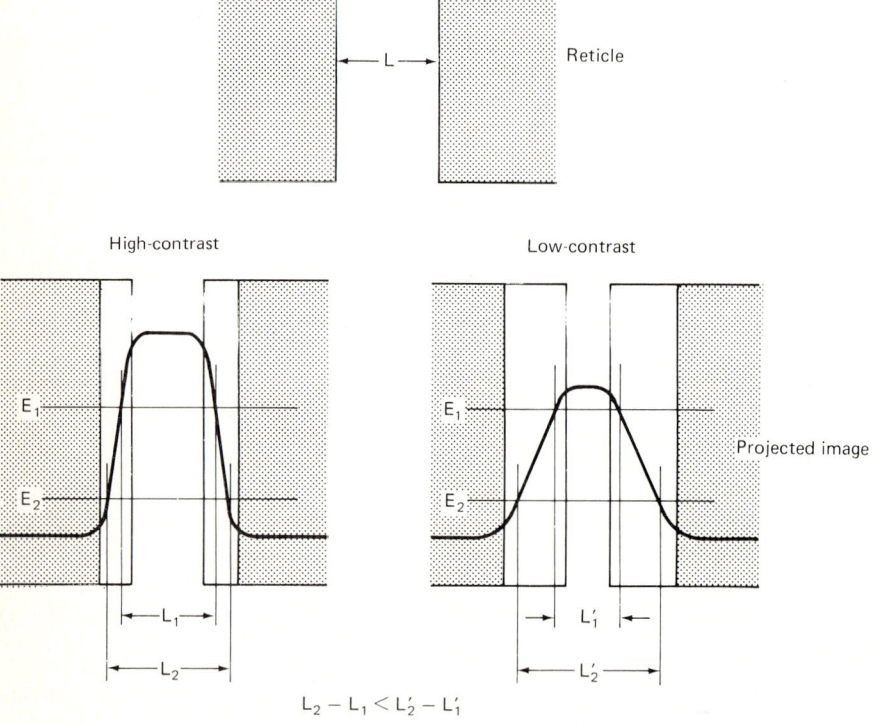

FIG. 4-35 Projected-image contrast versus line width.

contrast signal is shown at two different energy levels (E_1 and E_2), as is the low-contrast signal. The resultant changes in line width are drawn in the figures as L_1, L_2, L_1', L_2'. These variations in pattern dimension show why high-contrast images are preferred to low-contrast images and also why it is important to keep the energy constant while the emulsion or resist is being exposed and uniform over the mask area. Many production operations run two and three shifts and keep exposure systems at a uniform intensity and area. Uniformity requires constant quality-control testing on the line.

Modulation Transfer Function

Imaging with optical systems can be explained in terms of the modulation transfer function (MTF). The MTF is expressed as the ratio of the contrast in the image to the object contrast and is plotted as a function of spatial frequency. In exposure situations where chrome on glass masks are used, the object contrast is almost 1. If the object contrast is theoretically or nearly 1, the MTF will be equal to the image contrast (projected). Figure 4-36 shows the plot of MTF against spatial frequency in lines per millimeter for two hypothetical optical systems.

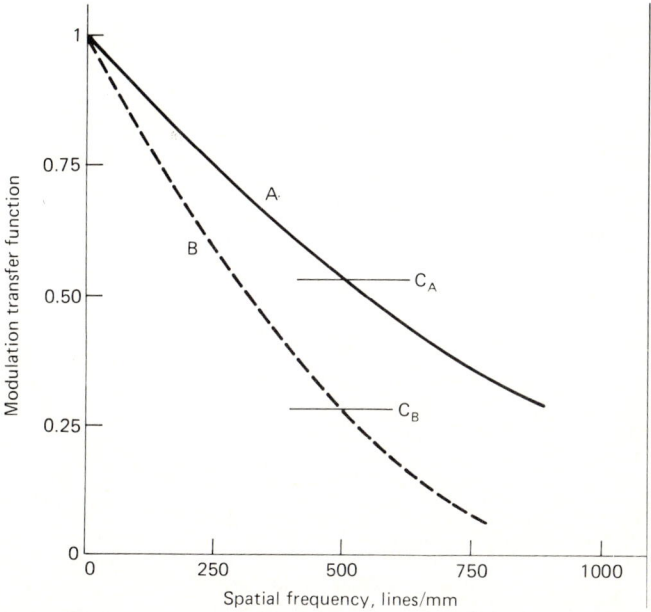

FIG. 4-36 Modulation transfer function plotted against spatial frequency.

Most resist systems require an MTF signal of 60 percent (0.60) or better to form a high-resolution image with good resist sidewall angles (over 75°). A 60 percent modulation will still result in reproduction of the mask image in the resist. Signals modulated below 60 percent by the optical-imaging system will not, with most resists, result in a faithful reproduction of the patterns in the reticle or mask.

Studies have shown that the slope of the exposure characteristic curve is inversely proportional to the MTF. This relationship is useful in predicting the amount of process latitude in a given resist system. The characteristic curves for AZ-1350 are plotted in Fig. 4-37. The graph shows line width versus relative exposure dose for three types ($f1.8$, $f1.7$, and $f1.6$) of $10\times$ reduction lenses. This particular study compared characteristic curves for a 1- and 3-µm line width. Note that the slopes for the 1-µm lines are slightly greater. However, the 1-µm images show various slopes depending on the lens used, while the 3-µm images all

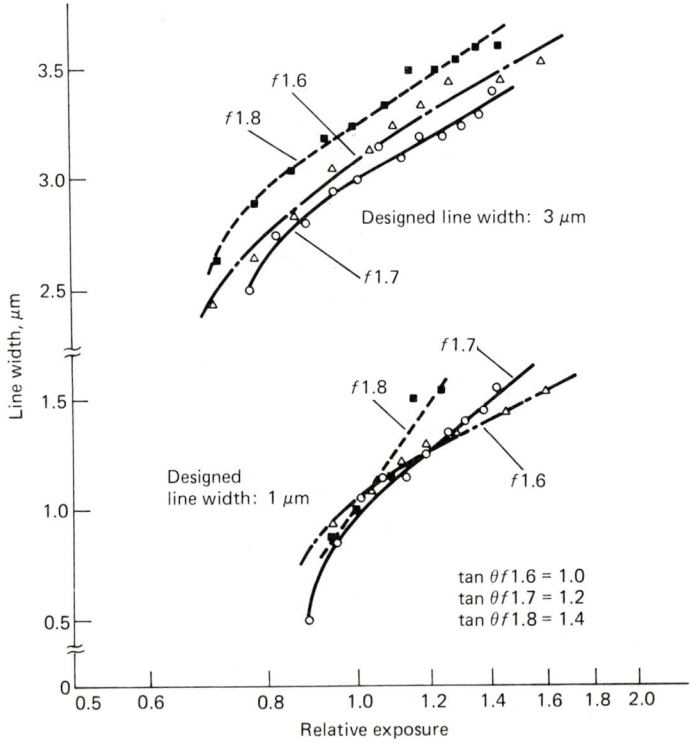

FIG. 4-37 AZ-1350 exposure characteristic curves; relative exposure plotted against lens type.

have the same slope. The $f1.6$ lens with 1-μm images was the worst case (smallest slope). Ideally, the lens-resist combination results in a very steep slope so that variations in relative or actual exposure have only a small effect on pattern width. In the experiment shown in the plot of relative exposure versus line width, the $f1.8$ lens showed greatest drift or deviation from the designed or optimum (1:1) pattern dimension. In general, these test results show that smaller pattern geometries are more difficult to control than larger ones.

The need to provide increasingly smaller MTFs for shrinking geometries places pressure on both the optical and the resist systems. There is little one can do to make major changes in the MTF response of a given resist system without making basic changes in the resist chemistry. The easiest change is to improve the MTF by improving the optical system. The characteristic curve data given above showed the advantage of the $f1.6$ lens over the larger-aperture $f1.7$ and $f1.8$ lenses. The differences in aperture size between the $f1.6$ and the $f1.8$ accounted for the 40 percent improvement in MTF of the smaller aperture ($f1.6$) compared to the $f1.8$ lens. Looking back to the MTF curves, we can see that a 40 percent change in MTF results in a significant corresponding change in spatial frequency or potential resolution. Thus, lens improvement from $f1.8$ to $f1.6$ can provide substantial gains in obtainable resolution.

Depth of Focus

One of the main factors in obtaining maximum line-width control in mask and reticle production is the depth of focus on the lens used. In previous chapters we have shown the various sources and degree of nonflatness that exist in mask-making as a result of substrate nonuniformities, temperature excursions during plate processing, and exposure equipment variables. The problem of having nonuniform flatness is only complicated by focus changes in the projected image during resist exposure. Since the focus depth is relatively shallow for most lenses used in microlithography, nonflatness approaching or exceeding the lens depth of focus will change image sizes recorded in resist. The improvements in automatic flatness compensation in exposure equipment have helped reduce this source of variability. Automatic focus has also reduced line-width control problems by refocusing each die pattern before exposing. However, in many cases the production throughput will not permit the additional time spent for this operation, and focus will be made only at the beginning of each individual array pattern.

Focus drift occurring while the active area is being printed will cause the pattern to shift if the drift exceeds the focal depth of the lens. Hence, the importance of lens depth of focus; it exists as a dimensional window within which all patterning ideally occurs.

Rayleigh's theorem is used to show the focal depth of a perfect lens as

$$\Delta x = 2\lambda f^2$$

where Δx = depth of focus
λ = wavelength of light
f = aperture number of lens

This formula points out the reduction in depth of focus as the f number of the lens is reduced. Thus, while the smaller f number of the lens helped provide a higher MTF, the cost is a reduction in depth of focus. Figure 4-38 shows the change in resolution as a function of focus shift for $f1.6$ and $f1.7$ lenses. Note the wider latitude of the $f1.7$ lens. A focus shift of ± 4 μm can change pattern sizes by more than 0.2 μm, an amount that will be beyond the specification of many VLSI mask designs. Since critical dimension control is typically about 10 percent of the minimum line width, a 2-μm line requires ± 0.2-μm control.

Geometries below 1 μm are increasingly sensitive to focus changes. Figure 4-39 shows how much more sensitive a 1-μm line is than a 3-μm

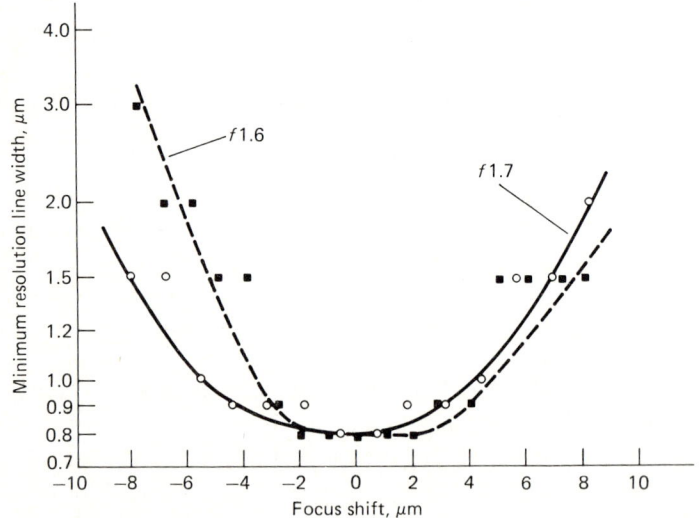

FIG. 4-38 Focus shift versus resolution change.

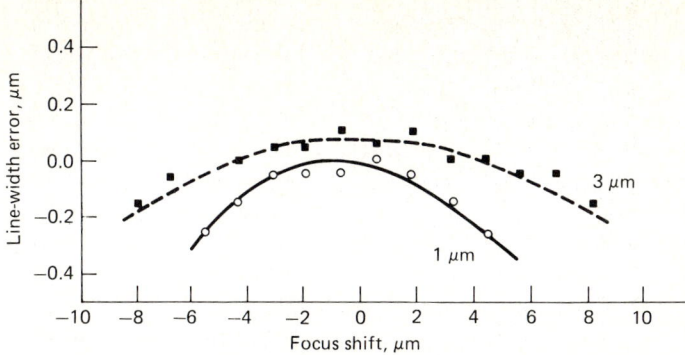

FIG. 4-39 Line-width error plotted against focus shift.

line to depth-of-focus changes. Note that the focal depth with the $f1.6$ lens used to produce the data is about 2 μm, and the theoretical figure would be

$$\Delta x = 2(0.45 \text{ μm})(1.6^2)$$
$$\Delta x = 2.304 \text{ μm}$$

The 2.304-μm theoretical value is within 10 percent of the actual figure, showing good correlation. Depth of focus of a lens then trades off with MTF, but selecting an f number with a high MTF ($f1.6$) and controlling focus to within the limit shown (2 μm) will provide the control and resolution potential needed to image 1-μm geometries. This assumes a "cooperating" resist and etch system. Optimizing each step of the imaging process is needed to keep all variables under control, and selecting a resolution level to meet is a necessary part of this process. Imaging 1-μm geometries is pointless unless an etch process is provided that will reliably etch the 1-μm patterns with the necessary control.

Reflectance versus Resolution

Reflectance data for several types of glass-blank coatings were given in previous chapters. The effects of reflectance on resist-imaging latitude and image resolution are given here to aid in designing a process for maximum line-width control and optimum pattern resolution. Images passing through an optical system are affected at all stages by the diffusion of light in air, the absorption of light by various lens elements, and the internal reflections occurring on optical surfaces and on some nonoptical ones. Lenses are coated with antireflection materials, and lens housings are made flat black to minimize reflections. Once the image reaches the resist surface, further attempts to preserve its quality are made by reducing reflectance of the material onto which the resist is coated.

The light reflected back into the "arriving" image at the resist-chrome interface causes serious line-width control and resolution problems. Unwanted positive-resist exposure caused by reflections reduces pattern resolution in a nonuniform manner relative to pattern sizes. Reduction of exposure latitude adds more problems, and thin (0.02 μm) chrome oxide films must be added on top of the bright chrome to reduce these problems. The resulting antireflective substrate compares very favorably with the bright chrome as shown in Fig. 4-40. This figure shows the relationship between line width and exposure for 3- and 1-μm lines using standard chrome with 65 percent reflectance and antireflective chrome with only 6 percent reflectance. The data point out the ability

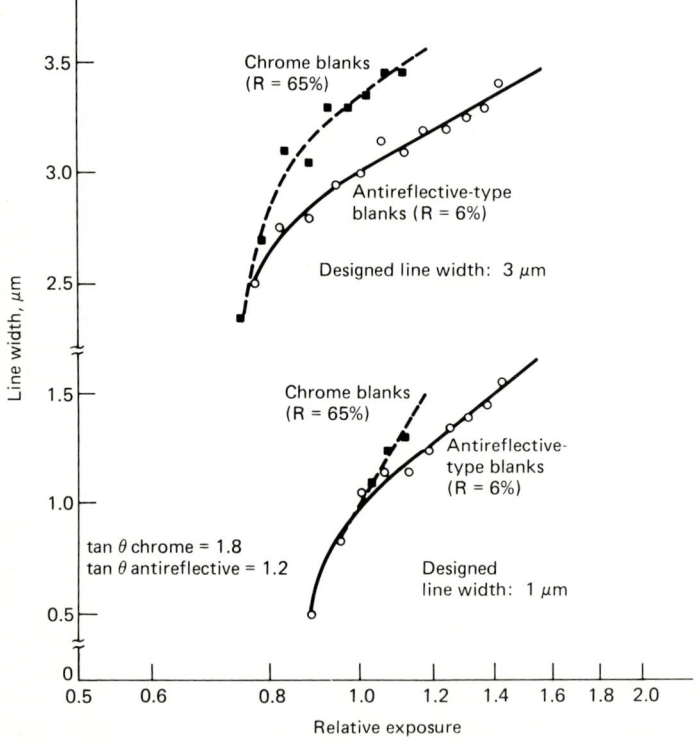

FIG. 4-40 Line width versus exposure for the reflection of different substrates.

of the antireflective chrome to match the designed line width better and also be more controllable at a given line size, compared to the standard bright chrome.

Measuring the effects of reflected light on MTF is possible by using the following formula:

$$C' = \frac{1}{1 + R} C$$

where C = contrast when reflectivity is zero
C' = contrast when reflectivity is R

In practice these values work out so that the antireflective chrome at a reflectance value of zero leaves the bright chrome with a value of 1.56. The effect of reduced reflectivity is also an increase in MTF, since the reflected light, interfering with the incoming incipent projected image, reduces the contrast or MTF values.

MTF versus Resist and Developer Parameters

Having considered the impact of the lens system and the substrate reflectance on MTF, we must also calculate the resist system impact on MTF. Most hard-surface masks are imaged with a positive optical resist, typically AZ-1350 or Microposit 1450B. This system is used for its high differential solubility (approximately 100) and wide imaging latitude with good resolution. The various resist parameters and their effect on each other and on the final imaged result are not discussed in detail here.[2] Here we will consider specific aspects of resist processing that most strongly impact MTF. These parameters are the resist thickness and the developer concentration. The other parameters are generally fixed by the process constraints or by supplier recommendations. For example, the resist softbake is usually 85 to 105°C, and development time is 30 to 60 sec for immersion. Development times are fixed to a certain extent by the rate of resist dissolution in the developer and the resist thickness.

The resist film thickness should be the minimum needed to give etch protection and a 10 to 15 percent addition to allow for overdeveloping and process variation. The absolute thickness used will vary since plates have different degrees of surface uniformity and etchability. The different glass or quartz coating materials, such as iron oxide, silicon, and chrome oxides, etch at different rates and have varying resist thickness needs for pinhole protection. In general the thinner the resist, the better the MTF, so the objective is to arrive at a "safe" minimum.

One additional factor in establishing resist film thickness is dust and

160 INTEGRATED CIRCUIT MASK TECHNOLOGY

handling resistance. Submicron particles are a frequent "visitor" to resist-coated blanks, and coatings below 0.5 μm are more susceptible to pinholing when particles either cause dewetting or bridge their way to the substrate interface. Resist coatings as thin as 800 Å have been used to image and etch (dry and wet) chromium. While this thickness may be used under highly optimized conditions, a much thicker layer is more practical and will not greatly sacrifice any optical contrast or resolution.

The thickness range used for positive optical resist on mask surfaces is 0.6 to 0.2 μm. The thinner the resist layer, the lower the MTF. Empirical testing of resist thickness versus line-width control shows, in Fig. 4-41, that variations in line size run on the order of 25 percent for 0.2-μm-thick resists and 40 percent for 0.5-μm-thick films, both measured on 1-μm line widths. Considering all the relationships shown in the figure, it is probably safe to assume a compromise between 0.2- and 0.5-μm-thick resists to optimize all parameters including reproduction

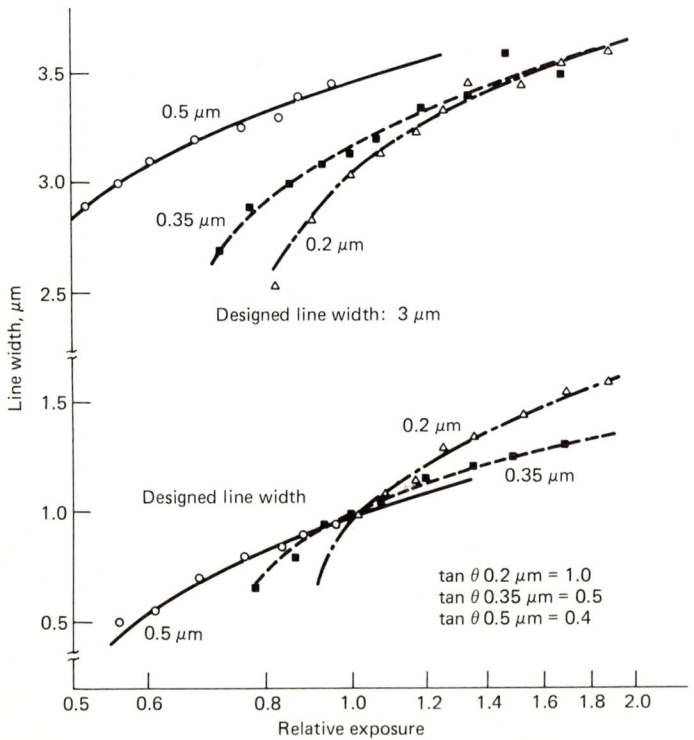

FIG. 4-41 Resist thickness plotted against line-width control.

relative to the original mask, pinhole protection, line control, and resolution.

Developer concentration is another key parameter in controlling the MTF in the imaged substrate. The AZ-1350B and Microposit 1450B resist systems, using AZ Developer at a 1:1 makeup with deionized water, result in about the best MTF obtainable for this system. Attempts to use stronger developer concentration will reduce the MTF and also make the 1-μm-range pattern geometries more difficult to control. Also, higher developer concentrations beyond 50 percent (for AZ Developer) reduce the differential solubility and therefore reduce image resolution. In processes where extreme control is desired, this developer can be made up at a 40 percent concentration with comparable imaging results to the 50 percent bath makeup.

Parametric MTF Improvement

The various parameters that affect the MTF have been discussed individually, but of course they are integrally related and function as a unit in producing a single MTF value. The area of impact, along with the imaging system changes discussed and the amount of MTF improvement, is shown in Table 4-7. These parameters were studied and implemented in a mask fabrication process at the Musashi works of Hitachi Limited in Japan.

PHOTOREPEATERS

Where the pattern generator produces the VLSI pattern on a reticle or mask from digital data, the photorepeater generates arrays of the IC images. Photorepeaters typically image directly onto resist-coated chromium. The system described below is a GCA Type 3696, shown here in Fig. 4-42. The GCA Type 3696 photorepeater is a laser interferometer–metered step-and-repeat microreduction camera. This system operates at $5\times$ (20-mm² image area) and $10\times$ (10-mm² image area). The laser-metered xy stage has an exposable area of 150 × 150 mm (6

TABLE 4-7 Parametric MTF improvement

Area of Improvement	Parameter Change	MTF improvement
Lens (10×)	$f1.8$ to $f1.6$	1.4
Depth of focus	±5 to ±2 μm	2.1
Blank reflectance	65–6%	1.5
Resist thickness	0.5–0.35 μm	0.8

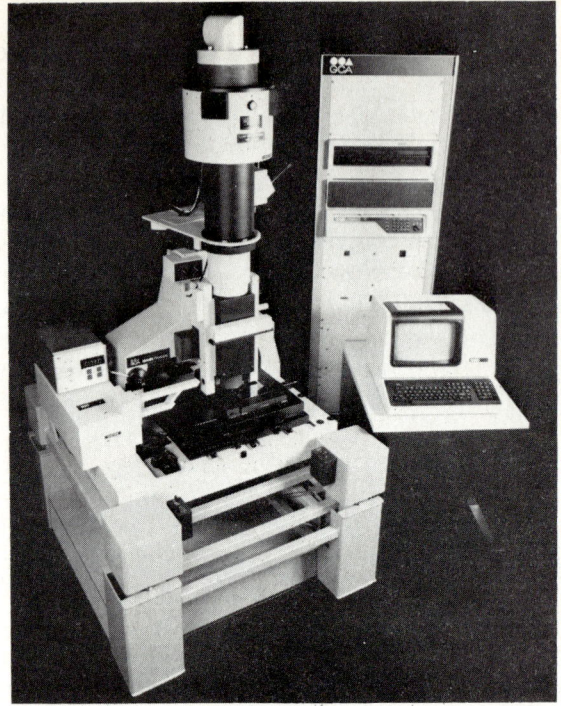

FIG. 4-42 GCA Type 3696 photorepeater. *(GCA Corp.)*

× 6 in), with a stage speed of 50 mm/sec. The laser that controls the stage is directly referenced to the optical column. The accuracy of the stage is ±0.6 μm on both the x and the y axis for the full distance of the stage travel, and positional precision is ±0.2 μm with the recommended environmental control. The least count of xy motions is $\lambda/16$ with 1-μin data input (0.1 μm). Finally, the stage orthogonality is ±0.5 arc second with software correction.

Control of most photorepeaters is by computer wherein a terminal with video or disk input can be made. The computer will be used to establish major parameters of the images, including array size, stepping intervals, measurement units, array origin, drop in test pattens, orthogonality scaling, and exposure values. Typically the software will allow arrays in a variety of shapes including squares, rectangles, and circles. In the GCA Type 3696 photorepeater, the laser system includes velocity-of-light (VOL) compensation for environmental variations.

Photorepeaters are powered by mercury arc lamps. The GCA Type

3696 system has a number of lenses as shown in Table 4-8. These lenses have different reduction capabilities and various field sizes, and while most are used at 436-nm wavelengths, optical variations result in different resolution capabilities. For example, numerical apertures run from 0.20 to 0.35 for 5× lenses with production resolutions of 1.75 and 0.8 μm, respectively. Other lens properties tested and supplied as part of a customer specification include tested field distortion, rotation error, tested field reduction error, and tested field trapezoid, all at a specified magnification, wavelength, field size, and numerical aperture. Lenses can, of course, be custom built to provide a combination of specific physical parameters to match a given application.

Aligning the reticle in a photorepeater calls for several key mechanical features to ensure accuracy, precision, and good parallelism between the two stages. Reticles used in the industry range widely in thickness and dimension, so platens or reticle holders need to be able to accommodate a wide range of plate dimensions. For example, the GCA Type 3693 photorepeater accepts plate thicknesses ranging from 0.060 to

TABLE 4-8 Reduction lenses and specifications for the GCA Type 3696 photorepeater

Lens type	Zeiss 10-77-82	Zeiss 10-78-06	Zeiss 10-78-06 Restricted field	Zeiss 10-78-37	Tropel* 597-G	Tropel* 597-H
Magnification	1:10	1:5	1:5	1:5	1:5	1:5
Numerical aperature	0.28	0.20	0.20	0.30	0.35	0.35
Wavelength	436 nm	436 nm	436 nm	436 nm	436 nm	405 nm
Field size	10-mm square	20-mm square	15-mm square	20-mm diameter	14.5-mm diameter	14.5-mm diameter
Reduction error (tested field)	±0.25 μm (8 mm)	±0.4 μm (16 mm)	±0.35 μm (11 mm)	±0.25 μm (11 mm)	±0.25 μm (8 mm)	±0.25 μm (8 mm)
Trapezoid (tested field)	±0.35 μm (8 mm)	±0.5 μm (16 mm)	±0.45 μm (11 mm)	±0.35 μm (11 mm)	±0.35 μm (8 mm)	±0.35 μm (8 mm)
Rotation error (tested field)	±0.25 μm (8 mm)	±0.25 μm (16 mm)	±0.25 μm (11 mm)	±0.25 μm (11 mm)	±0.25 μm (8 mm)	±0.25 μm (8 mm)
Distortion (tested field)	±0.2 μm (8 mm)	±0.4 μm (16 mm)	±0.35 μm (11 mm)	±0.2 μm (11 mm)	±0.2 μm (8 mm)	±0.2 μm (8 mm)
Production resolution	1.0 μm	1.75 μm	1.5 μm	0.9 μm	0.8 μm	0.8 μm

* Exposure field quoted is that which is diffraction-limited. Additional field is available at reduced performance.
SOURCE: GCA Corp., Bedford Mass.

0.120 and 0.25 in. Reticles in this system are held in the platen by a vacuum chuck with a 100-mm² viewing area and alignment fiducials spaced at 103-mm intervals in the platen, permanently aligned with the x axis of stage travel.

Reticle alignment in photorepeaters is typically accomplished with an optical microscope. The GCA Type 3693 touches the reticle only outside the active area, with a vacuum-chuck micromanipulator assembly that is screw driven for x, y, and rotation adjustments. The reticle alignment precision is ±0.5 μm using the recommended fiducials for both positive and negative polarity patterns. Exposure to make an array on the GCA Type 3696 is made with a 350-W mercury arc lamp with illumination uniformity of ±2.0 percent at the image plane. Automatic and manual exposure of resist is made to within ±5 percent control, also at the image plane. Since emulsion materials have much greater sensitivity, a smaller, 200-W lamp is used for exposure. A typical emulsion material requires different safety filters for alignment prior to exposing an array. Exposure time is adjustable in 1-msec increments over a range of 100 msec to 20 sec, all with keyboard command.

Focus is automatic on most photorepeaters, and reticle cartridges are generally provided to automatically change reticles. Photorepeaters provide automatic focus by means of laser or photoelectric detection. The reticle is focused to the image plane at the center of the depth of focus to allow for drift in parallelism. On the 3693 keyboard control of focus adjustment is made in 0.25-μm increments over a range of ±20 μm. In order to ensure high-quality performance from a photorepeater, all reticles must be checked for flatness prior to loading. This will permit adjustment during the exposure process, if needed, to provide good line reproduction in the array. All photorepeaters should also be placed in environmentally controlled chambers with a minimum of Class 100 air, temperature, and humidity control. Temperature control of ±1.0°C (±0.2°F) is standard with the GCA Type 5630 environmental chamber used with the 3696. Red safelights are used for emulsion plates, and yellow safelights for photoresist.

RETICLE PRODUCTION

Reticles for wafer steppers can be produced in one of several ways, all beginning with CAD digital-tape information. One process begins with CAD tapes and uses a pattern generator to generate a reticle that is then placed directly into the wafer stepper. The pattern is generated at either 5× or 10×, depending on the reduction ratio of the stepper lens. This method is shown as process 1 in Fig. 4-43.

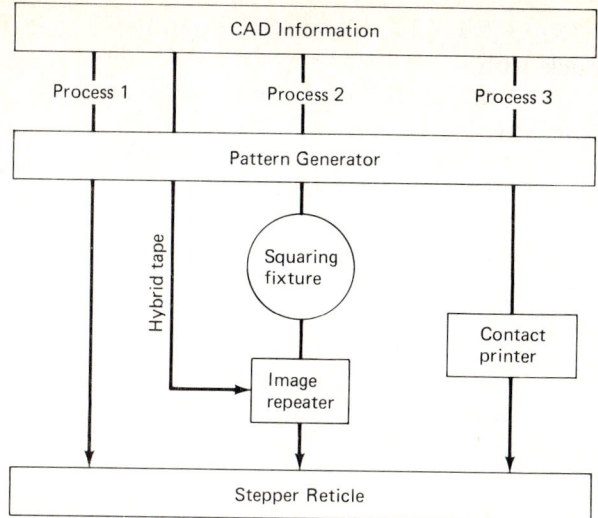

FIG. 4-43 Artwork pathways for stepper reticles.

Pattern generation is the simplest and most direct way to produce a wafer-stepper reticle. There are fewer steps than with processes 2 and 3 shown in Fig. 4-43. The pattern is produced on chrome or other suitable hard-surface materials. The process can accommodate either positive or negative photoresists, since resolution at 10 times the final image size is compatible with a good high-resolution negative resist. A positive resist is preferred for its higher inherent resolution. In a process facility where only a positive resist is specified, the digital tape can be made two ways to produce either clear- or dark-field reticles. Digitizing the pattern will result in a dark-field mask, and digitizing the background will produce a clear-field mask or reticle, all with a positive resist.

Pattern generation is most efficient for IC patterns that do not have large sections of repetitive elements, since these can be transferred more efficiently with image repeaters. Antireflective chrome reticles direct from the pattern generator are high in quality due to the fewer defects to be expected from a simple, one-step process. Added operator handling in the other processes shown means greater incidence of reticle defects, either from handling or from particulates.

Process 2 shows the additional step of image repeating, useful for frequently repeated pattern information. Image repeating fits well into those designs where a few basic types of structures are used, such as a calibration reticle or memory array. Memory cells, for example, can be digitized at the size they will be on the wafer and are then pattern generated at 50 to 100 times this size. If the stepper reticle is to be 10×, then these cells are imaged at 100× in the pattern generator. A 5× reticle would then call for 50× cell pattern generator.

The hybrid tape shown in the diagram in Fig. 4-43 is for use with the TRE Semiconductor Equipment Corporation Criss-Cross System. This system uses both the pattern-generator and image-repeater tools interchangeably on the same pattern data to produce a reticle for the stepper. The inherent efficiency of using one or the other for various pattern elements saves reticle production time. The hybrid computer tape positions the image-repeater stage in x and y for each of the larger (50 or 100×) cells mentioned earlier. In the image-repeater mode, the x and y stage data are entered from a cassette job tape or keyed in at the computer terminal. The 50× or 100× cells can be in chrome or emulsion, the emulsion offering the flexibility of generating both dark and clear fields (reversal emulsions and negative emulsions). These cells are registered to all of the other cells to maintain positional relationships. The image repeater referenced here contains a 1:10 reduction lens, which produces the stepper reticle at 10× or 5×.

The third process shown in the diagram in Fig. 4-43 is similar to process one, except that a hard-surface master mask is dropped from the pattern-generated images. This variation accommodates the reversal of mask polarity and permits an all-positive resist process. This process uses a digitized circuit pattern, and the use of negative (normal) or reversal emulsion pattern-generated plates provides any field orientation

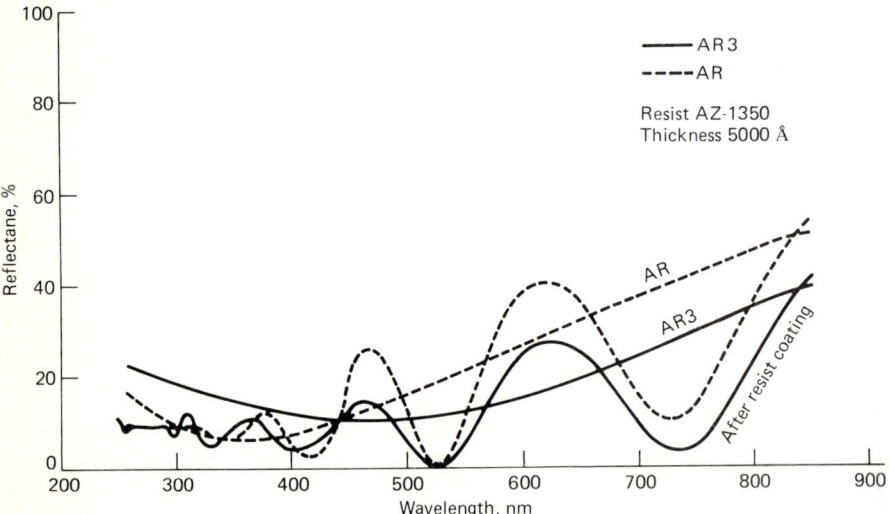

FIG. 4-44 Substrate reflectance before and after coating.

desired. The final chrome reticle is then contact-printed from this emulsion original, taking care to maintain reference edge to reticle alignment pattern spacing. This process is probably the least preferred of the three due to the use of contact-printing step, which introduces defects.

SPECTRAL REFLECTANCE

Spectral reflectance is especially important for masks that are made by using the photoresist image on glass or quartz as the final mask. The chart in Fig. 4-44 plots reflectance percent versus wavelength in nanometers and shows the spectral reflectance of a blank (in this case a Hoya LRC plate) before and after coating. The resist used was AZ-1350 at a thickness of 5000 Å.

REFERENCES

1. Bartlet, K., et al.; *SPIE Proc.*, vol. 39, p. 49, March 1983.
2. Elliott, D. J.: *Integrated Circuit Fabrication Technology,* McGraw-Hill, New York, 1982, Chap. 3.

5
Etching

INTRODUCTION

The etching step in photomask fabrication is the last major hurdle in the process that results in a usable mask. Prior to etching, imaged masks can be stripped and repatterned with resist at a nominal cost. Once etched, however, mask reworking becomes very expensive. Considerable care is taken to ensure that the dimensions formed in resist patterning are faithfully reproduced in the etched-chromium (or other mask-coating) structures.

This chapter deals with the various treatments that patterned masks undergo in order to deliver a production mask for wafer patterning. The major pathways that both emulsion and hard-surface masks follow *after* image development are outlined in Fig. 5-1.

The imaging steps required for a completed emulsion mask are covered in Chap. 4. The major steps covered in this chapter are all for hard-surface materials. These are postbaking, wet and dry etching, resist removal, and mask inspection. Chapter 6, "Pattern Measurement," covers the step after etching and inspection: measuring the etched structures. Inspection after etching catches overetched and underetched conditions, along with problems including resist lifting, resist attack, scratches, or image defects not found in the postdevelopment inspection step.

Thus, each major step in the process is preceded and followed by an inspection step. This type of process "gating" catches defects early and sends parts back through rework when possible. This minimizes the in-process costs and maximizes part yields. Each year, new mask inspection equipment appears on the market to provide greater defect-detection speed and accuracy. Smaller geometries mean that smaller defects must be detected. This in turn raises the cost of capital equipment in an

170 INTEGRATED CIRCUIT MASK TECHNOLOGY

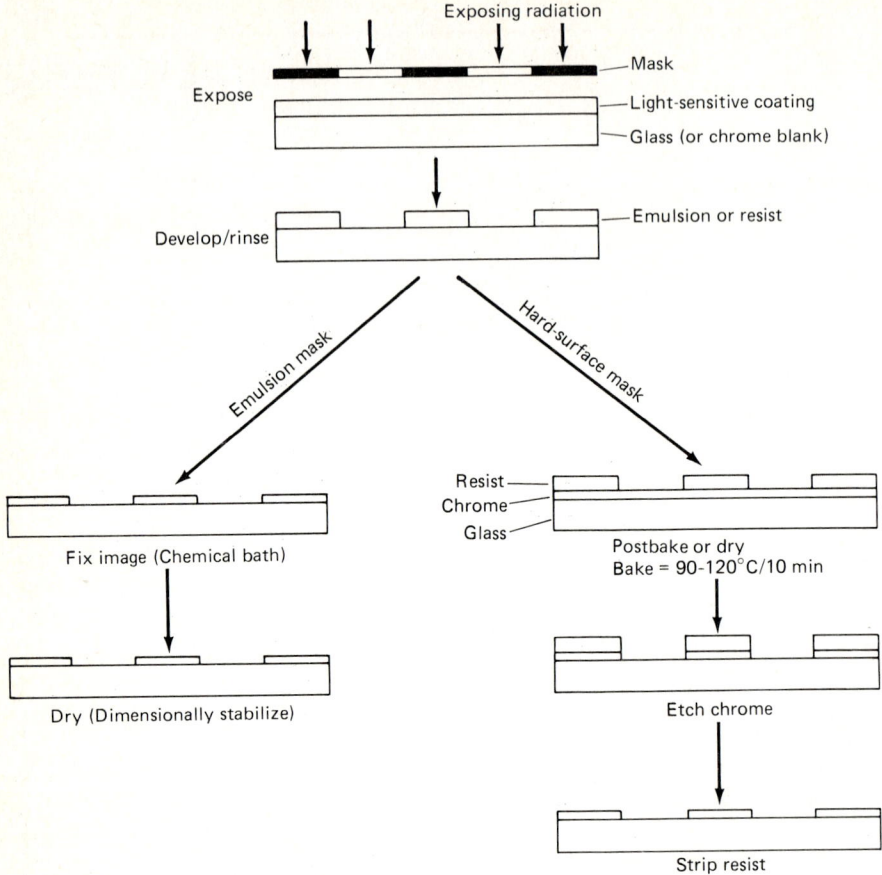

FIG. 5-1 Postdevelopment processing steps for emulsion and hard-surface masks.

industry already burdened with high capital investment costs. These costs, however, must be absorbed as technology advances, and passed on in the price of the finished mask.

SURFACES TO BE ETCHED

Hard-surface masks were originally made with sputtered chromium. Today, the number of mask surfaces has increased considerably to include the following:

1. Chromium
2. Antireflective chromium

3. Iron oxide
4. Silicon
5. Other metals and nonmetal oxides

Chromium continues to dominate, and iron oxide and silicon share a smaller part of the market in applications requiring see-through capability. Chromium possesses the major functional properties needed for VLSI mask fabrication. These include

- Adherence to glass and quartz
- Deposition possible in uniform layers without excessive stress or other physical or chemical nonuniformities
- Good bonding to resist materials
- Good etchability
- Opacity to exposure sources
- High-resolution potential (grainless)
- Relatively low cost
- Good cleaning resistance

RESIST IMAGES AS MASKS

Some masks can be produced without etching. These are masks made by using a resist that either is dyed or contains enough natural contrast or color to block the exposing light. Positive resists based upon diazo sensitizers typically are amber to light red. They darken with age through oxidation and a chemical reaction called "dark decay." In most cases, these resists can be used directly as masks without the addition of a dye. Since resists are functionally degraded by dye additions, a naturally red or orange-colored resist is ideal.

The process for making a resist-image mask is simple. The resist is applied directly to the glass-mask blank and imaged as in a standard process. The natural color of the resist image then serves as a mask for the mercury or other exposing wavelength. Tests should be run to determine the transmission properties of the resist and the amount of bleaching that takes place as a function of time. The resist can be "fixed" by high-temperature baking not only to darken the image for better opacity but to reduce bleaching.

Resists that are clear or too light in color to permit resist-image masks can be dyed. The average concentration is between 3 and 6 vol percent dye. Depending on the resist chemistry, dye additions up to 30 percent have been used without serious effects to the resist resolution properties. One of the main advantages of the resist-image mask is low cost.

Elimination of the metallization step and the etching step make the process extremely simple. Also, if the resist image is scratched or contains a defect, the mask blank is simply dipped in acetone or a suitable resist stripper and re-imaged. The process steps for resist-based masks are shown in Fig. 5-2.

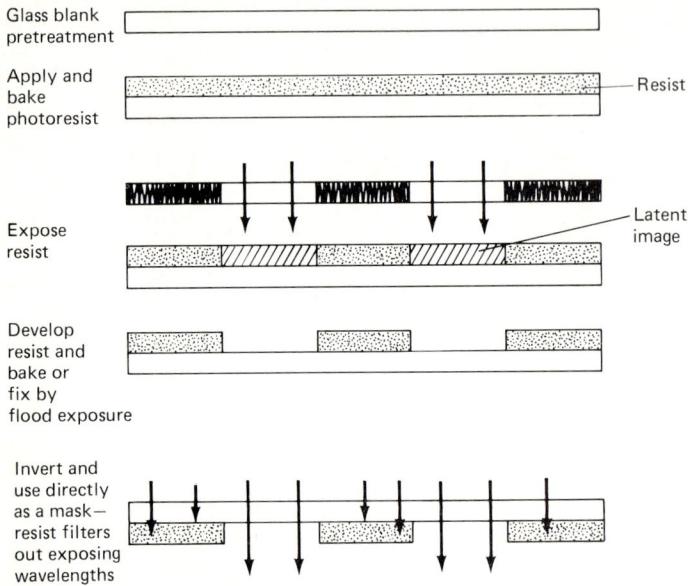

FIG. 5-2 Process outline for resist-image masks.

Most optical and nonoptical resists require postbaking before etching. Postbaking conditions the resist images to reduce undercutting in wet- and dry-etch processes. Since the dry-etching processes are inherently more anisotropic, lower bake temperatures and times can often be used, depending on the etchant gas.

Whether for wet or dry etching, the resist images must provide "resistance," as implied by the name. The list of etchants that currently available resists must withstand increases every year. New resists, however, are constantly being researched and marketed that offer better chemical and physical compatibility with the etchants. Masks are now made with several types of materials, as discussed earlier. Each of these materials has its own etchant, wet or dry. The primary job is to be sure that the chemistries of the resist and the etchant are sufficiently compatible through the etch process so as to leave the original resist geometries intact, including good edge sharpness.

Postbaking helps to increase the desired chemical inertness between resist and etchant. In addition to sheer etch resistance, the resist images must pass through the etch process without pinholing or redepositing resist residues or other contaminants in the nonimage areas through which light must pass. Last but not least, the resist must be able to be completely removed with a material that will not adversely affect the underlying substrate—a tall order! Actually, no single resist system is expected to do all this.

The trend in resist-technology development laboratories seems to be the "flavor-pack" approach: several different photoresists or electron resists, each customized in the direction of specific end-use requirements. The days when a positive optical resist had to be a panacea are over.

While there is still a shortage of specialized resists, several new materials are now in the field-testing stage. A number of these are designed for high-temperature processes, especially for wafers. The advantage of these for mask-making may be higher post-baking temperatures for better etch resistance. This in turn will deliver better resolution, especially on silicon and other hard-to-etch mask materials.

IMAGE HARDENING

Several techniques besides postbaking have been used to render resist images more durable in subsequent wet- or dry-etching processes, including ion milling and reactive-ion etching.

One approach is to subject the image to a 50-keV ion beam (arsenic) for a dose of $5 \times 10^{15}/cm^2$, as referenced in U.S. Patent 4,201,800 (IBM), issued May 6, 1980. A hardening solution of sodium 2-diazo-1-naphthoxy-4-sulfonate also may be used, in which the resist image is immersed for 2 to 5 min at room temperature.

Resist-surface cross-linking also will increase the resistance of an image layer, and a short plasma-gas exposure will cause the resist to link. All the preceding techniques also greatly increase the solvent resistance of the image, permitting a second resist layer to be applied without redissolving the first.

With positive resists as masks, prior to sputtering, removal of excess nitrogen (which causes outgassing problems in the sputtering chamber) is done by exposing the resist for up to 8 times the minimum exposure level. This reacts the photoactive compound (PAC) and not only eliminates outgassing but also makes resist removal much easier.

Most of the preceding treatments will result in a tough resist image, requiring the use of harsh removal techniques after etching. The safest and most aggressive dry-removal technique is a 30-min exposure to oxygen plasma at 300 W in a reactive-ion etch chamber.

POST-BAKE PARAMETERS

Postbaking resist images in mask fabrication is a relatively straightforward proposition. Postbaking is a postdevelopment step whose primary function is to improve the etch resistance of the resist. In mask-making there are only two areas where postbaking is somewhat critical: the hardening of the resist to prevent attack by wet- or dry-etching materials and the improvement of the adhesion of the resist prior to wet etching to minimize undercut. In all post-baking operations, there is a time-temperature relationship that must be evaluated and optimized for each resist and each mask-surface material. Various resists react differently to high-temperature postbaking.

THERMAL FLOW

In Fig. 5-3 we can see the relationship between postbaking and the thermal distortion that takes place in the photoresist. This plastic flow or physical change may affect the way in which a wet etchant clings to the photoresist image and, in fact, initiates etching at different rates. Generally speaking, the plastic flow of the resist is primarily a surface phenomenon and does not greatly affect the width of the photoresist images. This is important since any change in the photoresist line width will naturally change the final etched dimension in the photomask. Fortunately, most mask materials being etched are very thin, and in many cases resists used for mask fabrication do not require more than a low-temperature postbake in order to provide the necessary etch resistance and minimize undercutting caused by poor adhesion of the resist.

Another aspect of postbaking involves the chemical change that resists undergo during high-temperature baking. In many cases, photoresists are cross-linked by reacting with oxygen-forming species that are difficult to remove in photoresist strippers. This aspect is important since the removal temperature and type of solution should not be corrosive enough to the mask material so as to react with it.

Resist Shrinkage

In postbaking different resists, careful measurements should be taken of the resist-image dimensions before and after the bake step. This can be done with scanning electron microscopy or special image-measuring equipment as explained in Chap. 6 of this book. Postbaking may also cause a certain amount of shrinkage in the resist film, especially at the resist-mask-surface interface. This shrinkage may result in stresses being

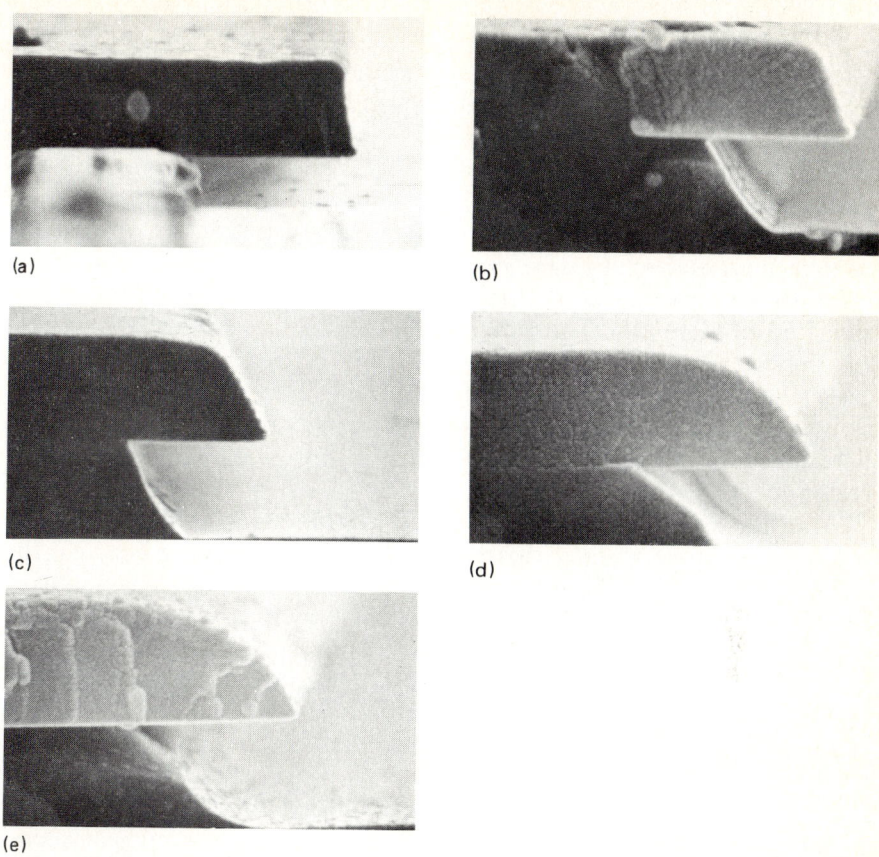

FIG. 5-3 Post-bake temperature versus thermal distortion: (*a*) 100°C, (*b*) 110°C, (*c*) 120°C, (*d*) 130°C, (*e*) 140°C.

built up in the resist film that can cause cracking, crazing, and embrittlement of the resist, leading to undercutting during etching. In many situations it is recommended that postbaking be kept below 120°C so as to avoid all the negative effects postbaking often causes. By baking at a low temperature such as 90°C the photoresist remains relatively flexible and will not break down in any way during etching.

Studies have shown that the positive resist used for mask fabrication typically shrinks around 110°C, so baking just below this temperature, which is usually also below the thermal-flow temperature of the resist, would seem to be an ideal range to use. Post-bake temperatures above 125 to 130°C combine the problems of resist embrittlement, plastic flow, and chemical reactions in the resist that harden and make it difficult to strip after etching.

ETCH-RESISTANCE TESTING

Since there are a number of factors that affect the adhesion of the resist to the substrate, we will discuss these separately and suggest that they be studied prior to implementing a mask fabrication process. The primary relationship in postbaking is between the temperature of the postbake and the amount of chemical resistance provided by that bake. A simple plot showing bake temperature versus degree of resistance to commonly used etchants for chromium and other mask materials will serve to demonstrate this relationship. Samples should be baked at a range from 90 to 180°C and then immersed in either the wet etch used for chrome or iron oxide or placed in a plasma reactor and exposed to the etchant gas for the normal etching time. Following this test, parts should be checked for loss of resist thickness, and in this way one can determine the proper level of postbake to provide a given amount of resistance.

Another aspect of postbaking is the relationship between the postbake temperature and the degree of adhesion or bonding between the resist and the mask film to be patterned. In this case, the test is one of subjecting a series of samples to post-bake temperatures between 90 and 160°C and then etching these test samples for the same time in either a wet or a dry etchant for chromium, iron oxide, or other suitable mask material. The optimization of adhesion as a function of postbake is then derived by measuring the line widths after etching. It is typically noted that the amount of undercutting is directly related to the temperature of the bake and the amount of the adhesion and that there is always a profile showing a gradual change in adhesion or a correspondingly proportional change in undercutting as a function of postbake temperature. Moreover, post-bake temperatures that are too high can actually disrupt or break the bonds of adhesion between some resists and the underlying mask material. Profiles of this kind of test have actually shown a gradual increase in adhesion to a certain point, followed by a decrease in adhesion through a certain temperature range, and then followed by an increase again in the adhesion as the temperature continues to rise. In short, it is critical that the relationship between resist adhesion and postbaking be established prior to setting up a production mask-making process.

POSTEXPOSURE BAKING

Another technique used to improve the resistance of resist images to the wet or dry etching is postexposure baking. This is a step wherein the photoresist coating, after exposure, is subjected to a 10-min bake at 90°C. This treatment has been shown to improve the resistance of the resist to lifting during development as well as improving its etched characteristics. Postexposure baking is particularly useful on mask surfaces, since they are typically very smooth and often difficult to bond to. Postexposure baking increases the adhesion of the resist to the chromium or iron oxide, and also builds in better resistance for subsequent chemical or dry processing. The only possible negative effect of postexposure baking will be a slight reduction in the rate of developing, assuming a positive optical resist is used.

One particularly good advantage of postexposure baking is the elimination of standing wave patterns that have formed during exposure and are part of the latent image prior to developing. These standing wave patterns can essentially be eliminated, according to the theory that the sensitizer in the resist is redistributed by the heat that the resistor is subjected to during postexposure baking. In mask fabrication, standing waves are a common problem due to the high reflectivity of substrates used.

POSTDEVELOPMENT EXPOSURE

Another technique that is of concern prior to etching has to do with the exposure of the resist after developing and of course prior to postbaking. Postdevelopment exposure will release nitrogen before the post-bake step, and this may permit the resist to seal itself during the post-bake step. Eliminating the nitrogen prior to the postbake removes the possibility of pinholes forming from nitrogen escape during postbaking. Small pinholes in the resist film can be easily penetrated by both wet- and dry-etched materials. Typically, the postdevelopment exposure is done by flooding the wafer for 5 to 15 sec using a short mercury arc lamp. A rule of thumb is to use an exposure time equivalent to the standard exposure used to image the photoresist. A particularly useful advantage of exposing the resist prior to postbaking is the effect it has on resist removal. Several studies have shown that exposing positive optical resist prior to postbaking greatly simplifies the removal of the resist by reacting the photoactive compound.

In most cases the use of a low-temperature softbake will be sufficient to provide the degree of adhesion and chemical resistance of positive optical resist to the wet or dry etchings. Seldom is it necessary to postbake resists higher than 110°C in order to achieve excellent etch resistance and good reproduction of mask geometries after etching. In fact, in many cases, chrome plates are processed directly from the developer, rinsed, and processed *wet* through the chrome wet etchant, followed by a rinse, resist-removal step, and nitrogen blow-dry. This "all-wet" process has worked satisfactorily in the industry for some years. In more critical-geometry masks for VLSI processes, the use of dry etching is almost mandatory, and in these processes a postbake will generally assist in achieving better etched results.

Figure 5-4 shows the added thermal resistance provided by postdevelopment exposure. Note the difference between the unexposed and the exposed resist images.

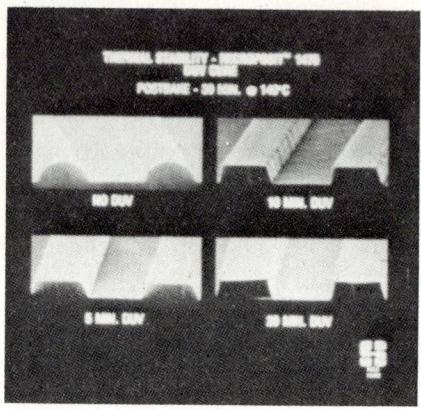

FIG. 5-4 Effect of postdevelopment exposure on thermal resistance.

WET ETCHING

Wet etching of photomasks has for years been the standard etching technique. As mask geometries have continued to shrink, the problems associated with wet etching have made this approach less favorable and have made dry-etching techniques much more attractive to the mask manufacturer. Until the 1970s practically all photomasks were wet etched in manually controlled etching production environments. Since all wet etching was manually performed, there was a tremendous amount of variability in the etched techniques used. Each operator had a particular way of etching photomasks, and process uniformity was extremely difficult. Wet etching, however, has played a significant role in the growth of photomask technology since virtually all masks have been wet-etched until very recently.

The etching of chrome, iron oxide, and other mask materials can be done very easily with wet etching in an immersion or spray mode. In recent years many types of equipment have become available to permit in-line spray or batch etching of chromium and other types of photomasks. Batch processing smooths out some of the nonuniformity problems associated with manual etching in an immersion mode. Also, it permits independence from operator variability, a common problem with early wet etching.

The main problem associated with wet etching is typically one of undercut and disposal of the spent etchant solution. However, since photomask films are typically very thin, this problem is not as serious as it is with wafer etching. The thickness of the chromium or other mask-material layer is typically below 1000 Å, so the amount of undercut is very minimal. Furthermore, the use of post-bake treatments and other image-hardening techniques practically eliminates all forms of undercutting during mask etching.

Overall then, the most serious limitation of wet etching for photomask production seems to be that of process control, specifically line-geometry control. This problem can become severe with VLSI geometries approaching 1 μm in width. It is mainly for this reason that photomask manufacturers have turned to dry etching as a solution to line control and high mask-part yield in production.

Chrome Etching

Chromium is by far the most common material used for mask fabrication, as discussed previously. There are a wide variety of wet etchants used for chromium; the most common are those composed of ceric ammonium nitrate with an oxidizing agent. The oxidizing agent is typically acetic, perchloric, or nitric acid. Another type of etchant used for chromium is potassium permanganate. The most popular of these types of etchants, however, is ceric ammonium nitrate. While it is difficult to monitor the strength of ceric ammonium nitrate etches, there are a variety of process techniques used to identify the relative activity of an etching bath. The etching time used is typically determined by calculating the thickness of the chromium and the etching time of the chrome, along with density or thickness variations in the chrome layer. Chrome etchants should always be filtered to 0.5 μm with an absolute filter to eliminate particles that may interfere with the etching process.

Generally, a sample part is run from each lot prior to etching a batch of plates in production. The amount of time required for the etchant to remove the chrome, or clear time, is checked visually. Then the rate of chrome removal is computed for the specific etchant being used. The removal rate of the etch is used to compute a clearing time for the thickest or highest-optical-density chrome substrate material to be used. This clearing time is established in light of the fact that the optical density from substrate to substrate will vary nearly 10 percent. An etch time is then computed by adding 40 percent of this time. A 40 percent clear-time factor is typically selected to reduce line-etch-profile slope variation. Reflective chrome or chrome oxide plates require a 30 percent past clear minimum etch. Line edges can appear rough or ill-defined should the plate receive inadequate etching. If the chrome-etching mechanism is anisotropic in nature, then slopes should be reduced with an increased etch time, although a certain degree of photoresist undercut will be incurred. This undercut should be uniform and consistent provided that the chrome substrate has no significant adhesion problems.

Etch Profiles

Figure 5-5 shows the profiles of etched chrome of two different densities that were etched past the clear point. Notice the difference in the slopes. An etch that is not long enough will typically result in a mask with greater variations in line-width dimensions along with poor edge acuity. This is shown in the graphs. Conversely, etch processing that is continued to the proper completion time will show straight and sharply etched edges and will have more consistent line-width profiles. The graphs show profiles of the same lines, where they are etched to 40 percent past the clear time. Note that high-density chrome has better stability through overetching. While the chrome has been undercut slightly more beneath the resist, the normal chrome-resist and chrome-glass adhesion factors should hold the degree of undercut constant, the slope of the actual undercut being reduced even though the chemical etching and inward movement of the chrome have been increased.

Immersion etching of chrome and other mask blanks is a simple but

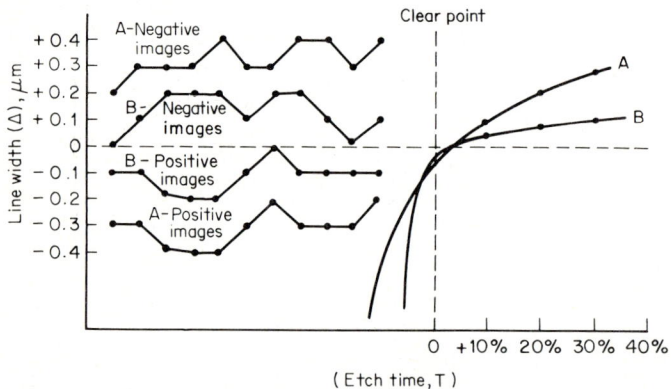

FIG. 5-5 Etch slope plotted against chrome density. Key: A = low-density chrome; B = high-density chrome.

FIG. 5-6 Immersion wet etching of photomasks. *(Fluorocarbon.)*

time-tested method that provides good results. An example of this technique is shown in Fig. 5-6.

Wet Etchants for Chrome

There is a wide variety of etchants for the various mask materials. The etchant used will depend on the resolution requirements of the process and on the type of resist used. Commercially available etchants from Cyantek are listed below according to the type of etching required.

- CR-4 chromium photomask etchant: A nitric acid–based photomask etchant designed to etch chromium at 23 Å/sec at 21°C with minimal undercutting.
- CR-7 chromium photomask etchant: A perchloric acid–based photomask etchant designed to etch chromium at 20 Å/sec at 21°C with minimal undercutting.
- CR-8 chromium photomask etchant: An acetic acid–based photomask etchant designed to etch chromium at 17 Å/sec at 21°C with minimal undercutting.
- CR-9 chromium photomask etchant: A concentrated perchloric acid–based photomask etchant designed to etch chromium at 30 Å/sec at 21°C.
- CR-12 chromium etchant: A high-speed perchloric acid–based chromium etchant designed to etch chromium at 50 Å/sec at 21°C. Due to its speed, it is recommended for chromium-photomask retouching and spot removal.

- CR-14 chromium photomask etchant: An acetic acid–based photomask designed to etch chromium at 24 Å/sec at 21°C.
- CR-18 chromium photomask etchant: A sulfuric acid–based etchant designed to etch chromium at 11 Å/sec 21°C.
- UTE-1 chromium photomask etchant: Ultraprecision perchloric acid–based photomask etchant designed for maximum speed, maximum etch uniformity, minimum undercutting, and maximum dimensional control.

In addition to these general categories of etchants for chromium there are a wide variety of generic and proprietary solutions used. These are included in Table 5-1, as well as etchants for iron oxide and silicon.

TABLE 5-1 Etching solutions for various masks

Mask substance	Solution (source)	Comment
Chrome	HCl + Al, Fe, Zn etc.	Activation
	Alkaline etch (Kodak 1966)	
	50 g NaOH ⎫ 1 part	
	100 mL H_2O ⎭	
	100 g $K_3(Fe(CN)_6)$ ⎫ 3 parts	
	300 mL H_2O ⎭	
	Ceric sulfate (Woitsch 1968)	
	9 parts saturated $Ce(SO_4)_2$ solution	
	1 part concd HNO_3	
	Ceric sulfate (Balzers 1970)	If milky deposit is formed on mask during rinse, dip mask after etching first in 10 vol % H_2SO_4 and rinse afterward.
	100 g $Ce(SO_4)_2 \cdot 4 H_2O$	
	50 mL concd H_2SO_4	
	1000 mL H_2O	
	Ceric ammonium nitrate (Kodak 1969)	
	164.5 g $Ce(NH_4)_2 \cdot (NO_3)_6$	
	43 mL $HClO_4$	
	1000 mL H_2O	
	Ceric ammonium nitrate (EMC Inc.)	
	310 g $Ce(NH_4)_2 \cdot (NO_3)_6$	
	120 mL concd HNO_3	
	1970 mL H_2O	
	Ceric ammonium nitrate with organic acid	
	a. 150 g $Ce(NH_4)_2 \cdot (NO_3)_6$	30-sec etching time
	35 mL CH_3COOH 98%	
	1000 mL H_2O	
	b. 100 g $Ce(NH_4)_2 \cdot (NO_3)_6$	100-sec etching time
	50 mL CH_3COOH	
	1000 mL H_2O	

TABLE 5-1 Etching solutions for various masks (*Continued*)

Mask substance	Solution (source)	Comment
	c. 60 g Ce $(NH_4)_2 \cdot (NO_3)_6$ 67 mL CH_3COOH 1000 mL H_2O	7-min etching time
	Ceric ammonium sulfate 64 g Ce $(NH_4)_4 \cdot (SO_4)_4 \cdot 2\,H_2O$ 500 mL $2N\,H_2SO_4$ 500 mL H_2O	3-min etching time
Fe_2O_3	H_3PO_4 heated to 60–90°C	
	Corning, old 1 part 97% HI 3% HPO_3 1 part HCl concd	
	Corning new, Towne Labs 575 mL HCl 285 mL H_2O 150 g $FeCl_2$	
	Mettler I 530 g $AlCl_3 \cdot 6H_2O$ 630 g CaBr 110 g $SnCl_2 \cdot 2H_2O$ 850 mL H_2O 260 g HBr	
	Mettler II 100 g $MgCl_2 \cdot 6H_2O$ 200 g $CaCl_2 \cdot 2H_2O$ 25 g $SnCl_2 \cdot 2H_2O$ 165 g H_2O 60 g 32% HCl	
Si	70 g $FeCl_3 \cdot 6H_2O$ 9 mL concd (38–40%) HF 220 mL H_2O	Room temperature, 1 μm/min
Indium-tin-oxide (ITO)	LCE-11 indium-tin-oxide etchant	Designed to etch ITO films of varying thickness in LCD manufacturing.
Iron oxide	FE12-cc11 iron oxide photomask etchant	Used primarily with thinner or softer iron oxide materials. Approximate etch rate is 40 Å/sec at 21°C.
	FE12-cc13 iron oxide photomask etchant	Used primarily with thicker or harder iron oxide materials. Approximate etch rate is 40 Å/sec at 21°C.

TABLE 5-1 Etching solutions for various masks (*Continued*)

Mask substance	Solution (source)	Comment
	FE12-cc15 iron oxide photomask etchant	Used with both hard and soft materials, where a universal etchant is desired.
	FE12-cc19 iron oxide photomask etchant	Stabilized iron oxide etchant for general use and CVD films.
	37% HCl	Acid is filtered to 0.2 µm and is used in manufacturing iron oxide etchants.
	FE-12 ferrous chloride crystals $FeCl_2 \cdot 4H_2O$	Used to manufacture iron oxide etchants.

NOTE: For plasma etching $Cl_2 + O_2$ must be present in order to form CrO_2Cl_2 (chromyl chloride). This is the only chromium compound which is volatile under the process conditions (boiling point 116°C).
SOURCE: *Proc. IGC Conference* 1980.

Since both positive and negative photoresists are used in mass fabrication, we will include separate processes for etching chrome masks with these types of resist. Table 5-2 shows the basic chromium-photomask process utilizing positive resists.

The next process for etching chrome (Table 5-3) is that using a negative photoresist. Note the differences in the stripper for the resist as well as the type of etching and etched parameters that will be different. While negative resists are rarely used in photomask fabrication, there are applications where the negative working aspect is an advantage. For example, in a process where only a small area of the resist is used to form the image, a negative resist would provide an advantage since only a small amount of exposure area would be used, and the balance of the resist washed away. This would tend to eliminate the possibility of pinholes in a mask, and a mask made with positive resist of the same orientation would statistically have more pinholes. This specific issue is covered in more detail in Chap. 4, "Substrate Imaging."

TABLE 5-2 Basic chromium photomask process (With positive photoresist)*

Step	Procedure
1. Expose	The correct exposure must be determined empirically.
2. Develop	Develop 30 to 60 sec with gentle continuous agitation with CC200, diluted 1 part CC200 to 1 part water at 21°C.
3. Wash	Wash vigorously for 60 sec in DI water.†
4. Etch	Etch until images are clear visually, then 15% additionally in CR-4, CR-7, UTE-1, etc., at 21°C.
5. Wash	Wash vigorously for 60 sec in DI water.†
6. Strip	Strip 2 min in RS-2, RS-4, etc., with continuous agitation at 21°C.
7. Wash	Wash vigorously for 60 sec in DI water.†

8. Dry	Dry in conventional manner such as
	  a. Isopropyl alcohol dip followed by vapor drying in same
	  b. Water rinse and spin dry
	  c. Water spray and blow-dry or bake dry

OPTIONS:
1. Developer strength may be increased to decrease exposure times.
2. A pre-etch step with PEH-1 or PEN-1 can be used before the etch step if wash effect is inadequate. A 15 to 20-sec dip in pre-etch will improve the uniformity of etching.
3. Wash times may be increased if water flow is inadequate or if water temperature is too low. Wash temperature should be 21°C.

* Multibath process may be desired to maintain integrity of chemistry.
† DI denotes "deionized."
SOURCE: *Cyantek Chemicals, Mountain View, Calif.*

TABLE 5-3 Chrome etching utilizing negative photoresist*

Step	Procedure
1. Photoresist application	Coat negative photoresist on chromium photoblank. Bake out solvents to dry coating per resist manufacturer's specifications.
2. Exposure	Exposure must occur in an oxygen-free environment. Complete exposure of resist is desired to maintain adequate resist thickness and image resolution.
3. Develop	Develop 30 to 60 sec in CC600 negative photoresist developer.
4. Rinse	Rinse developer off for 30 to 60 sec with CC611 negative photoresist rinse.
5. Dry	Dry photoresist images quickly upon removal from rinse.
6. Postbake	Postbake plate per photoresist manufacturer's specifications.
7. Etch	Etch until images are clear visually, then 15% additionally in CR-4, CR-7, UTE-1, etc., at 21°C.
8. Wash	Wash vigorously for 60 sec in DI water.†
9. Strip	Strip in negative photoresist stripper with intermittent agitation at 90°C for 5 min.
10. Wash	Wash vigorously for 60 sec in DI water.†

11. Dry	Dry in conventional manner such as
	  a. Freon or alcohol dip followed by vapor drying in same.
	  b. Water rinse and spin dry.
	  c. Water spray and blow-dry or bake dry.

* Multibath process may be desired to maintain integrity of chemistry.
† DI denotes "deionized."
SOURCE: *Cyantek Chemicals, Mountain View, Calif.*

Iron Oxide Etching

The next process using wet etching is that for iron oxide photomasks, and this process uses a positive photoresist. The steps for resist development are shown in Table 5-4.

Equipment for Wet Etching

There are many kinds of equipment for immersion and spray etching or wet etching of chromium. An example of the batch (spray) chrome-etch equipment is shown in Fig. 5-7 along with the typical parameters used in a photomask process.

This type of batch equipment can be used in both an immersion and a spray mode, and a variety of nozzles and spray-etch agitations can be used to derive different kinds of effects in the etch blank. For example if it is desirable to control the overetching to very precise limits, a very fine spray of the etchant at a selected temperature would be used along with a very slow rate of chrome removal. This would permit more precise control of etching and allow the operator to stop the etching within ± 100 Å.

TABLE 5-4 Basic iron oxide photomask process (With positive photoresist)

Step	Procedure
1. Expose	The correct exposure must be determined empirically.
2. Develop	Develop 30 to 60 sec with gentle continuous agitation with CC200, diluted 1 part CC200 to 1 part water at 21°C.
3. Wash	Wash vigorously for 60 sec in DI water.*
4. Etch	Etch until images are clear visually, then 15% additionally in FE12-cc11, FE12-cc13, etc., at 21°C.
5. Wash	Wash vigorously for 60 sec in DI water.*
6. Strip	Strip 15 to 60 sec in RS-4 stripper with continuous agitation at 21°C.
7. Wash	Wash vigorously for 60 sec in DI water. *

8. Dry	Dry in conventional manner such as
	  a. Isopropyl alcohol dip followed by vapor drying in same.
	  b. Water rinse and spin dry.
	  c. Water spray and blow-dry or bake dry.

OPTIONS:

1. Developer strength may be increased for decreasing of exposure times.
2. A pre-etch step with PEH-1 or PEN-1 can be used before the etch step if wash effect is inadequate. A 15 to 20-sec dip in pre-etch will improve the uniformity of etching.
3. Wash times may be increased if water flow is inadequate or if water temperature is too low. Wash temperature should be 21°C.

* DI denotes "deionized."
SOURCE: *Cyantek Chemicals, Mountain View, Calif.*

FIG. 5-7 Batch spray-etching equipment for photomasks showing the Megasonic cleaning system tank, two rinse tanks, and a rinse-dryer. *(Fluorocarbon.)*

One potential problem area to avoid in spray etching is the clogging of nozzles in the spray equipment. A clogging condition can be checked by taking a substrate that is exposed without any pattern and then developed and etched to approximately 80 percent of the clear time. The plate is then examined using backlighting and will produce a pattern with some kind of symmetry if the spray orifice has been clogged.

Wet etching of chrome is also done with in-line equipment. A typical in-line wet-etch system for chrome plates is shown in Fig. 5-8.

Wet versus Dry Etching

Wet-etch technology prevailed for many years because of the inability of dry etching to provide uniform removal of chromium or other materials being etched. Dry plasma etching not only was nonuniform but also gave nonreproducible results. However, in recent years major problems have emerged causing wet etching to fall behind dry etching in terms of production use. Primary problems associated with wet-etch technology in mass manufacturing are the corrosion caused by wet etchants in clean-room areas, disposal difficulties, toxic fumes, and the

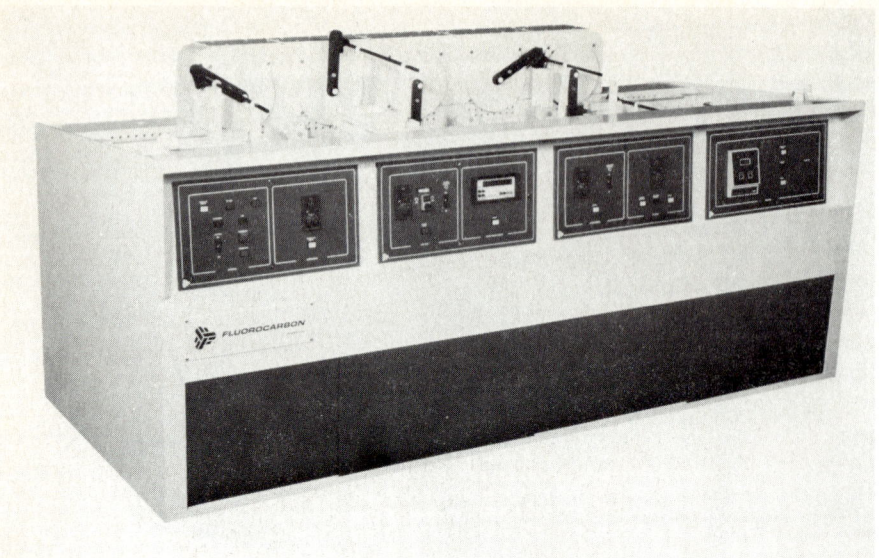

FIG. 5-8 In-line etching equipment for photomasks. *(Fluorocarbon.)*

splattering of acids, which creates a human safety problem. In addition, chemical costs are high, as are costs for equipment and etch hoods required for wet etching. Special drains, special tooling, and administrative headaches caused by government safety (OSHA) and pollution (EPA) regulations are additional disadvantages. The idea of dry etching is appealing for these reasons as well as for some serious technological reasons.

Plasma dry etching not only simplifies the process by reducing the number of steps required but also improves the resolution and yield of parts in a production process. Further, dry etching can be used as a precleaner for the glass prior to deposition, a selective remover of chromium without undercutting, and a cleaning environment for masks after photoimaging.

DRY ETCHING

Advantages of Dry Etching

The innovation in plasma equipment and refinement of plasma techniques to improve uniformity have made dry plasma etching extremely competitive with wet-chemical methods for the fabrication of photomasks. Plasma etching improves the resolution for a given process, especially when used with a positive photoresist. The combination of dry etching and positive-resist imaging gives rise to higher mask densities.

The major benefits associated with the use of dry plasma include

1. Easier resist removal
2. Elimination of resist postbaking
3. Increased resolution and etch sharpness
4. ±1 to 2 percent uniformity in etching
5. Increased device electrical uniformity (threshold voltage)
6. Plasma de-scum etching and resist removal in a single step
7. Ecology and safety benefits compared to wet processing

The most significant advantage of plasma etching for mask fabrication compared to wet etching is the improved resolution capability. It is extremely difficult to fabricate geometries below 1 μm with wet-etch techniques, while this can be done routinely with dry plasma etching. Also, the sheer growth of the semiconductor field has put production pressure on many companies and created throughput requirements. Dry plasma etching in the past has had serious limitations compared to wet-etch processing, which was done in batches. However, very recently the advent of in-line plasma etching has removed that barrier and has permitted dry processing to be technologically superior as well as competitive from a throughput standpoint. The safety feature of dry etching is somewhat better than wet etching, although there are some gas species that are considered highly toxic and must be handled with extreme caution. Overall, however, plasma etching provides a reduction in danger to operators simply because the volume of chemicals used is less and operator exposure to them is indirect.

Cost has become a major issue in recent years, when comparing wet and dry processes. Plasma etching of course does not require water rinsing whereas wet etching typically involves a significant amount of water, which is relatively expensive. The repeatability provided by dry processing also tends to improve yields, which is a significant cost benefit.

One breakthrough that accelerated the use of dry etching for chrome-mask manufacturing was the announcement by LFE Corporation of the Equi-Etch* technique. Prior to this, the nonuniformities in etched profiles, caused by perturbations of the electric discharge (typically ±10 to 15 percent), resulted in severe limitations for the use of dry plasma in advanced mask processes. The Equi-Etch system decreased the temperature of the substrate during etching and permitted the use of the system on thermally sensitive devices. The uniformity provided by this system was made possible by employing an inductive rf power

*Equi-Etch is a trademark of LFE Corporation.

coupling and a perforated metallic material-handling zone within which the masks are exposed to evenly disbursed electrically neutral active species. By allowing the preferentially electrically neutral active species within the perforated metallic envelope, there is a reduction of the temperature during etching and extremely uniform etching throughout the batch of materials in the presence of the ever-present electrical field nonuniformities.

Overview

The emergence of hard-surface masks has taken place gradually over the past 10 years, and emulsion masks have now been left with only a small portion of VLSI production. Conventional emulsion masks are inexpensive, but they suffer from poor resolution and etch quality in the generation of fine patterns. They also have a relatively short life span and cannot uniformly provide the accuracies of the IC pattern over the entire surface of the mask plate with low defects. Etching chrome is not an easy task either, but it is possible to generate extremely high-resolution, high-quality masks with very good yields using wet- and dry-etching processes. The primary advantages of dry versus wet etching have already been discussed, and as we have seen, a key factor is the lower mask cost provided by dry etching.

Mask plates used today in production range from 4 to 6 in square, and are typically coated with a thin layer of chrome or antireflective chrome ranging in thickness between 600 and 1000 Å. In the case of antireflective chrome, a thin layer of chrome is deposited onto the glass, followed by a 200-Å coating of chrome oxide. The illustration in Fig. 5-9 shows the cross-sectional structures of a chrome and an antireflective chrome plate.

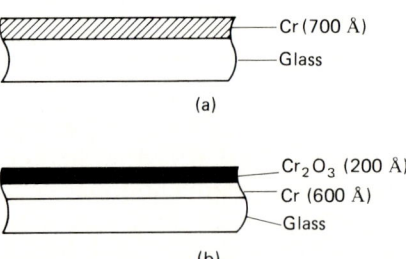

FIG. 5-9 Cross sections of chrome and antireflective chrome substrates.

Etch Duration versus Temperature

One of the important parameters in dry etching of photomask substrates is the reaction temperature. Since photoresists and electron resists deform at different temperatures depending on the resins used, one should establish both the thermal-flow temperature of the resist and the maximum reaction temperature during the dry etching. There are several types of plasma environments used, including capacitive plasma, inductive plasma, and an inductive Equi-Etch medium. The capacitively excited plasmas stabilize at about 430°C after 6 to 8 min of etch time. Inductively generated plasma reaches an equilibrium temperature of around 320°C within the same time period. The Equi-Etch medium, cited earlier as a development from LFE Corporation, reaches a temperature of about 215°C and stabilizes at about 250°C after 15 min using 350 W of rf power. The bulk of etching applications in photomask application involves removal of thin (1500-Å) films. Figure 5-10 shows the relationship between the etching duration in minutes and the reaction temperature in degrees Celsius for the different types of plasma just mentioned.

One of the inherent advantages of dry etching is the absence of impurities and dust particles that are typically contained in liquid etchants. Also, the solvents used in wet etching can cause mask defects whereas gases are filtered and cleaned to a much higher degree. The

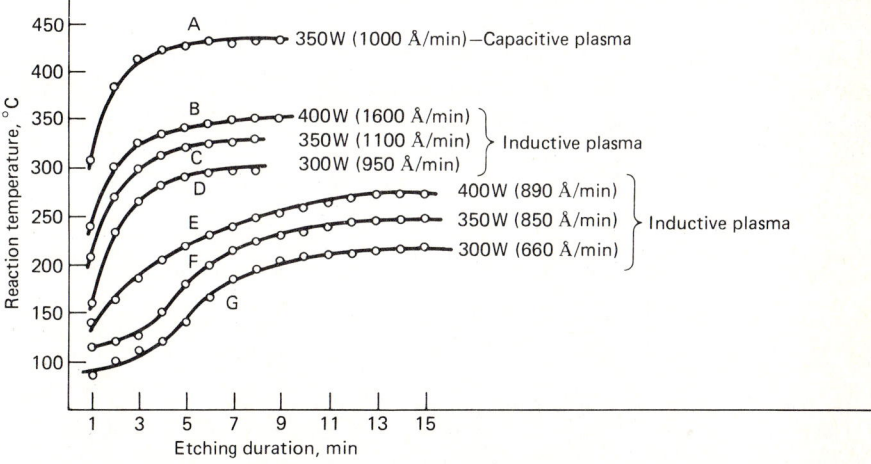

FIG. 5-10 Reaction temperature as a function of etch duration. Experiments were performed for a quartz reactor of 8-in ID and 8-in length at a pressure of 1.45 torr. Plots A, B, C, and D represent etching without a perforated metal cylinder; plots E, F, and G represent etching with a perforated cylinder. *(LFE Corporation.)*

overall simplicity of gas plasma etching also helps to reduce defects on high-density masks.

Etch Rate versus Pressure

The etch rate of chrome and chrome oxide is a function of the gas pressure, among other parameters. Figure 5-11 shows the relationship between the etching rate in angstroms per second and the pressure in torr. These data are taken for an rf power level of 160 W. As the data indicate, the etch rate reaches a maximum at a particular gas pressure, and this maximum is different for each type of plasma. Note that there are separate plasmas indicated in the figure. Of particular interest is the mixed-gas plasma containing helium, which provided a weak dependence of etch rate on pressure. The greatest etch rates of the chrome as well as the antireflective chrome films were found to be at about 0.3 and 0.15 torr, respectively. Also note that the etching rate of the chrome is greater than that of the chrome oxide films at the same power level even though different gases are used.

Etch Rate versus rf Power

Figure 5-12 shows the relationship between etching rate of chrome and chrome oxide in angstroms per second and the rf power level in watts. Once again, several plasmas are used at different gas pressures as noted.

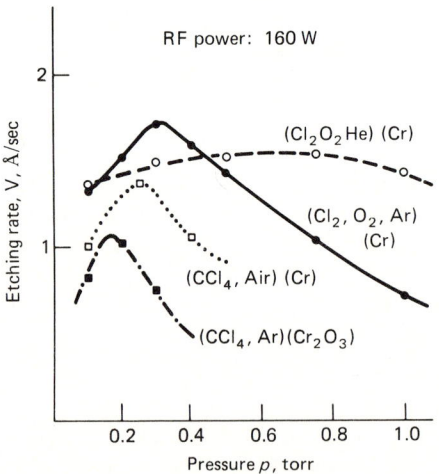

FIG. 5-11 Etch rate plotted against pressure. *[Ref. 1.]*

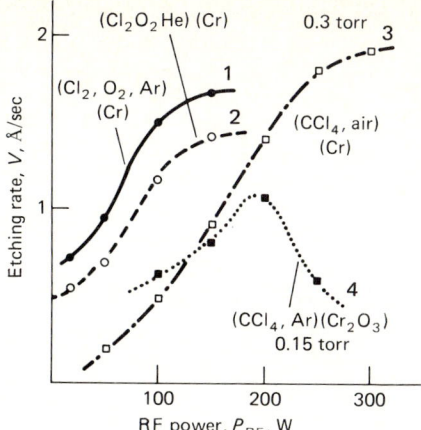

FIG. 5-12 Etch rate plotted against rf power. *[Ref. 1.]*

Chrome films were etched at 0.3 torr using gases containing argon and air (gas mixtures 1 and 3, respectively), and antireflective chrome was etched at 0.15 torr using gas composed of CCl_4 and argon (gas mixture 4). Note that the etch rate tends to increase along with the rf power and reaches a maximum at a given point depending on the type of gas. Gas mixture 3 (CCl_4, air) etches chrome with a saturation point of about 300 W. This same peak for the other plasmas is reached at as low as 160 W for the argon-chlorine-oxygen mixture and the helium-chlorine-oxygen plasma (gas mixture 2). The antireflective chrome has a maximum etching rate at 200 W. Once again, the chrome oxide film etches at a lower rate than that of the chrome films even at their saturated values.

Etch Rate versus Oxygen Gas Concentration

Another important parameter in determining the process for chrome plasma etching is the percent of oxygen in the gas mixture. Figure 5-13 shows the relationship between the etch rate in angstroms per minute and the volume percent of oxygen in the gas plasma. These gas plasmas use a mixture of CCl_4, Ar, and O_2. The chrome layers used in this experiment were sputtered, and the antireflective chrome coatings of CrO_x and CrO_y were vacuum-deposited. Note that in the data the etched rate of the chrome films applied by sputtering and the antireflective chrome films are increased as the oxygen concentration increases in the gas mixture. When the oxygen concentration reaches approximately 40 percent, a maximum sputtering rate is achieved.

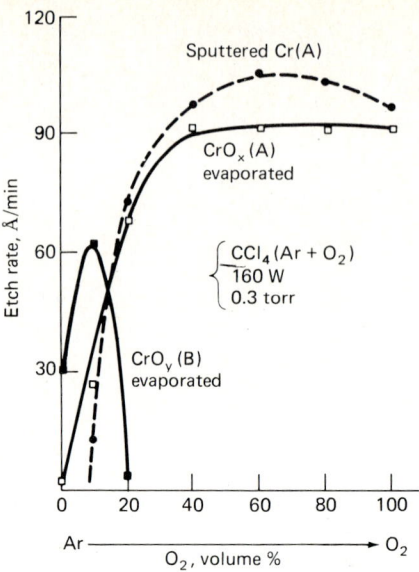

FIG. 5-13 Etch rate plotted against oxygen gas concentration. *[Ref. 1.]*

Of particular interest here is the similarity in etch rates of the two materials, a factor not observed in the earlier experiments with pressure and power level. A significant difference, however, is that the etch rate of the antireflective chrome or chrome oxide increases rapidly as percent oxygen increases up to about 10 percent. At concentrations above 10 percent the etch rate drops off rapidly as oxygen concentration increases and reaches nearly zero at a 20 percent oxygen concentration In this experiment there are two different antireflective chromes, noted by A and B, supplied by two different companies. The significant difference in their etch rate behavior is difficult to explain. From this experiment it was concluded that the plasma-etch characteristics are extremely sensitive to the stoichiometry of the deposited chrome oxide layer as well as the structure on the surface and beneath the surface of the metallic film.

RF Power versus Etch Rate for Mixture of CCl_4 and Air

Figure 5-14 shows the practically linear relationship between etching rate and rf power for chrome films. This example illustrates the chromium etched with the CCl_4 and air mixture. Note the linear increase in etch rate as the rf power or sputtering increases. The variation of the sputtering power causes variation in the deposition rate of the films. This leads to a variation in the grain size of the chromium as well as a

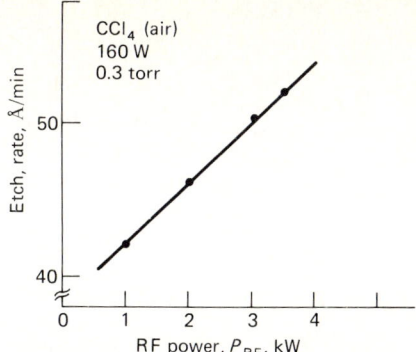

FIG. 5-14 Etch rate on sputtered chrome versus rf power, for a mixture of CCl₄ and air. *[Ref. 1.]*

change in the surface structure of the metallic film. Other experiments have indicated that the etching rate of chromium films deposited by sputtering is generally larger than that of vacuum-deposited chromium films. In short, it is evident that the etching of chromium films by gas plasmas is a function not only of the etching environment and its parameters but also of all the parameters that are involved in getting the chromium applied to the glass surface. Factors such as grain size, surface condition, and temperature will have varying effects on the etching properties later on.

Pattern Width of Master Mask versus Copy Mask

One good way of comparing the etching results of wet- versus dry-etching techniques is to plot the variation and line widths that occur from the master mask to a copy mask. Figure 5-15 shows the difference between the readings on both positive- and negative-working master masks and those of both negative- and positive-working copy masks. The data also show the difference between wet-etched masks and dry-etched masks. As would be expected, the dry-etched masks result in a more faithful reproduction of the original masters compared to wet-etched masks. There is very little difference between the original and the copy of dry-etched masks, due to the elimination of undercutting, a factor that works to the advantage of both chrome and antireflective chrome films.

Etch Time versus Line-Width Change

An examination of the reason for the small amount of undercutting plus matching has been made and is illustrated in Fig. 5-16. In this

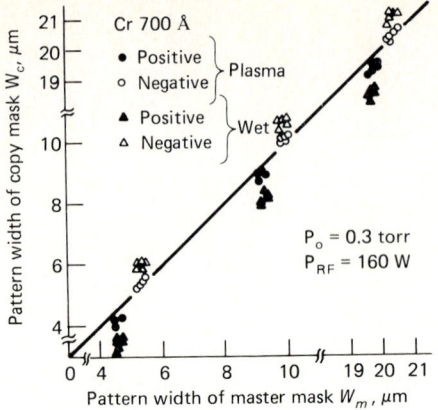

FIG. 5-15 Image fidelity with the dry-etching process. *[Ref. 1.]*

examination, the relationship between the resist pattern width and the etched pattern width is calculated for gas-plasma-etching versus chemical-etching techniques. In the figure, $\Delta W = (W_e - W_r)/2$ is the amount of undercutting and is measured as a function of etch time in two different kinds of gas plasma etchant. The etching time (T_0) shown in Fig. 5-16 means the amount of time to etch a 700-Å-thick chrome film

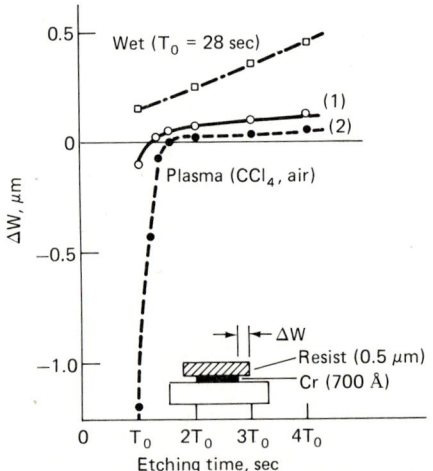

FIG. 5-16 Etching time versus line-width change: (1) 0.3 torr, 160 W, T_0 = 4.32 min; (2) 0.3 torr, 30 W, T_0 = 48 min. *[Ref. 1.]*

down to the chrome-glass interface. In the test the chrome is etched using a plasma-gas mixture of CCl_4 and air. As is indicated by the data, in wet-chemical etching the amount of undercutting is always a positive figure and increases in the linear fashion with increased etching time.

This characteristic undercutting is common to all wet-etching techniques and has been well-documented. With plasma dry etching note that despite the increase in etching time, there is very little increase in the amount of undercut. The actual value of the line width in the case of dry etching is a negative figure and only becomes positive with an increase in etching time. The size of the line width of the etched patterns is actually larger than that of the original mask pattern. This characteristic can be referred to as negative undercutting. As you can see from the figure in the positive range of line-width change, the values of ΔW for glass plasma etching are much smaller than those for conventional wet-chemical etching. This happens despite the fact that the values of line-width change increase with increasing etch time. Additionally, in the dry plasma etch the slow etch rate causes a very large negative line-width change and a small positive line-width change.

The characteristic "cutoff" of line dimensional change in dry etching is a major advantage for VLSI mask fabrication. It provides the lithographer with the opportunity to overetch by a fairly wide margin without severely changing the line-width dimensions according to process specifications. On the other hand, the wet-etch process is very critical and a slight amount of overetching will change the line widths such that they fall outside of the process specifications. It is therefore easy to see why dry plasma etching has become a major etch technique for high-resolution chromium photomasks.

Undercut Profiles

There is generally a predictable pattern of resist and chromium undercut for wet *and* dry etching, as long as the process variables are held reasonably constant. In Fig. 5-17 we can see the cross section of the resist and chrome layers and their dimensions. These calculations permit us to know the percent transmittance along an etched chrome edge. At $T = T_0$ the chrome is just completely etched, with zero *overetch*. At $T = 2T_0$, the etch time is doubled. Note that at $T = T_0$, the undercut is a negative value (larger feature size than the mask).

One problem associated with microimaging is proximity effects. As the pattern widths get smaller and more closely spaced, the shadowing and reflection of light between various pattern elements affect imaging parameters. Since the relationship between the pattern size and shape and the resultant optical effect (shadow, reflection) vary, so does the

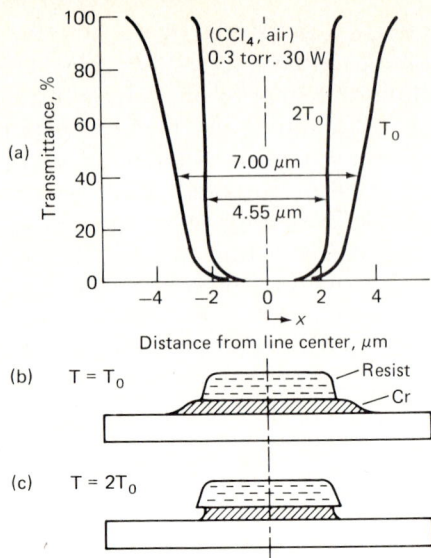

FIG. 5-17 Cross-sectional profiles after etching. *[Ref. 1.]*

optimum resist exposure dosage. Optimum exposure doses are therefore given for a specified image size *and* configuration.

In the case of etching, proximity effects are also a factor, especially in wet etching. First, in the wetting of the etchant to the surface, the variation in pattern configuration acts as a variable. Surface tension will vary between the long, closely spaced conductor traces and the larger, more widely spaced bonding pads or contacts.

The initial stages of etching, when the etchant first contacts the surface, are critical. Also, when etching is complete, dewetting often occurs in large, wide-open areas, but etchant (and therefore the etching reaction) remains in the areas where pattern density is high and surface tension holds the solution.

Fortunately, dry-etching processes operate with a significantly smaller dependency on proximity effects. The relative closeness of one pattern element to another has little bearing on when the active plasma species begins dissolving or combining with the surface to react it into another form. Even variations in pattern shapes that cause major image differences in wet etching are left unchanged by gas plasma or other dry-etching mediums. For example, inside corners of pattern elements are much less sensitive to overetch in wet etching than outside corners. Also, in resist exposure, the outside corners are often free from any shadowing and capture maximum reflectance. The result is that "blanket" processes, such as resist exposure, resist development, and etching, should be optimized on the basis of pattern configuration. In the case of wet etching, this is highly impractical and maybe even impossible.

Figure 5-18 shows the relationship between the change in pattern width (ΔW) as a function of pattern-element size. These data show how relatively insensitive the etched chrome patterns are to variations in shape or size. Pattern widths ranging from 5 to 20 μm are essentially unaffected by their size over a 15- to 18-min etch cycle. These samples were chromium, and both "windows" and "doors," or clear and opaque areas (respectively), were tested. The photoresist used was A2-1350B, and the undercutting factor (negative) remained constant as depicted in the cross sections at the the right of Fig. 5-18.

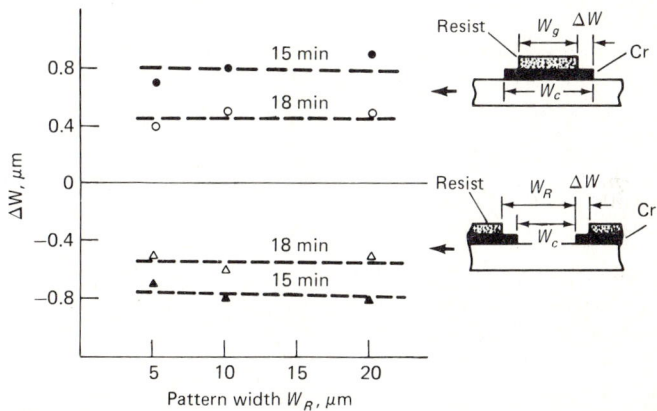

FIG. 5-18 Line-width change plotted against line width in plasma etching of chromium. *[Ref. 1.]*

Pattern shift, or the difference between the size of the mask original (master) and the copy (submaster), is precisely controlled in mask manufacturing. In the etching step, where imaged masks become finished masks, measurement for pattern shift is essential. Pattern shift can be expressed as

$$\Delta S = W_c - W_m$$

where ΔS = pattern shift
 W_c = pattern width of copy mask
 W_m = pattern width of master mask

In most dry-etching processes, the amount of pattern shift is negligible, whereas positive undercutting in wet etching produces very measurable differences. Figure 5-15 showed this relationship for positive and negative images in both wet- and dry-etch environments. Figure 5-19 shows pattern shift as a function of gas pressure. The materials etched here are antireflective chrome where gas mixtures of CCl_4 and air are used to etch the chrome and gas mixtures of CCl_4 and argon are used to etch the chrome oxide.

The reflective chrome layers in Fig. 5-19 were etched with $Ar\text{-}Cl_2\text{-}O_2$ mixtures. The pattern change or shift of the antireflective chrome is much smaller than that for the reflective chrome. Note that both positive and negative images were evaluated. Even reflective chrome, in plasma etching, can hold pattern shifts down to as little as 0.20 μm, where wet etching usually produces pattern shifts close to 1.8 μm overall, or ±0.9 μm.

OVERETCHING

In all areas of mask processing, variations are encountered that require compensating in order to maintain reasonable part yields. In etching, the thickness of the deposited metal layer will vary, requiring a certain overetch to keep the process under control in a production mode.

Since some images will be etched before others, the question of pattern-dimension change versus overetch arises. Figure 5-20 shows the relationship between pattern shift and etch time for antireflective

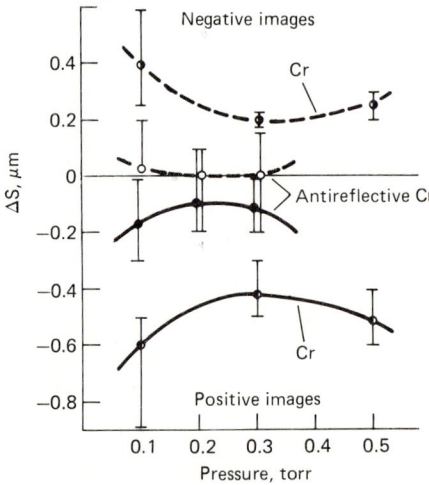

○● Antireflective Cr: (CCl_4, Ar) for Cr_2O_3 and (CCl_4, Air) for Cr; 160 W

○● Cr: (CCl_4, O_2, Ar) for Cr; 160 W

FIG. 5-19 Change in a mask's line geometry plotted against gas pressure. [Ref. 1.]

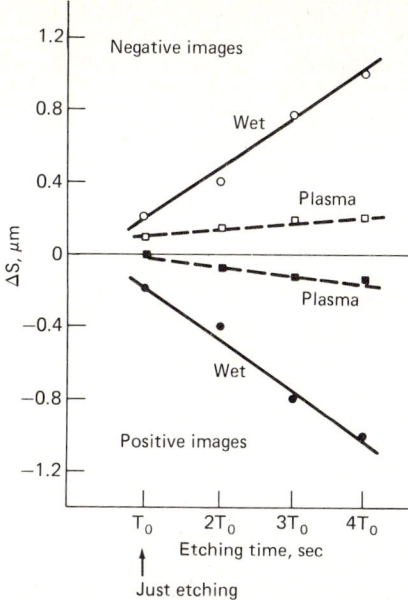

FIG. 5-20 Change in the mask's line geometry plotted against etching time for an antireflective chromium mask. *[Ref. 1.]*

chrome. In these data, overetching up to 4 times the clear time ($4T_0$) is tested for both wet and dry etching and positive versus negative images.

The plasma-etched images showed considerably greater stability in the dry-etched rather than the wet-etched samples. The difference between positive and negative images was small, and overetching apparently affects these areas equally. New end point–detection instrumentation is being employed to further control the overetch time and keep it to a minimum. In some processes, design engineers enlarge geometries and plan for a calculated reduction of geometry by controlled overetching. Obviously, close attention to controlling the thickness of chrome and other mask-film layers will simplify the problem of overetch control.

REVERSE ETCHING

Reverse etching is removal of the chrome and chrome oxide areas *under* the resists' images *before* the nonimaged mask areas are etched. Figure 5-21 compares conventional and reverse etching. The primary difference is a doubling of the power level. The breakdown of the resist in the high-power-level plasma environment accelerates the etching of the

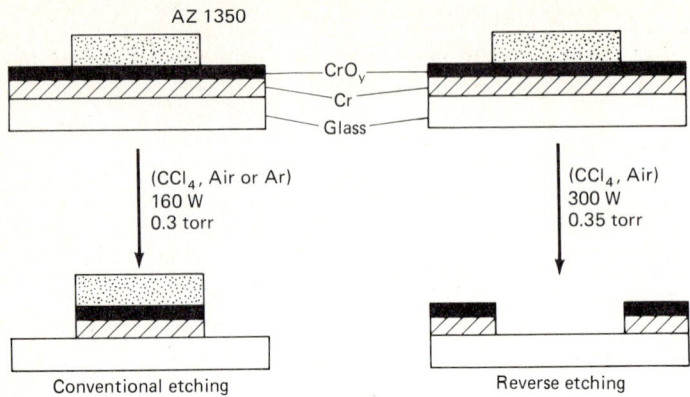

FIG. 5-21 Comparison of conventional and reverse etching. *[Ref. 1.]*

areas under the resist. The gas by-products of resist breakdown mix with the existing plasma to produce a new gas-plasma species. This "mixed" plasma is in high concentration immediately near the resist images, hence the rapid etching and reversing of the expected result. Different resists will produce changes in the nature of this etch phenomenon.

RESIST REMOVAL

Resist removal after etching can be accomplished in wet-stripping solutions, in dry plasmas, or in a combination of wet- and dry-stripping environments. The temperature level of postbaking and the ambient gas are the primary factors that affect removal. In most photomasking applications, only very thin films are being etched, and therefore the question of isotropy is almost academic. This removes one of the most severe requirements in most etching applications: maintaining line geometry dimensions and control through the etching cycle. In addition, the adhesion of mask resists to photomask and electron-mask surfaces is typically quite good, making it easier still to etch a given dimension without loss of image integrity. Finally, only very thin (1000 to 4000 Å) coatings of resist are needed to provide etch resistance in mask-making, simplifying resist removal.

In summary, resist removal from etched masks is fairly straightforward and easy, especially when compared to wafer processing. A major difference, however, is in the critical nature of the mask itself. Residual resist films, particles, voids, or other defects left in the mask after resist removal can potentially be reproduced many times on wafer surfaces if not caught in the mask inspection step.

Resist-Removal Criteria

There are several guidelines that all wet or dry resist strippers must adhere to in order to facilitate high yield. These include

1. *Complete,* residue-free removal of the resist coating.
2. Removal process is completely inert with respect to the mask surface.
3. Removal process economics do not adversely effect the overall process economics, i.e., yield per gallon of the liquid stripper or number of parts that can be dry stripped per hour.
4. Removal process is nonpolluting to meet environmental regulations and nontoxic safe handling to meet industry-approved safety guidelines.

Wet-Chemical Resist Removal

The most common technique for removing thin positive-resist coatings is immersion in liquid stripper baths. Recent in-line and semi-automated batch stripping equipment makes this approach productive and removes the process variability associated with "hand" operations. Typically, resist-remover solutions are plumbed into the same equipment as the etchant, and computer-programmed nozzles dispense the etchant, rinse, and remover solutions according to process needs.

Wet removal of resist coatings does pose some inherent problems of its own. For example, chips or small flakes of resist will stick to a chrome or glass surface and bond strongly enough to remain through rinse operations. Fibers and other airborne contaminants may also remain through etch operations, altering the IC pattern slightly. Problems related to surface tension and static charges in wet-chemical operations are not often overcome by even high-pressure jet-spray rinsing. Also, the active ingredient or strength of the resist-removal solution changes constantly if the solution is recycled. Recycling is often required to maintain process economics.

Good chemical resist strippers for positive resist on chrome include

- RS-1 positive photoresist stripper: A nonionic organic solvent stripper that is used to strip positive photoresist at 21°C.
  Recommended use is for 5 to 10 min at 21°C for 0.5-μm photoresist baked at 100°C or less.
- RS-2 positive photoresist stripper: An alkali-organic stripper designed to strip positive photoresist at 21°C.
  Recommended use is for 2 to 5 min at 21°C for 0.5-μm photoresist baked at 100°C or less. Upon heating to 40°C, the strip time can be decreased and chemical life extended.

- RS-3 positive photoresist stripper: A concentrated alkali-organic stripper designed to strip positive photoresist at 21°C.

    Recommended use is for 2 to 5 min at 21°C for 0.5-μm photoresist baked at 100°C or less. Upon heating to 40°C, the strip time can be decreased and chemical life extended.

- RS-4 positive photoresist stripper: An alkali-organic stripper designed to strip positive photoresist at 21°C with minimal effect on surface depositions, e.g., iron oxide.

    Recommended use is for 2 to 5 min at 21°C for 0.5-μm photoresist baked at 100°C or less.

- LCS-4 positive photoresist stripper: A positive-photoresist stripper designed to strip at 21°C with no effect on indium tin oxide.

- BA-1 nonionic positive photoresist stripper: High-purity γ-butyrolactone stripper used primarily in positive-photoresist lift-off processes at 80°C.

These products are commonly used in the industry for mask-making applications and are available from Cyantek Chemicals in Mountain View, California.

Remover 1112A (Shipley Company)[2] is also widely used to remove resists from mask surfaces, especially iron oxide. Iron oxide is particularly sensitive to attack by other chemical resist strippers, and Remover 1112A does not react with this material. Further, Remover 1112A may be heated without causing safety problems and will then readily strip or dissolve postbaked resist. Since some chemical etchants react with the surface of the resist to form high-molecular-weight species or structures more insoluble in strippers, a more aggressive chemical is needed.

Dry-Chemical Resist Removal

The major argument for using dry plasma removal of positive resist from photomasks is cost.[3] While environment and process reliability are also key factors, the cost argument gets people's attention. Plasma removal is an essentially self-contained process and is a simple oxidation reaction. The organic resist (C_xH_y) combines with active oxygen very readily, as follows:

$$C_xH_y + \text{active } O_2 \rightarrow CO, CO_2, H_2O$$

The stable by-products, in a gaseous state, are drawn off by the vacuum pump.

Masks are loaded into their holders or cassettes and, in a batch operation, placed in a vacuum environment of about 0.2 torr. The O_2

gas then is pumped in at a rate of several hundred milliliters per minute, followed by inductive coupling of rf energy to the gas at a specific frequency (13 MHz). This so-called excitation energy generates several active species, but the primary one is atomic oxygen.

Atomic oxygen essentially takes apart the resist, breaking it into its simpler components, which, by themselves, are volatile gases. The generation of active oxygen is mainly the result of dissociation of molecular oxygen. This may occur by excitation reactions due to initial electron impact:

$$e^- + O_2 \rightarrow O_2^* \quad \text{(in more than one state } +e^-; O_2^* = \text{excited oxygen)}$$
$$\rightarrow O + O + e^-$$
$$\rightarrow O^- + O$$

Various energic states of the resultant atomic oxygen are also possible.

Loss reactions of atomic oxygen within the discharge proceed either homogeneously (in the gas phase) or heterogeneously (on a solid wall). Of the reactions that involve neutral species the following are the most important:

$$O + O + O_2 \rightarrow 2O_2$$
$$O + \text{wall} \rightarrow \tfrac{1}{2}O_2$$
$$O + O_2 + O_2 \rightarrow O_3 + O_2 \quad \text{(usually on a cold wall)}$$
$$O + O_3 \rightarrow 2O_2$$

Theoretically, the initial attack of oxygen on resists results in abstraction of hydrogen to form carbon- and oxygen-containing free radicals and water. Subsequent attack of oxygen atoms on the free radicals yields CO, CO_2, OH, and hydrogen atoms. A possible sequence may be the following:

$$\text{Photoresist (e.g., } \sim\!\!CH_2-CH\!\!\sim) + O^* \rightarrow CH_3CHO, OH$$
$$\underset{\underset{CH_2}{\overset{\|}{}}}{\overset{|}{C-CH_3}}$$

1. $-CH_3 + O^* \rightarrow H_2CO + H$
2. $CHO + O^* \rightarrow OH + CO$
3. $CHO + O^* \rightarrow H + CO_2$
4. $OH + O^* \rightarrow O_2 + H$
5. $O^* + CO + M \rightarrow CO_2 + M$
6. $OH + H_2CO \rightarrow H_2CO + H_2O + HCO$
7. $O^* + H_2CO \rightarrow CO + H_2O$

The last two reactions have a lower probability of occurrence. The yield of CO_2 in these systems is only between 3 and 6 percent according to the slow, triple-collision reaction $CO + O + M \rightarrow CO_2 + M$ (M = third body). This reaction liberates the emission of blue visible radiation that is characteristic of electronically excited CO_2 molecules during photoresist stripping.

The yield of CO_2 is independent of pressure, temperature, and the presence of hydrogen atoms, suggesting a slow reaction between CO and O.

The rate of removal of organic polymeric material can frequently be increased in an oxygen plasma when small amounts of certain gaseous species are added to molecular oxygen before it enters the discharge zone. These entities increase the degree of dissociation of O_2. Water vapor and H_2 are typical cases. Such catalytic activity has been ascribed at least in part due to wall effects, i.e., rendering the inner walls of the reaction chamber more passive toward atom recombination processes. Results indicate a substantial catalytic effect for oxygen atom production in the presence of added N_2, NO, or N_2O, and H_2. No substantial effect was found for added He, Ar, and CO_2.

In summary, commercial-grade oxygen (O_2) is considered a good raw material for resist stripping since it contains a small amount of water. High grades (99.999%) of oxygen will strip the same resists, but the removal rate is less.

Dry gas-plasma removal of positive resists from mask substrates is certainly the more advanced method for VLSI device fabrication. Greater computer control over the process and less dependence on hand operations permit this operation to be more reliable and therefore reduce defects.

Results of the cost analysis of wet and dry resist removal are shown in Table 5-5.

TABLE 5-5   Costs of Wet-Chemical Stripping

Type of chemical	Gallons per week*	Cost per week, dollars
J-100	26	$ 300.00
Acetone	7.5	100.00
Alcohol	7.5	120.00
Methylene chloride	7.5	200.00
Sulfuric acid	26	450.00
Hydrogen peroxide	2.7	25.00
Emulsion DB-110	0.7	7.00
Total cost		$1202.00

* Based on 10,000 wafer starts per week.

The plasma (oxygen) cost for the same number of surfaces as in Table 5-5 would be about $2.00. The cost of the plasma equipment is such that a payback period of 20 to 30 weeks is calculated. The overriding factor in most manufacturing operations is yield. If a new or different technique contributes ever so little to improving part quality and therefore yield, the multiplying factors (number of better dies per part times parts per day times 365 days) handle the rest and prove the positive economics of the new approach. The difficult aspect of changing to new process technology is living through the initial stages of the learning curve when the return is either nonapparent, nonexistent, or negative. Experience indicates that new processes generate initial negative returns. The objective is simply to move quickly through that portion of the curve. The mask industry is still in the transition from wet to dry processing, for both etching and resist-removal operations.

REFERENCES

1. Abe, Haruhiko, and Kyusaku Nishiuka: "Microfabrication of Photomasks by Gas Plasmas," Kodak Publication G-47, 1976.
2. Technical Data Sheet on Remover 1112A, Shipley Company, Newton, Mass., 1982.
3. LFE Corporation: *Plasma Dry Stripping*, Process Control Division, Marlboro, Mass., 1979.

6
Pattern Measurement

INTRODUCTION

Integrated-circuit technology is predicated on the basis of controlled pattern reproduction and image-transfer processes. The flow of electrons through ICs, to work properly, must be contained by channels and "wells" of very precise dimensions. If these critical dimensions shift by a small percent, the circuit will simply not work. In essence, the science of microelectronics rests very heavily on the ability to create very predictable pattern geometries. Since patterns are all essentially microscopic, we rely entirely on measurement technology. VLSI dimensions typically run below the submicron level, where optical microscopes are unable to supply reliable information. The only tools left to reliably measure micrometer- and nanometer-range geometries are high-energy-beam devices such as scanning electron microscopes. The current optical methods that fractionate light waves are able to detect at some dimension that is a predictable section of a light wave. A key problem facing IC mask and wafer fabrication engineers is improvement of the measuring capability to keep pace with shrinking pattern sizes.

In this chapter we will explore the various techniques used to measure patterns and equipment that is dedicated to metrology. The variations in types of equipment give rise to variability in results from the same set of masks. Calibration standards have been developed to "even out" predictable differences in equipment and methods. There is still the major measuring variable to be addressed: the human operator. On a given day, the same operator can measure the same element on the same mask and get different results on the same measuring instrument. This scenario is almost the rule, certainly not the exception. Imagine how much variability can be incurred by adding in many *different* people, measuring with different instruments and using different mask specimens.

The need for removing the element of subjectivity is still evident and really grows as dimensions shrink. Operators are not to be blamed for the entire problem, however. Aberrations, diffraction, and other optical variables cause changes in the aerial images transmitted through microscopes. Diffraction will cause a very sharp edge on a chromium-pattern element to have a gradation from dark to light at the line edge. This transition region, similar to the Airy disk in an optical system (its diffraction-limited spot diameter), must then be measured using an optical theshold. In an optics system, the Airy disk has a 1.0-μm diameter in a 0.65 numerical aperture lens. Figure 6-1 shows the material or substrate profile along with its corresponding optical-image profile and the optical threshold. The threshold will vary considerably with the equipment used to perform the measurements. A 50 percent threshold will produce either a dark band or a line between the two images. In image-shearing microscopes, the profiles of the split image allow for the formation of a third "displaced" image and profile, shown in Fig. 6-2.

Other image profiles can be derived depending on the equipment used and method of illumination. A theoretical model of the relationship between a line object and its coherent spectrum is given in Fig. 6-3a. Taking this model into account, we see in Fig. 6-3b the calculated profile of a 2-μm clear-line-image object with coherent illumination at 500 nm

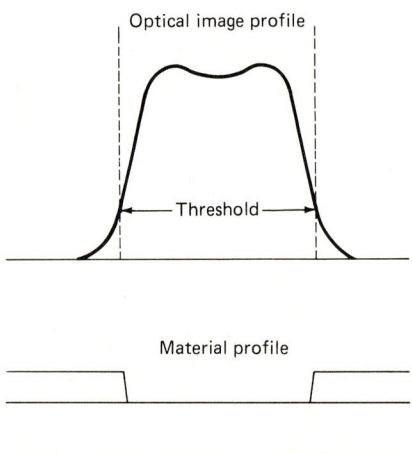

FIG. 6-1 Comparison of optical image profile and substrate dimensional profile. [Ref. 1.]

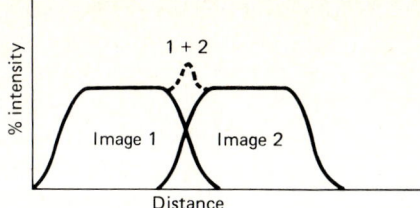

FIG. 6-2 Overlapping images, in an image-shearing microscope, creating a third, displaced, image. *[Ref. 1.]*

using a 0.95 numerical-aperture lens *(a)* without spatial filtering and *(b)* with optimal spatial filtering. It is essential to know the profile of image intensity and its correlation to the object *and* influence of the measuring instrument in order to derive a pattern measurement that is meaningful.

The measurement of geometries in mask and wafer fabrication is perhaps the least-publicized aspect in microelectronics. Metrology, the science of measurement, has the "last word" in determining the quality of work performed by the lithographer. All the processing that leads to the formation of patterns on superflat surfaces culminates in a predetermined set of geometries of precalculated line width. The relative success or failure of the entire process of microelectronic fabrication rests to a large degree on the ability to accurately and repeatably measure the geometries formed on semiconductor surfaces.

Pattern sizes in mask and wafer fabrication are now in the 1-μm region, and critical dimensional tolerances are therefore in the 0.2- to 0.4-μm range and still getting smaller. The continuing problem for

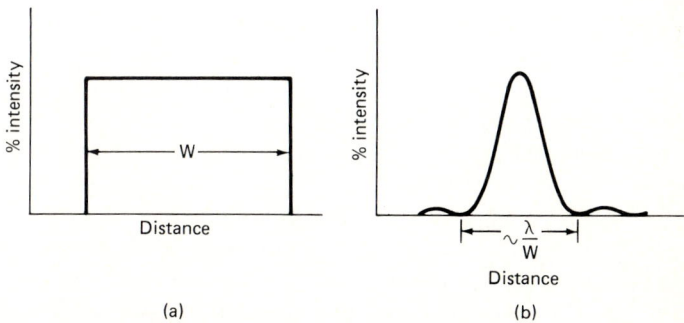

FIG. 6-3 Relationship between *(a)* an ideal line object and *(b)* its coherent spectrum. *[Ref. 1.]*

mask producers is generating patterns to greater accuracy and in larger-volume batch sizes. The equipment used to measure image sizes becomes more sophisticated every year, and in this chapter we will review the various approaches used to determine just how small things really are.

Various facilities have different needs for image measurement, and a key part of setting up the right measurement equipment is an accurate understanding of the real needs. Research departments need to have fairly well advanced measurement capability, since they typically work on leading-edge-image geometries. Their volume is extremely small, however, and this situation is quite different from the wafer production line where much larger geometries are measured for quality on a three-shift basis. We will review the various stages of the mask fabrication process and identify the types of equipment used for checking patterned substrates. The job begins with the original output from the digitized tapes and ends with final measurement of the etched metal and pad widths before the chips are final-tested and encapsulated.

OPTICAL MICROSCOPY

Optical microscopes are the most widely used measuring tools for photomasks. Measurement and inspection of masks occurs at several steps in the fabrication process, and many individual measurments and inspection checks must be made. Optical microscopes fit easily into production operations. They are relatively small and technicians quickly master the operations, including Polaroid and 35-mm slide-film documentation of results. Optical microscopes are also reasonably accurate and, dollar for dollar, are inexpensive measured against the function they perform.

Originally, optical microscopes were used with simple trinocular heads for both mask inspection and pattern-size determination. The development of image-shearing eyepieces, cathode-ray-tube (CRT) scanners, and other optical dividing systems became "add-ons" to the basic microscope, forming the basis of many current line-width measuring and inspection systems. Microscopes used for many of the critical-dimension (CD) measurement steps employ simple stage and/or eyepiece micrometers. These micrometer attachments are relatively inexpensive and can be used for line-width measurements down to about 7 μm.

Stage micrometers are simple glass microscope slides fitted onto the xy stage of the microscope and contain a ruling or set of patterns. The increments should read in millimeters, and a separate calibrated slide will be used for each individual magnification. Three such slides with a trinocular scope make a useful system and cover a wide range of inspection and measurement applications. A simple shortcut to having a separate micrometer scale for each magnification is to use one micrometer scale and simply recalibrate the microscope when changing magnifications.

The filar eyepiece is another optical microscope attachment for small-dimension measurements. Filar-micrometer eyepieces are capable of much greater accuracy than stage micrometers. The primary means of gaining accuracy in the filar micrometer is to divide the area to be measured into smaller units or a greater number of pieces. The mechanism used to accomplish this is a revolving drum that subdivides one revolution (360°) into 100 divisions, giving it good sensitivity. As the drum is hand-turned slowly while one views through the eyepieces, a cross hair is slowly moved across the field of view. The filar drum is always calibrated before each set of measurements is taken. A key advantage of filar-micrometer eyepieces is the speed at which measurements can be taken. Simpler eyepiece micrometers are less sensitive, since the calibrated scale is etched or printed onto the eyepiece and the *xy* stage must be moved to register a measurement.

Digital electronics has impacted optical-microscope measuring systems by providing readout counters. These not only reduce the strenuous job of visually discerning the image edge on every measurement, but also can be coupled to electronic printers for a hard copy of measurement results. Digital readouts and recording printers reduce operator eyestrain and greatly reduce the chance of incorrect measurements. Readings are even simpler to make with the use of closed-circuit TV screens, where the image is enlarged many times, allowing several people to view the image at once and greatly simplifying image measurement.

One type of optical microscope that is used widely in mask-processing and mask-handling areas is the comparison microscope. Mask comparators, as they are called, accommodate two masks from two different levels and permit level-to-level mask alignment. A photograph of this type of system in use in a production environment is shown in Fig. 6-4. Note the use of clean-room clothing with this type of operation. In the mask comparator, the two different sets of patterns are optically superimposed after being recorded by the individual microscope objectives. The separate objectives are shown in the close-up view of this instrument, portrayed in Fig. 6-5. The information provided by this type of optical microscope includes registration from one mask level to the next. Process operators can review an entire mask set *before* committing it to a production operation. The possible misalignment between layers or drift in the critical-dimension tolerances can be picked up here before costly mistakes are generated in the form of reject wafers.

214 INTEGRATED CIRCUIT MASK TECHNOLOGY

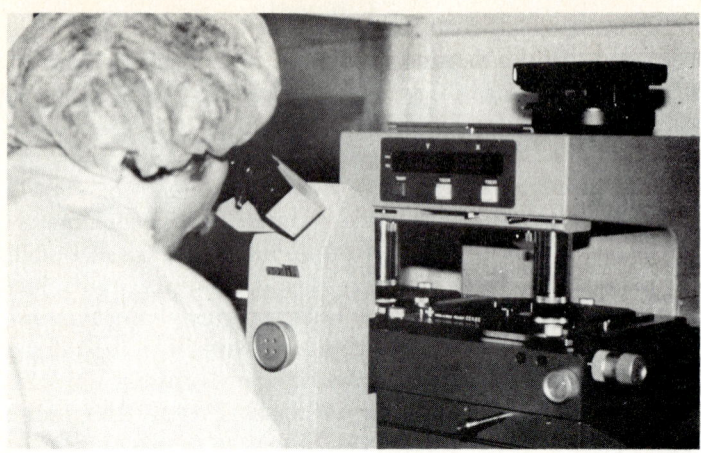

FIG. 6-4 Optical comparison microscope in production use. *(Photronics Labs, Brookfield, Conn.)*

Typically, problems like these are discovered well before final master masks are generated.

The other key function performed by this type of optical comparator is the referencing of a master mask against a copy for reproduction accuracy or the checking of a complete set of masters against a copy for reproduction accuracy, or the checking of a complete set of masters against a copy set of the same pattern. Figure 6-6 shows the superim-

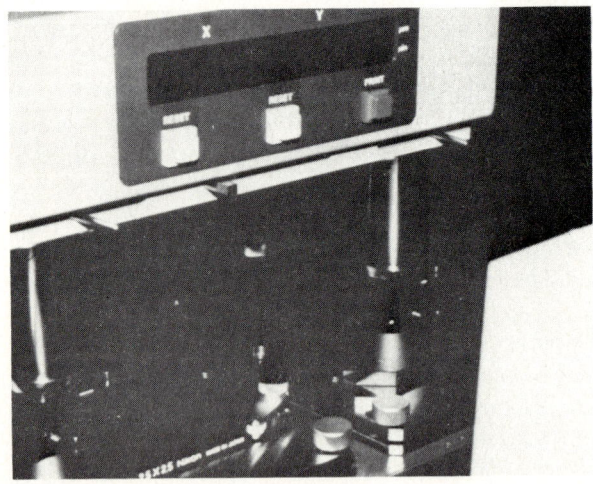

FIG. 6-5 Dual objectives of optical comparison microscope. *(Photronics Labs, Brookfield, Conn.)*

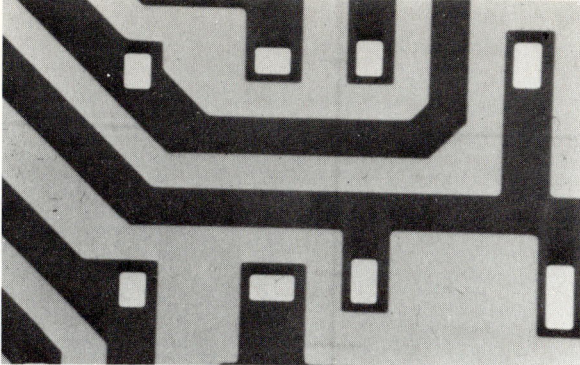

FIG. 6-6 Overlay image of two mask levels in an optical comparator. *(Photronics Labs, Brookfield, Conn.)*

position of two mask levels from the same set, being checked for registration, level to level. The design rules have already established a set of specifications for spaces and line widths for this part of the circuit. The operator will take measurements of these points to be sure they conform to the design rules.

There are several systems of this type commercially available, including the Leitz MVG 7 × 7 system, which operates on the same principle as described above. They typically use red and green images (one color from each mask) in overlay to bring out differences. The dimensional changes that occur are shown to the operator as optical fringes. The fringes are then measured with a micrometer (plane-plate or similar technique). The results of these readings are digitally recorded on a screen or simply portrayed in a digital readout for the operator to record. The overall stage control is either manually or automatically adjustable depending on the unit, and the entire mask area may be measured against a master or control in this fashion.

Since critical dimensions are getting smaller every year, increased sensitivity to this parameter is more important as new VLSI mask designs come "rolling out" of the photoplotters and digitizers. The reliance upon electronics to provide more and more of the sensing and measurement of microimages is a trend seen as necessary to process an increasing number of submicron- and micrometer-range pattern elements. The sheer job of counting thousands of points on a calibrated optical scale tests the patience of even the most seasoned production inspectors and engineers. Electronics, properly calibrated and programmed, can perform this essentially mechanical sensing and recording operation with far less fatigue and most certainly less chance of error. The optical microscope continues to be the nucleus for more electronic

216 INTEGRATED CIRCUIT MASK TECHNOLOGY

add-on devices to simplify and refine the measuring and inspection tasks for VLSI masks and patterned wafers.

Image-Shearing Microscopes

A good example of the electronic mechanization of functions to improve reliability and increase throughput is the image-shearing microscope. In essence this type of microscope performs the same type of operation as the filar micrometer but uses strain gauges instead of a micrometer screw. The image-shearing microscope, popularized by Vickers, uses a TV monitor, digital readout, and of course the basic microscope, all shown in Fig. 6-7. The image-shearing principle works by first dividing the mask pattern, resist image, or other element to be measured into two identical pictures. An operator then moves a sensitive rotating drum (as in the filar eyepiece) so that the very edges of the images barely touch each other.

There are at least two optical methods used to shear the images and thereby obtain a reading. One method involves pulling the edges together

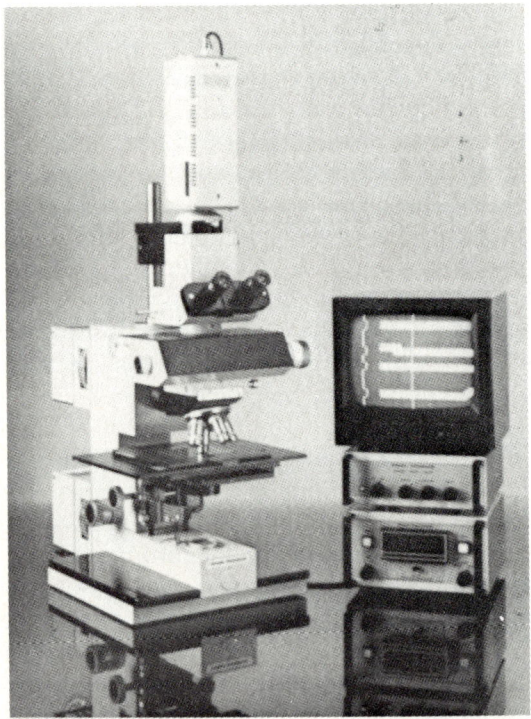

FIG. 6-7 Image-shearing microscope. *(Vickers.)*

so that the original split double images become one or coincident. In this approach the optical intensity as viewed by the operator remains constant, and this makes it easier to see the small edges and record changes in critical dimensions from image to image.

The other approach is to use polarizing elements on each side of the image and record the reading. This method has the disadvantage of requiring perception of varying intensities; however, some operators find this easier than the other technique. Prior to puchasing such a system, operators will need to spend some time testing actual samples on the system, and thereby discern the best approach for the type of application they have. There is no question as to the variety of image types, the variation in reflectance and texture, and overall appearance of images in these systems. One system will be ideal for measuring resist patterns on chrome, while another mode or entirely different instrument will be needed for different substrates.

Photosensing Devices

Photometers are devices used to sense absolute light-intensity values as well as different or changes in a signal. Obviously, this capability is easily applied to the measurement of reflected or transmitted light from a photomask. Most photometers will easily and accurately sense a pattern line or space edge.

In principle, a photometer operates as an attachment to an optical microscope by first getting a magnified image of the information to be sensed. The photometer principle is one of light detection of image intensity from a scanning slit. A motorized drive unit carries the scanning slit across the area to be measured, and a linear encoder makes the actual measurement once the slit has passed over the image. After the pattern has been measured and data have been transmitted via the encoder, the slit is reset into its "zero" position and is ready for another reading. Line-edge detection by optical encoding disks is a well-understood and equally well perfected technology. Image-sensing optical measuring systems have played and continue to play an important role in microelectronic image evaluation. Photometers of various types are available commercially, and some are completely automated.

Automation in optical measuring systems is essential for quality-control operations that require hundreds of measurements of the same element. Highly redundant measuring operations are easily automated and a perfect application for a photometer-based measurement tool. The use of data processing along with this equipment adds the capability of generating hard copy of the results over a period of time. The trend in the changes in CDs from a series of mask runs is an example of the type of data available from these systems. Figure 6-8 shows a binocular view seen through the Nanometrics Nanoline photometer.

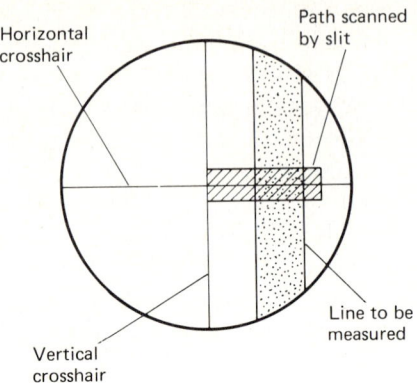

FIG. 6-8 Line-image profile from Nanometrics Nanoline microdensitometer. *(Nanometrics, Inc., Sunnyvale, Calif.)*

TV Scanning Microscopes

Moving still further away from operator-dependent measuring systems, TV scanners provide automatic image detection, data generation and memory storage, and automatic image-tracking capabilities. Like previous optical measuring and inspection systems, TV scanning systems generally employ an optical microscope at their "core." Working in tandem with the microscope is an automatic-focus mechanism, eliminating a time-consuming and eye-straining operator task. A video system provides the screen display, and an analog-to-digital converter is used to transform the pattern elements into digital information. Once digitized, the data are processed in a microcomputer, also housed in the system.

A typical TV scanning system is portrayed in Fig. 6-9. This particular system is an ITP System 80, which uses a $100\times$ optical microscope. The operator, in a standard measuring operation, places the mask under the scanning sensor on the microscope table and keys in the proper position information. The unit takes over at this point by automatically following the edge of a pattern element and recording data at the same time.

The principle of operation of this type of system rests on the ability to distinguish maximum opaque and maximum transparent areas of the sample, referred to as clear- or dark-field thresholds. Also employed is a mechanism referred to as peak detection, where the video signal

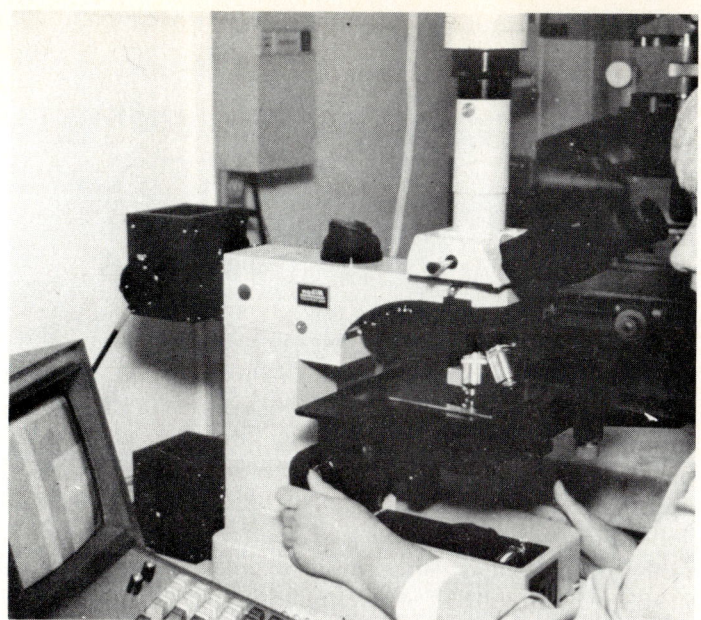

FIG. 6-9 ITP System 80 optical microscope with TV scanning. *(ITP.)*

emitted from the sensor is at the lowest point or minimum energy value. In research labs and on the production line, these systems provide a means to obtain hundreds of image measurements without unduly straining operators and incurring measurement error as a result. Advantages of the video scanning systems include small size, relatively low cost versus productivity, and reasonably good accuracy.

Laser Measurement

Lasers offer another accurate and semi-automated means of pattern measurement technology. Lasers are relatively low-cost, high-quality point sources whose beam is diffracted on the edge of the image to be measured. The scattered light is sensed by detectors that record and transmit the data. Unlike principally simpler optical microscope systems, the laser is insensitive to variations in the density of the image being measured since diffraction occurs at a physical edge or step. Optical systems are also likely to vary on measuring according to the intensity variation in the primary pattern illumination system. Laser systems operate independently of this parameter. A typical laser-based measuring tool is the Nikon XY-21, shown in Fig. 6-10.

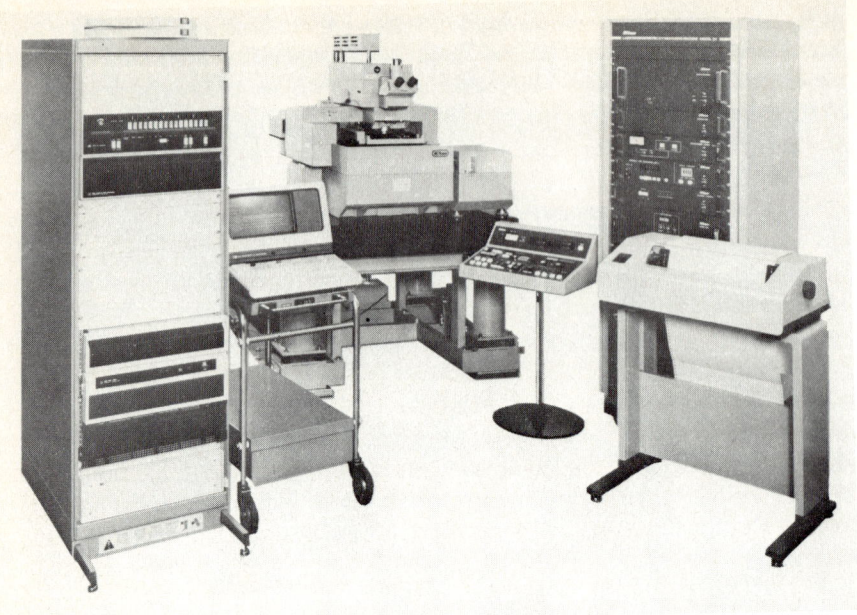

FIG. 6-10 Nikon XY-2I laser intrferometric measuring device. *(Nikon.)*

A more complex laser-based measuring tool is the Nikon incident-light micropattern analyzer Lampas-M2. This system is capable of submicron pattern measurement, using a scanning laser spot to detect pattern edges. Pattern widths varying from 0.8 to 100 μm are measurable with repeatability of $\leq \pm 0.05$ μm. The eye-fatigue problem is eliminated since this system, shown in Fig. 6-11 uses automatic measuring.

One of the shortcomings of earlier-mentioned optical microscope systems is variation due to substrate reflectance. Semiconductor oxides, nitrides, and polysilicon need to be measured in varying thicknesses. Chromium, emulsions, resist images, and iron oxide all occur in different thicknesses, have different reflectance values, and present an entirely different image to the optical microscope system. One immediate problem is adjusting for the optically changing conditions so that the same "real" measurements are taken each time. In other words, how can you be sure your system is always calibrated to accommodate the changes in specimens being measured?

Another key question to be asked of the optical microscope systems relates to the wavelengths used. In mask fabrication, the 436- or 365-nm lines are used to pattern resist on chrome. In mid-uv lithography, wavelengths in the range of 280 to 320 nm are used, and deep-uv

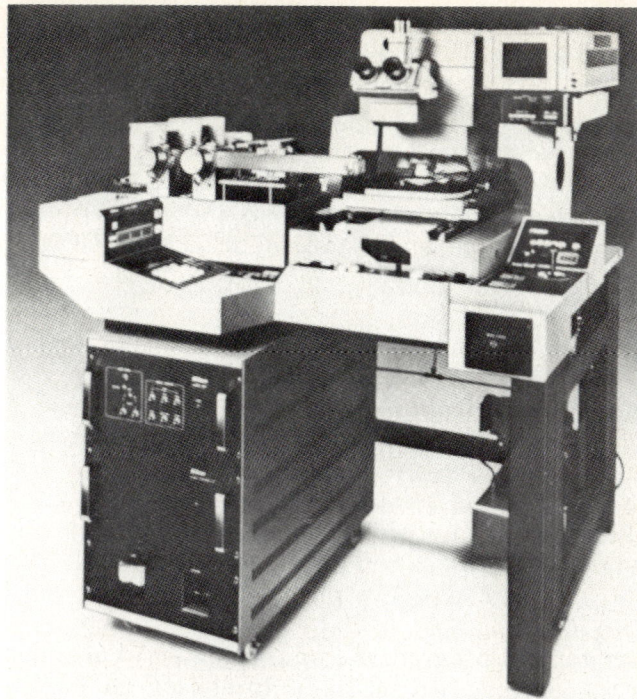

FIG. 6-11 Nikon incident-light micropattern analyzer Lampas-M2. *(Nikon.)*

imaging employs wavelengths between 200 and 280 nm. The question is simple: How can measuring systems, using lower-frequency (longer-wavelength) light, measure images that required higher frequencies (shorter wavelengths) in order to be generated? The answer is most likely they cannot, at least not accurately or repeatably. The general rule of thumb in metrology is to use a measuring energy frequency higher than the energy frequency used to form the image being measured; the greater the separation in frequencies, the more accurate the measurement is likely to be.

The Lampas-M2 system has a minimum readout unit of 0.01 μm over a wide range of substrate types. The specimens can be observed directly through the microscope at either 100× or 500×. Alignment takes place at 100×, and the image and laser-beam spot are seen together at the higher magnification. Conversion from 100× to 500× is simple.

The measuring system employs automatic pattern-edge sensing using a scanning laser microspot. Automatic line-width measurement is made with a laser interferometer, but it can also be accomplished with a regular reflection signal. The measuring speed is 2 μm/sec and can be switched to 10 μm/sec. A simple program of the coordinates on the mask or wafer will enable the system to automatically address, focus, and measure a succession of pattern elements.

The automatic measurement is carried one step further by the digital printer, which records the measurements and generates simultaneous computation of average and standard deviations. Other measuring functions of this system include

- Repeat scanning (of a single pattern)
- Automatic manual focus
- Screening out of background noise
- Range sensitivity (gain setting of edge detection pulse)

The basic principle of sensing detection is shown in Fig. 6-12. Note that the laser beam is bounced off a mirror, through a lens, and focused onto the edge of the pattern being measured. The signal is then broken into several parts and sensed by photodetectors, giving out the signals shown in Fig. 6-12.

The operator can program the unit with a set of acceptable critical-dimension values and then set the unit into an automatic measuring mode, telling it to display a "go" or "no-go" depending on the reading taken on the sample under test. Masks up to 6 in and wafers up to 5 in can be measured in this system.

SCANNING-MICROSCOPE MEASUREMENT

The highest level of precision in measurement technology is obtained with scanning electron microscopy (SEM). SEM analysis is needed for the high-magnification analysis of microelectronic structures. The scanning electron microscope provides resolution on the order of 50 to 100 Å, and will detail shapes of microstructures as well as their dimensions. Earlier scanning microscopes required that samples be broken into relatively small pieces before viewing in the chamber. The manufacturers of scanning microscopes have responded to the needs of the IC industry by providing the following capabilities:

1. Insertion of entire mask or wafer into vacuum chamber for observation
2. Provision to avoid damaging the substrate with the electron beam
3. Ability to see several specimens per hour
4. Ease of operation so that process personnel can be readily trained.

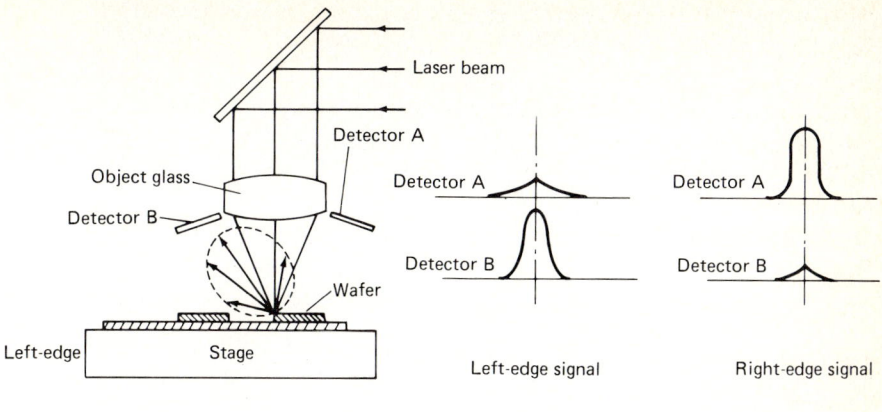

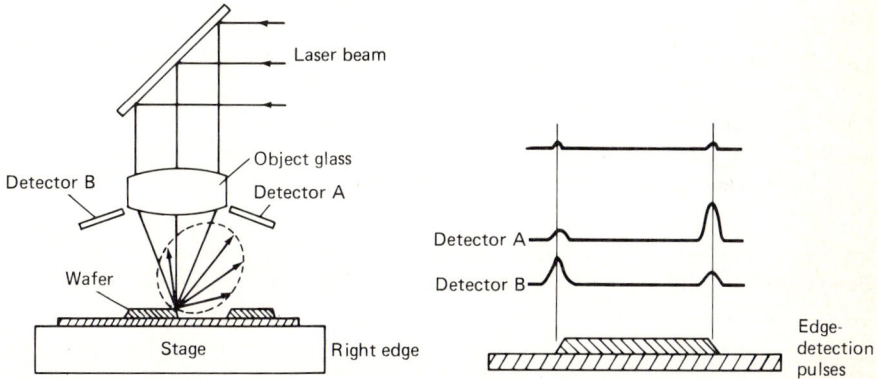

FIG. 6-12 Operating principle of Lampas micropattern analyzer. The distance between the edge-detection pulses of A and B signals is displayed in the lower left corner. (*Nikon.*)

A system that meets these parameters and will accept substrates up to 5-in square is shown in Fig. 6-13. The sample can be moved 100 mm in both the *x* and *y* planes, tilted up to 60°, and rotated 360° continuously. The working distance in the *z* plane is 10 to 48 mm. A special option (Auto Mag Correction Unit SM-MAC) will automatically correct the image to a predetermined magnification. This means, with focus adjustment, an image of specified magnification is obtainable regardless of the substrate thickness.

Protecting the sample from the potentially damaging beam is done by blanking (electromagnetic shuttering) the beam and using an optical microscope to search for areas of interest. A schematic drawing of the JSM-IC25S showing the way in which this is accomplished is presented in Fig. 6-14.

224 INTEGRATED CIRCUIT MASK TECHNOLOGY

FIG. 6-13 Scanning electron microscope for mask and wafer observation. (*JEOL.*)

After the sample has been viewed through the microscope, the prism is retracted, and the sample is irradiated by the electron beam. A special eucentric stage permits the specimen to be tilted from a horizontal position without changing the point at which the beam irradiates the sample. Thus, by focusing once, the sample can be viewed, measured, and then tilted and remeasured or photographed without refocusing or changing the sample position.

Focus time is a short 0.7 sec with the automatic-focus mechanism; vacuum pumping with a beltless oil rotary pump is automatic. The resolution on a 5-in mask is about 30 nm and down to 10 nm at a short working distance.

Another instrument performing the same type of task is the Nanometrics Cwikscan II field emission inspection line-width measuring scanning electron microscope. This system takes advantage of lower operating voltages to avoid damaging the samples in the system. High-voltage electron-beams used in scanning microscopy will create surface-doping effects, rearrangement of surface molecular- and heat-induced distortion, resist exposure or cross-linking in undesirable areas, and other unwanted effects. In times when scanning electron microscopes were not needed as measuring tools, many fine electronic adjustments were required, including accelerating voltage, signal-to-noise tuning,

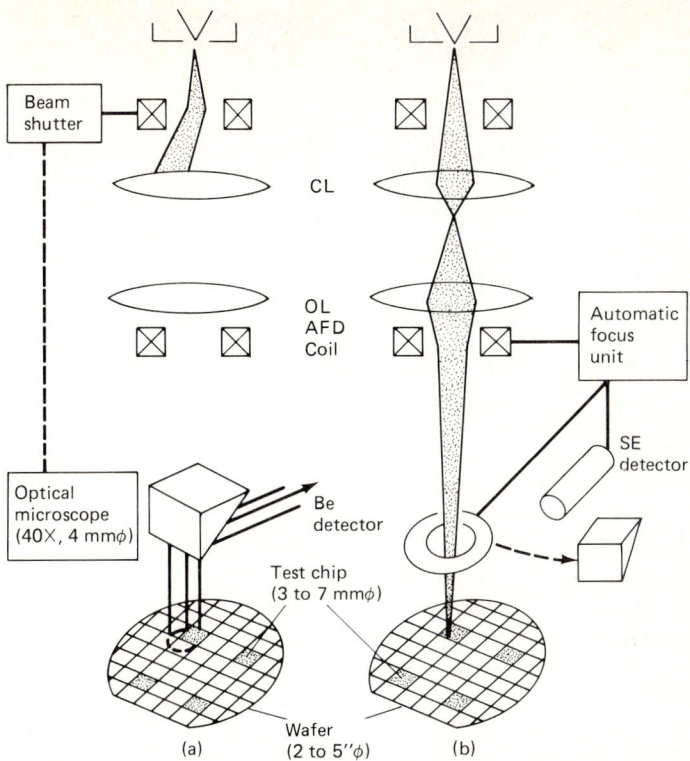

FIG. 6-14 Operating principle of JSM-IC 25S scanning electron microscope.

and many other "know-turning" exercises that took 20 to 30 min before a sample could be received. The majority of SEM systems now in use as measuring tools are easy to operate and can produce excellent photographs or measurements with only a few hours training.

Measurement on the Cwikscan II can be preprogrammed so that operators oversee the cassette that feeds parts automatically into the scanning electron microscope for resolution, line-width, or other critical-dimension checks. The repeatability of a scanning electron microscope is close to that of an optical microscope, although the scanning electron microscope beats all instruments for absolute resolution in practical measuring applications. In the Cwikscan, a joystick is used to select the points of interest, and a conical lens is available to permit a complete view of the mask or wafer surface at high magnifications. If an operator wishes to measure resist images *before* committing the part to the etch step, care must be taken to measure the dimension of the resist at the interface with the substrate. In a low-voltage scanning electron micro-

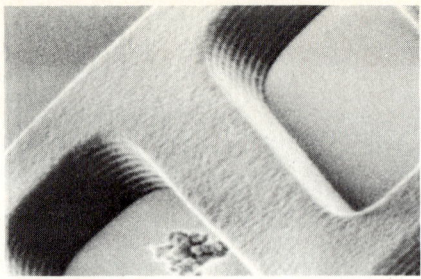

FIG. 6-15 Submicron resist images observed and measured with scanning electron microscope. *(Nanometrics, Inc., Sunnyvale Calif.)*

scope, secondary electrons are generated from the primary beam as it strikes the resist surface. The pattern of "secondaries" is such that with resist on glass or oxide or even chrome, a high-contrast image results, making it easier to see the dimension in question. A video cursor is then used to take the actual measurement.

Some examples of the quality of images coming from the Cwikscan II are shown in Fig. 6-15 and 6-16. Figure 6-15 shows some submicron resist images in excellent detail, complete with standing-wave patterns. This photograph was taken at 18,000× magnification with 1.5-kV electrons. Of particular importance is the fact that it *did not* require a conductive-metal coating step, was processed without breaking the substrate, *and* can be sent back to the production line, unaffected by electron exposure.

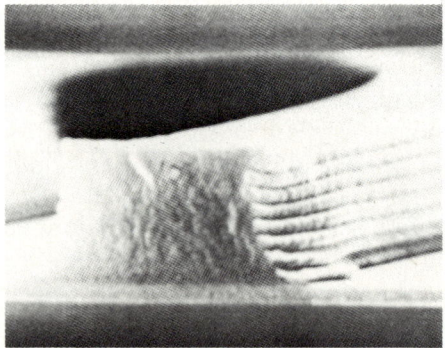

FIG. 6-16 Scanning electromicrograph of resist structures made at 33,000 magnification on a Cwikscan series scanning electron microscope. *(Nanometrics, Inc., Sunnyvale, Calif.)*

Figure 6-16 shows a cross-sectional end view of a resist line at 33,000 × magnification. This was taken with 20-kV electrons and portrays incredible detail of the very fine standing-wave patterns in the resist sidewalls. These structures are small as 800 Å and are very clearly resolved. A very close look at the point where the resist touches the substrate is often used to check for pattern dimension, cleanliness of resist development, and for adhesion to the substrate.

The scanning electron microscope, with automatic features and simpler operation, is truly a first-rate measuring tool. Its advantages can be summed up as follows:

1. Automatic focus
2. Programmable to specific points
3. Good productivity in production and quality checks
4. Eucentric stages for easy tilt and accurate magnification
5. Low noise
6. No metallization
7. Five-inch plates on wafers loaded intact
8. Resolution good to 100 nm

While scanning electron microscopes that are fast and fully automated on the production floor are still needed, they are rapidly approaching that stage of development. One of the major problems facing the industry in terms of measurement science is standardization. The National Bureau of Standards in Washington, D.C., has studied this problem intensively with regard to the semiconductor industry. They have explained *why* differences exist between various measuring systems, but the solution as to how to reach agreement or standardization remain to be found. The need for a consistent or repeatable relationship between the image edge and the edge detection threshold is fundamental. Calibration of various measurement systems rests on this need. The control of all the variables encountered in optical imaging microscopes is also essential if a uniform standard is to be accepted. These variables include numerical apertures (NAs), focus, edge-detection technique, wavelengths of light used to illuminate specimens, and refractive index of films measured. In their publication, *Optical Linewidth Measurement— A Basic Understanding*,[1] Diana Nyyssonen and John M. Jerke of the National Bureau of Standards explain that "for systems which cannot measure the proper optical threshold, a calibration curve of measured known linewidths must be established over the range of interest and subsequent measurement data must be corrected."

In the next section of this chapter we will discuss the use of an optical line-width standard.

STANDARDS

The challenge of setting down a standard is difficult enough with several different types of measuring systems, but it is further complicated by the use of several types of masks. The line-image threshold that is used to determine the image edge when measuring through an optical microscope is different for the different mask types. Chrome and antireflective chrome have different reflectance and transmittance values. Since antireflective chrome is typically used in the most demanding situations relative to image resolution and CD control, this type of mask is a good choice as a candidate for an optical line-width standard.

The National Bureau of Standards (NBS) has evaluated such a standard (SRM 474) and published extensively on its use. This standard was evaluated on four different types of line-width measuring systems and on three different chrome thickness layers. The various measurements were then corrected using the SRM 474 and measured against readings taken on the NBS optical line-width calibration system. On bright chrome with low transmittance, all values were within ±0.05 μm as checked in the NBS system and other measuring systems using the SRM 474. However, the calibration curve *did not* correct all systematic measurement errors for see-through antireflective chrome. As reported by John M. Jerke (NBS) and Charles E. Wendell (University of Rochester) in their report on this subject,[2] these results confirmed the theoretical expectations that the amount of correction for systematic line-width errors is a function of the measurement system as well as of the chrome-mask transmittance value.

The types of measuring systems compared in this study were image shearing (optical display), optical filar, video image scanning, and coincidence shearing.

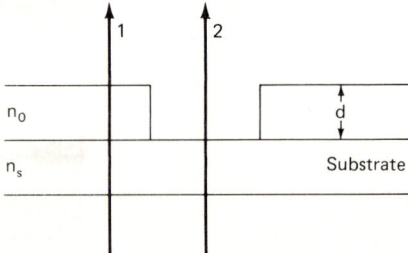

FIG. 6-17 Optical path difference (OPD) used to calculate phase difference: $\Delta\phi = k$ (OPD); $\Delta\phi = \phi_2 - \phi_1 + kd$. *[Ref. 2.]*

The variations in optical transmission of different mask types cause different readings of the optical threshold or image edge where measurements originate. This threshold or edge image can be broken down into its component parts and studied from the difference in optical phase, a parameter calculated by the formula given with Fig. 6-17.

The optical phase difference $\Delta\phi$ for phase-transmitted light is calculated from the optical path difference between rays 1 and 2 in Fig. 6-17. The formula is broken down as follows:

$$\Delta\phi = \phi_2 - \phi_1 + kd$$

where d = chrome layer thickness

$k = \dfrac{2\pi}{\lambda}$

n_o, n_s = indexes of refraction for chrome and glass

λ = illumination wavelength

The overall pattern, shown in Fig. 6-18, is repeated 8 times over the mask areas, and a close-up of the pattern shapes is shown in Fig. 6-19. Note that pattern elements C3 and D6 are submicron in size and may not reproduce well in the photograph shown here. The SRM 474 is a very useful tool for checking the differences between measuring systems, and the reader is advised to contact the National Bureau of Standards in Washington, D.C., directly to obtain such a calibration device for use in production.

In the exposure of resist and in the measurement of images, nonco-

FIG. 6-18 National Bureau of Standards Pattern SRM 474. *(Courtesy W. Smallwood, NBS.)*

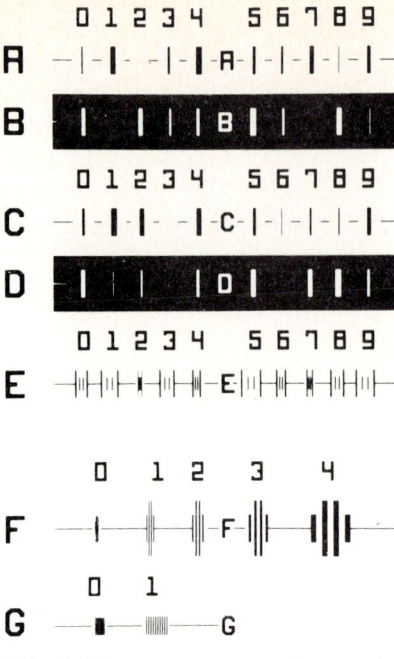

FIG. 6-19 Basic pattern of the NBS SRM 474 test target.

herent illumination and coherent illumination are used, and each presents a different energy profile and corresponding different optical measurement point. The calculated optical-image profiles for microscopes with both coherent and noncoherent light are shown in Figs. 6-1 and 6-2. The relationship to the optical threshold is discussed in this section. In practice, noncoherent light will not be available through a high-numerical-aperture microscope objective. All measurements should be made with coherent illumination. The resolution range of the NBS SRM474 is recommended at 0.5 to 12 μm using transmitted light.

In summary, parameters affecting line-edge determination and overall measurement of patterns on chrome masks include

1. Mask material
2. Measurement system
3. Line-edge optical phase difference
4. Background transmittance

The calibration curve discussed is useful when using opaque bright chrome but is not recommended for see-through antireflective chromium.

THICKNESS MEASUREMENT

A major part of measurement technology is concerned with determining the thickness of various oxide, metal, and resist layers used in mask- and silicon-device fabrication. The primary area of interest is in the 1-μm-thickness region, even for the coatings used on optical surfaces, such as antireflection layers and special dye absorbers. Many techniques are used to measure thin-film layers including[7]

1. Coulometry
2. Beta-ray backscatter
3. Magnetics
4. X-ray fluorescence
5. Eddy currents
6. Optical microscopy
7. Scanning electron microscopy
8. Ellipsometry
9. Profilometry
10. Multiple-beam interferometry
11. Channel spectra
12. Guided-wave methods

In the area of mask fabrication the more common methods involve optical and mechanical approaches, and we will discuss these in detail. More recent use of scanning electron microscopy has increased the resolution at which microstructures are viewed, and SEM analysis as a thin-film measurement method is becoming practical as equipment is modified to suit this application.

Interferometry

Tolinsky beam (dual, multiple) interferometry is widely used in microelectronics for film-thickness measurement since it is accurate and nondestructive. The specimen must present a "step" or some type of topography with this method. The principal mechanism is one based on the interference of coherent light (or other radiation) reflected back from the sample being measured. A reference flat is also used, as light is reflected from this to generate a series of fringes. The schematic diagrams in Fig. 6-20 show the principle of operation. The interferograms derived from the two basic types of systems are also shown with the diagrams. The fringes shown in these photographs each represent one-half the wavelength of the illuminating radiation. The reference flat shown in the diagram is tilted so that the fringes run at right angles to the step in the specimen. The lateral shifting of the fringes is caused by the change in specimen topography where the step exists.

Calculation of the step height is made by measuring the fringe spacing (w) and lateral shifting of fringes across the substrate topography (Δ); the step height (h) or thickness of the layer to be measured is then calculated as follows:

$$h = \frac{\lambda \Delta}{2w}$$

It is important that the illuminating wavelength be kept highly collimated and at right angles to the surface of the substrate, since changes in either of these parameters will affect the validity of the step-height equation. Since nearly all microscope objectives provide well-collimated

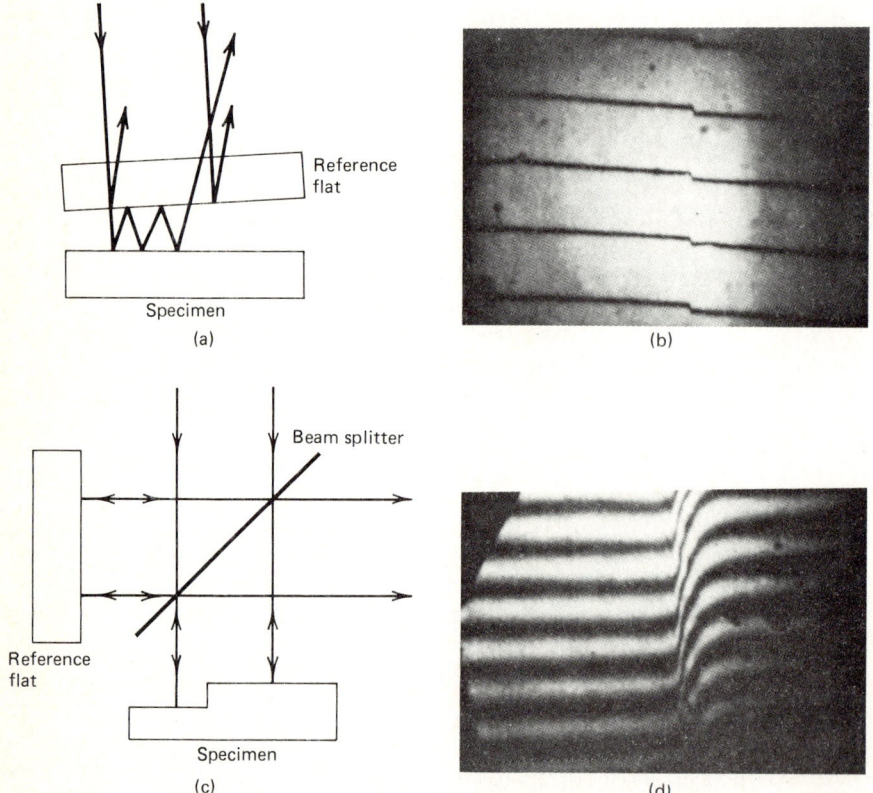

FIG. 6-20 Schematic diagrams and interferograms of (a), (b) multiple- and (c), (d) dual-beam interferometers. *[Ref. 4.]*

light, this should not be a problem. Almost all commercially available microscopes accommodate interference attachments or screw-on interferometers.

In checking resist layers, there may not be sufficient optical density in the resist layer to cause the reflectance needed to get a good fringe pattern. The sample can be overcoated with a thin layer of evaporated aluminum, a technique that renders the resist pattern unusable. The need for overcoating is especially great in dual- and multiple-beam interference methods where the fringe patterns are considerably sharper.

The standard dual-beam interferometer method of thickness measurement has a predictable accuracy of 20 to 30 nm, and multiple-beam interference methods will improve this by almost 10 times! A standard industry reference for this technique is ASTM Standard F388-77, obtainable through the American Society for Testing and Materials, Philadelphia, Pennsylvania.

Stylus Profilometry

Measuring the thickness of a thin resist layer is performed quickly and accurately with surface-profile devices. The method is destructive in the sense that a small scratch is left on the resist, oxide, chrome, or glass layer. Similar to the interferometer method, stylus-profile methods require an exposed edge or step of the layer to be checked. One method of performing stylus measurements is shown in the diagram in Fig. 6-21. The Tally Surf and Dectac measuring instruments are based on "riding" but gently weighted diamond or similar styluses that track the specimen and record the variation in topography. The printout of one of these instruments on a thin resist layer is shown in Fig. 6-22. Note the small "bumps" where the instrument faithfully recorded "radial striations" or surface irregularities of less than 300 Å where rapid drying caused the coating to dry nonuniformly, before it could "relax" and slowly release its solvents.

Experiments have been run at the National Bureau of Standards using stylus-measuring methods and are published in the form of Technical Note 902, available from the NBS in Washington, D.C. The standard developed at NBS for calibrating thickness-measuring equipment is an optical flat made of silica and partially coated with a 2.99-μm film of silicon monoxide, overcoated with aluminum to promote reflectivity, and finally, coated with silicon monoxide again for mechanical resistance to the diamond stylus tip used to measure. Dual- and multiple-beam interferometry is used to calibrate this standard, and estimates from NBS place the 3-σ error of calibrating the 2.99-μm film at approximately 25 nm.

234 INTEGRATED CIRCUIT MASK TECHNOLOGY

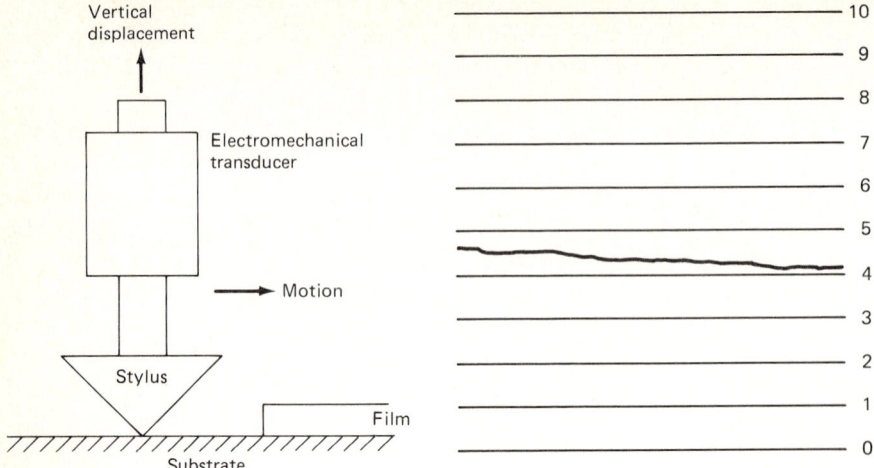

FIG. 6-21 Surface-profiling stylus-measuring principle. *[Ref. 3.]*

FIG. 6-22 Stylus surface measurement of a resist coating (XP-2138 photoresist striation-free coating, Dectac trace, 200 Å per division). *(Dectac.)*

Stylus profilometry is extremely useful on the production line since specimen measurements can be made rapidly and with sufficient accuracy for VLSI processes. There are several good instruments commercially available for stylus-thickness measuring, one of which is shown in Fig. 6-23. This particular unit is being used to measure positive photoresist thickness on a mask just after exposure and development. Checks are also made to ensure good resist uniformity across the entire mask or wafer surface. A series of resist-thickness measurements taken on a 5-

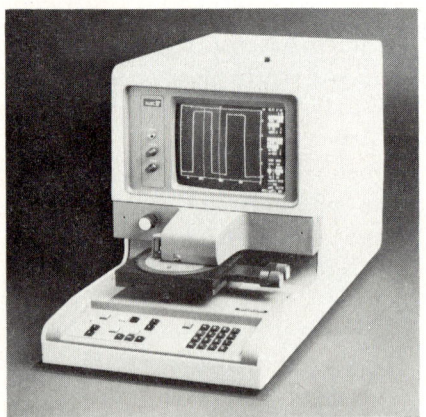

FIG. 6-23 Stylus profilometer. *(Tencor Instruments.)*

PATTERN MEASUREMENT 235

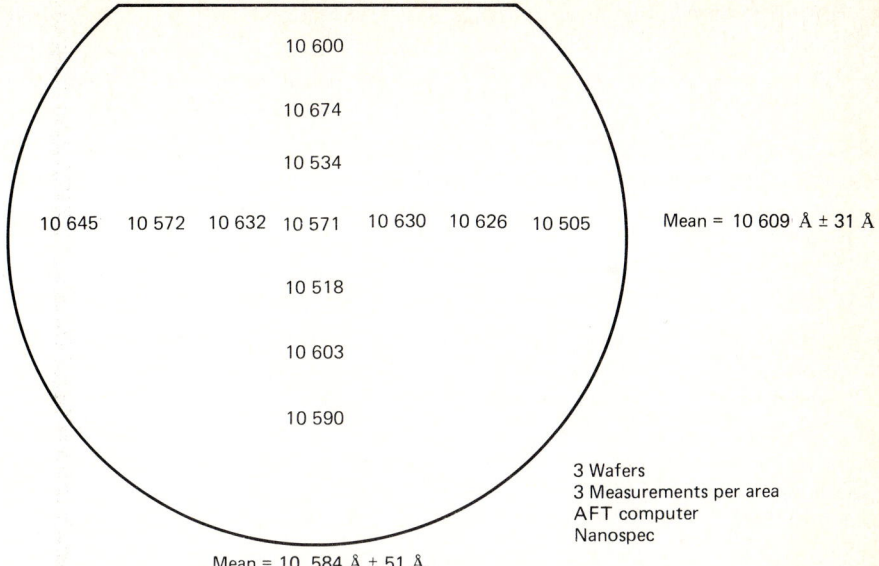

FIG. 6-24 Measurements of thickness variation of XP-2138 coating across a 5-in wafer or mask surface. *[Ref. 8.]*

in wafer are plotted and displayed in Fig. 6-24. Note the small percent of resist deviation from the mean, based on several sample runs. This degree of uniformity is required in order to maintain the control of micrometer-range geometries being patterned in the resist from the mask. The only critical measurement left to perform on a mask or wafer after resist thickness is known (along with the variation in thickness across the wafer) is the slope angle of the resist sidewall. A scanning electron micrograph of this important topographical detail is shown in Fig. 6-25.

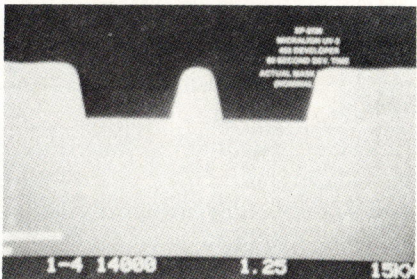

FIG. 6-25 Measurement of photoresist sidewall angle. *(Shipley.)*

The sidewall angle in resist images will vary according to the contrast inherent in the resist and in the signal exposure energy. The combination of these factors, along with the refractive index of the resist, the reflectivity of the substrate, and the nature of exposed-resist erosion in the developing solution, produces a characteristic resist sidewall. Thus, careful measurement and observation of resist sidewalls serves not only as a predictor of etch results but also as an indication of what is happening in the other aspects of the imaging process.

If, for example the exposure energy is poorly collimated, a relatively low sidewall angle (less than 60°) can result. On the VLSI alignment systems, typical resist sidewall angles range from 75 to 90°, and an 80° angle sidewall is considered indicative of good optical imaging.

Resist-sidewall measurement on masks is somewhat less critical since the coating is very thin and the amount of undercut during etching is almost unmeasurable. However, it is still recommended that process operators take the time to scanning electron micrograph the resist-sidewall angle.

The last technique for obtaining good SEM pictures is to image a series of lines and spaces across the mask or wafer surface. After development, simply break the specimen at a 90° angle to the resist images and shoot the sample on end, looking directly at the fractured end of the substrate. Stylus measuring of resin-based resists, for either sidewall angles or thickness measurements, should be done carefully to ensure that the stylus does not partially pierce the coating and thereby render an inaccurate measurement.

Prism-Coupler Measurement

Prism-coupler measurements are useful for accurate measurements of thin films. Typically these films are semiconductors, such as silicon, silicon dioxide, iron oxide, and silicon nitride, and have very uniform mass. The technique involves placing a prism (with a refractive index higher than the film to be measured) directly on top of the film or substrate. The substrate is then supported by two points, and a small force carefully applied to the prism will result in optical coupling between the prism and the substrate.

The mechanism of this behavior is explained by A. Feldman and T. Vorburger[3] as follows: "Laser radiation incident on the region of optical coupling would normally be totally internally reflected at the base of the prism." However, the coupling is a result of the angle of incidence of the laser beam (relative to the prism base) corresponding to a reflected beam in the film, at an angle synchronous to a propagating mode. When this occurs, power is drawn from the incident beam and coupled into the film via the evanescent field. Due to the optical scatter within the oxide, silicon, or other layer, and at the film boundaries, light from the propagating mode also couples into all other possible modes of propagation. The light that couples *back out* of the film and into the prism provides the basis for this measurement technique.

This light is imaged, as it exits the prism, on a screen and appears as streams. Figure 6-26 shows the prism on the substrate with the light coupling out, and a picture (or *M*-line spectrum) of the streaks is shown on the right of the figure. These streaks are called "*M*-lines." By measuring the maximum brightness points of the *M*-lines, the synchronous coupling angles can be determined. The minimum brightness of the reflected beam will also serve as a measurement parameter. A least-squares fit of measured mode angles to the mode propagation equations will produce the thickness value and the refractive index. Errors in measuring are a function of the refractive index match between the substrate and the film. The worse the index match, the lower the measuring error.

The prism coupler method has the advantage of high accuracy and is nondestructive. Opaque chromium cannot be measured, but anti-reflective transparent and see-through chrome as well as all other transparent film materials such as resists can be measured.

Ellipsometric Measurement

The use of ellipsometers is well known in the semiconductor industry, mainly as a tool to check the thickness of thin films and determine their refractive index. Ellipsometry is based on the principle of light being polarized into different states. A change in the state of polarization occurs as the light is reflected from the surface to be measured at a known angle of incidence. By measuring the ratio of the amplitude-

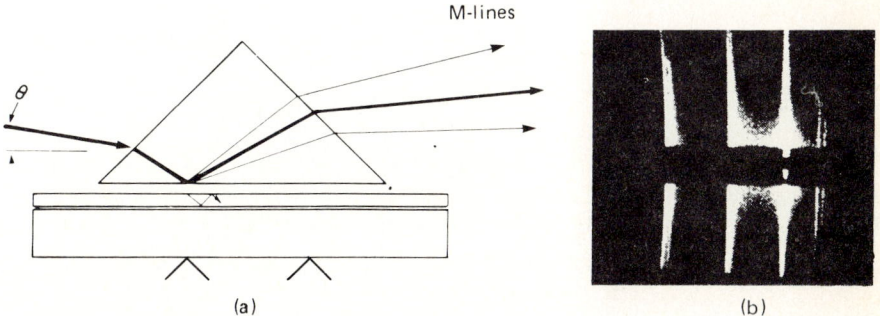

FIG. 6-26 Prism-coupler principle and photograph of *M*-lines. *[Ref. 3.]*

reflection coefficients and using published computer programs to plug in some of the known parameters (angular settings of polarizers and compensators in the ellipsometer), measurements can be derived. Ellipsometry is nondestructive and noncontacting and can allow for rapid film-thickness determination. A typical ellipsometer is shown in Fig. 6-27.

A key difficulty in production is that surface contamination on the substrate being checked will interrupt measurement accuracy. Be sure parts are well-cleaned before this operation.

Channel Spectra

A scanning spectrophotometer is used to measure film thickness with this technique. Both transparent and opaque films are measured by placing them into the spectrophotometer and observing the fringes that result. In the case of transparent substrates (resist images on glass) an extra set of complementary fringes is seen. The name "channel spectra" is synonymous with "fringes." Applications in use currently are for dielectric films on glass.

Equipment for this technique is commercially available and typically incorporates microprocessor control. The scanning beam in a computerized system will "look" at the visible reflectance spectrum and derive the layer thickness (after calibration) in less than 15 sec. Coatings as thin as 500 nm can be measured with 5 percent accuracy.

FIG. 6-27 Ellipsometer used in thin-film measurement. *(Goertner Scientific Corporation, Chicago.)*

All the optical and mechanical measurement methods reviewed here are used in semiconductor processing for the thickness determination of films in the 1-µm-thickness range. Some methods are relatively new, such as prism coupling, and will benefit greatly from the development of simple production-oriented equipment. The methods cited are all accurate within a few percent and are therefore suitable for most VLSI processes.

APPLICATIONS FOR PATTERN MEASUREMENT

The importance of reliable and accurate measurement tools in mask fabrication is well-understood when considering the number of operations that depend on these measurements. The primary application we have dealt with is the mask dimensions. The mask shop must check the critical dimensions on a finished mask after all the artwork steps are completed. The mask then travels to the wafer fabrication line where critical dimensions are double-checked again on the mask. The mask is then used in the exposure aligner, and the resist images are measured after development. If the resist images are not within tolerance, the mask in question is checked again, and the wafer may need to be re-imaged due to a process problem. The imaged wafer is then etched, and CDs are once again measured for conformance to the specifications. Final electrical tests will confirm acceptability of the pattern dimensions. Overall, several different surfaces are involved in the measurement processes, many requiring different equipment. In addition to CD measurement, many other areas and aspects of the mask and wafer fabrication process involve measurement technology. Figure 6-28 identifies some of these areas for a MOSFET process, including process variables.

The measuring equipment for VLSI patterns includes both absolute and relative values. The absolute systems incorporate a primary standard, including the NBS photometer and laser interferometer, the NBS scanning electron microscope and laser interferometer, and the Nikon mask system with photometer and linear encoder. Relative systems are calibrated with a relative standard, and then samples are compared to this standard. The relative equipment include the TV systems, filar eyepieces, image-shearing microscopes, and photometric apparatus. Despite the refinement in standards and improvement in resolution of measuring equipment, measurement errors are a major problem. Some of the sources of measurement error include

1. Variability in operator judgment of edge location and focus
2. Inadequate training in measurement parameters and influences
3. Predetermined ideas about measurement technique

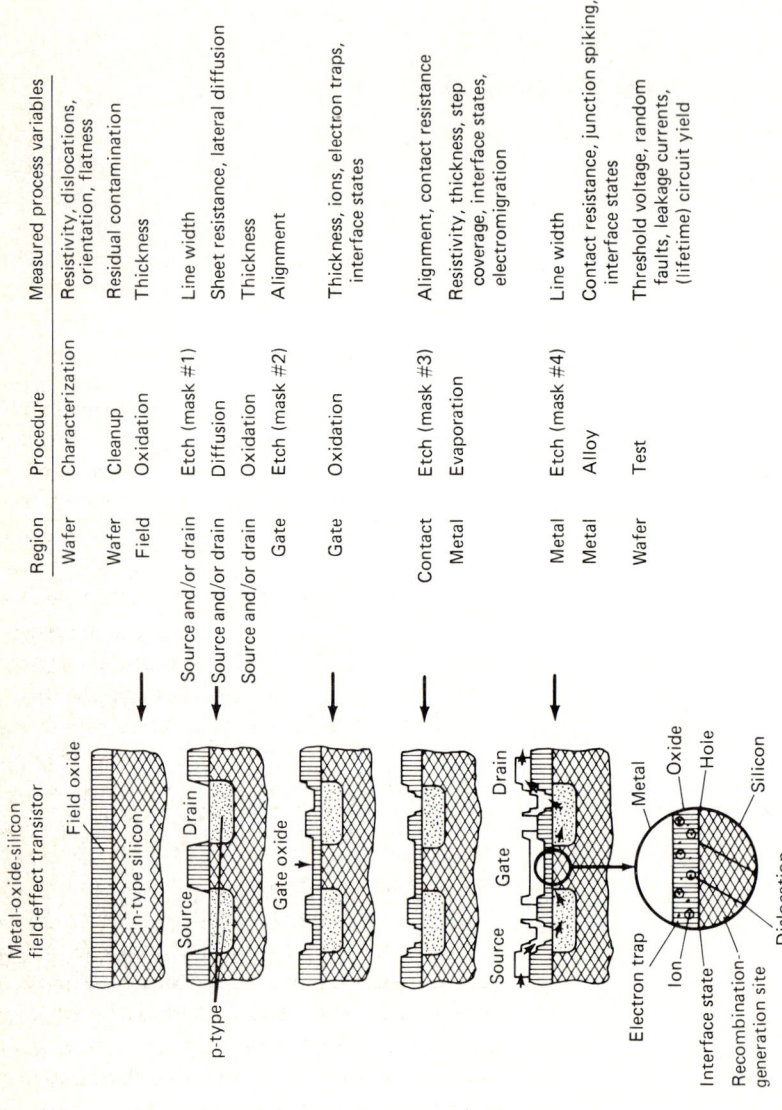

FIG. 6-28 Measurement application in a MOSFET process. [Ref. 6.]

4. Misalignment in the measurement system
5. Vibration
6. Variability in the photo- or electron-optic system (energy intensity, focus-element movement, etc.)
7. Electrical variability
8. Nonlinearity of the measurement system with respect to the standard used
9. Poor translation of measurements from one instrument to the next

Proximity effects, various or unknown thresholds used for edge location, and other measurement phenomena lead to the conclusion that line-width calibration should be performed for both lines and spaces separately using many widths over the range of interest.

REFERENCES

1. Nyyssonen, D. and J. M. Jerke: *Optical Linewidth Measurement—A Basic Understanding*, National Bureau of Standards, Washington, D.C., October 1978.
2. Jerke, J. M. and Charles E. Wendell: "Use of the NBS AR-Chromium Optical Linewidth Standard for Measurements on Other Types of Chromium Photomasks," *SPIEJ.* **342** (1982).
3. Feldman, Albert and Theodore Vorburger: "Comparison of Optical and Mechanical Methods of Thickness Measurement," *SPIEJ.* **342** (1982).
4. Rose, Mitchell: "Masks and Wafers: Linewidth Measurements in a Submicron Industry," *Test and Measurement World,* September 1982.
5. Nanometrics product brochure on Cwikscan II scanning electron microscope, January 1983.
6. Nyyssonen, D.: "Process Control Metrology for LSI's," *IGC Conference,* June 1981.
7. Schram, R. R.: "Measurement Technology for Critical Dimensions on Masks and Wafers," *IGC Conference* Sept. 24–26, 1978.
8. Alvarez, F. P., D. J. Elliott, H. F. Sanford, and M. W. Legenza: "Improved Novolak-Based Photoresist system for Very Large Scale Integration (VLSI) Lithography," *SPIEJ.* **394** (1983).

7
Masks in Production

INTRODUCTION

The description of mask fabrication, starting with raw silica and glass melts and ending with final inspection, presents the world of the mask up to its time of use. Perhaps it is analogous to the life of a person up to the point where a career begins. The many mask-preparation steps only serve to make the product as ready as possible for the production line. In the volume production lines, masks are subjected to an entirely new world. Many different environments that test all the capabilities of the mask are part of its useful life. The subject of this chapter is a description of the various aspects of masks used in production. These subjects are divided into the following categories:

1. Inspection of the finished product
2. Protection while in the exposure aligner
3. Periodic cleaning to maintain quality
4. Mask handling, storage, and identification
5. Reworking mask defects

INSPECTION

Inspection is a rapidly changing area. New types of automatic inspection equipment are being applied to the problem of inspecting increasing volumes of masks. The masks are becoming larger in area and more complex in terms of pattern elements. Quality improvements are essential to maintain good device yields, and quality checks are needed to find defects, determine their origin, and either correct them on the mask being checked or make changes in the process from which the problem originated. The changes in die sizes, with dice becoming bigger, also make the masks and wafers more defect-sensitive. A smaller number of individual larger die areas will produce a higher statistical defect percent than a larger number of smaller dice. Figure 7-1 shows the relationship between yield-per-mask level and die size.

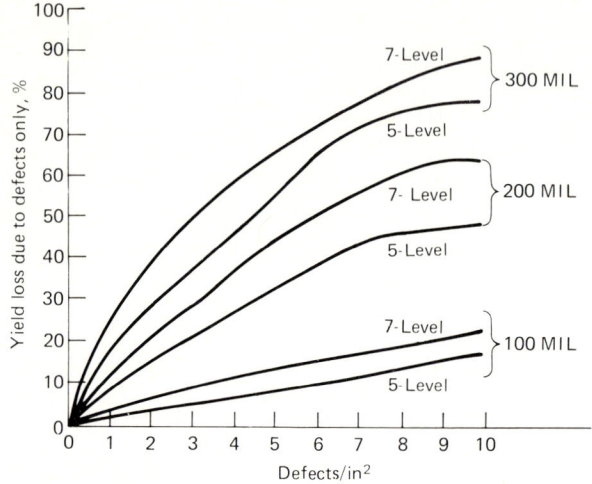

FIG. 7-1 Yield per mask level versus die size: 5- or 7-level process.

Die size is not the only reason for providing thorough mask inspection. Perhaps the largest burden on the fabrication process is the cost of lost time and material as a result of defective masks that make it into the production line. The inspection step ideally serves to screen out all the defective masks before they are used to print a single wafer. There are also problems with masks that are not defects in the form of pattern description. These can be runout errors, mask-overlay problems, and substrate irregularities.

Defects

The primary areas of mask inspection can be divided by the type of defect or problem. The most obvious type of problem is a defect in the pattern area. Defects can be random or repeated, and inspection operators as well as automatic inspection equipment will generally pick up both the defect and its regularity if any exists. Gross microscope inspection of masks at 125–500× is generally sufficient to see this type of problem. However, the size of the masks and the sheer number of parts to be inspected at a 100 percent level really require automated mask inspection. For example, 100 percent manual inspection of the active area of a 4 × 4 in mask would require a minimum time of 5 to 8 hr. The same mask in an automatic inspection system can be checked in 20 min.

Defects located at the inspection step are often reparable. The computer printout from automatic inspection will locate the sites and plot the area of the defect. In the section of this chapter on reworking mask defects, the treatment of this area is discussed. There are several ways to fix defects on masks. Since most defects are either pinholes or voids in the chrome (or other mask material) or chrome spots, repair is simply a job of adding opacity to, or removing opacity from, the glass plate.

Registration Errors

Registration errors are not uncommon and come in several varieties. These can be runout, image-placement errors, overall image dimensional errors, or mask-to-mask-overlay errors. Measuring accuracy on the order of ±0.15 μm is needed to detect these types of errors.

The types of equipment used to detect registration errors are linear digital comparators, optical mask comparators, and the automatic mask inspection system. In optical comparators, common geometric registration patterns are superimposed and viewed optically. This vertical stacking technique also serves to identify parts of the pattern that may have been omitted during the artwork preparation stage. In the automatic inspection and linear digital comparators, the complete pattern dimensions are plotted by horizontal comparison of the entire mask set. The computer then prints out the data, identifying the actual mask data against the original specifications.

Critical-Dimension (CD) Checking

Critical dimensions are the most closely watched areas of mask patterns. CD tolerance runs about 10 percent of the line width and refers to the dimensions of both lines and spaces, as well as variations along a given pattern geometry, for the most critical aspects of the pattern. Critical dimensions are often checked with high-power image-shearing microscopes or SEM measurement. They are also monitored in an automatic inspection system. The calibration standards referenced in Chap. 6 are used to zero the instrument that checks critical dimensions. The size of many critical dimensions on VLSI masks almost eliminates manual inspection with conventional microscopes. The use of electronic measurement is essential in this area. Automatic focus and image detection eliminate possible operator error and greatly speed up the process of checking these very important pattern elements. CD checking in an automatic inspection system is quite fast, and an entire mask can be checked in a few minutes with this equipment.

Mask-Quality Checks

The overall quality of a mask and its constituent elements must be measured in terms of array centering and rotation. Title, sizing marks, and orientation are other examples of overall quality checks. There are special templates used in simple microscopes to check for array rotation, as well as software in automatic inspection systems to find this problem. These types of flaws are regarded as "gross" and will be typically caught before the mask reaches the production line or even the final inspection step.

Overall Inspection Criteria

The benchmarks noted above for inspecting VLSI masks must be quantified. The amount of precision and accuracy needed in critical-dimension control will run between 0.3 and 0.1 μm depending on the line size. A 2-μm line will typically have a tolerance of ±0.3 μm. Pattern registration runs between 0.1 and 0.5 nm on a 4-in wafer, and fatal defects per layer (of approximately 1.0 μm) are measured in percent yield with figures between 95 and 99 percent. Many specifications call for 100 percent yield in the fatal-defect category. Since the inspection step is responsible for determining mask quality, a set of specifications must be given to differentiate between an acceptable mask and a reject mask. For example, the specification for a defect would call out no more than 2 defects/in^2, and the defect diameter should not exceed 1.5 μm. If three defects are found, all having a dimension greater than 1.5 μm, the mask is rejected back to the repair station. In general, a defect will be an unintentional opaque spot in a clear field or a clear spot in an opaque field. Figure 7-2 shows the most common types of defects and their general appearance.

In establishing overall inspection criteria for a given mask set, it is important to understand the most likely source of these defects. For example, registration errors, where positional errors are incurred from one mask level to the next, are caused by stepper-table-position problems. They can also be caused by errors in loading the reticle in the step-and-repeat camera or by nonflat blanks. The critical-dimension tolerances that can be held to about 0.25 μm are smaller in direct proportion to the reduction in line widths. Variations in CDs come from artwork-

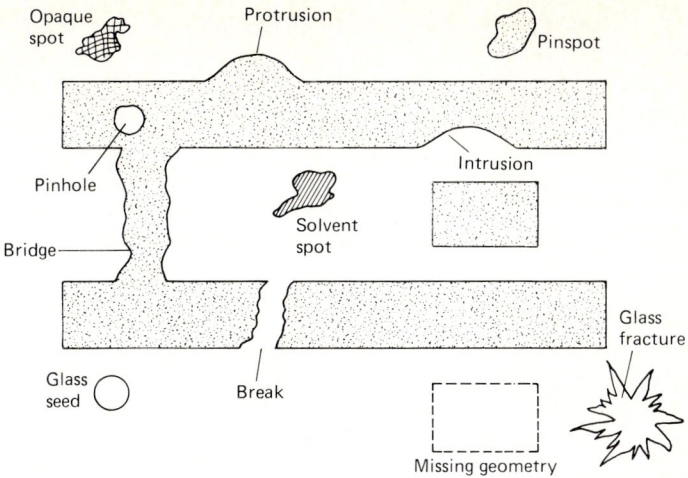

FIG. 7-2 Typical photomask defects.

generation equipment as well as shifts in the glass blank. Finally, the random defects that become part of the inspection criteria are caused by environmental contamination, handling, and glass defects. Increasing die sizes increases the probability of any defects causing a failure. The overal sensitivity of the die to random defects is greater *both* as a function of diminishing feature size and increasing die size. Thus, random visual defects are the largest single cause of poor yield in microlithography. Registration errors and CD tolerances are affected only by the size of the pattern elements and therefore are not as serious in impact on photolithographic yield.

Definition and Sources of Defects

Defects can be broken into distinct categories of shape, size, and source in an attempt to identify mask problems and correct them. The following is a list of some common mask defects and their likely point of origin.

1. *Break:* A break is caused when unexposed resist that should protect a chrome area is removed before etching, leaving the chrome bare, to be then etched away. A break in a pattern is generally caused by poor adhesion of the resist or a contaminant in the resist causing it to dissolve in the developer when it would normally remain. Also, a thin spot in the resist film or a dirt particle under the resist ends up leaving the chrome unprotected in the etch, thereby causing the break.

2. *Bridge:* A bridge is caused when resist that should be removed by exposure is left on in the etching step or, if the resist is removed from all areas, when something in the etch process prevents the etchant from reaching and dissolving the chrome. Causes can be chunks of resin not totally dissolved in the resist solvent and sensitizer mixture, a cross-linked spot in the resist not soluble in the developer, dirt stuck in the resist, poor wetting of the etchant to the chrome surface, or objects in the etchant preventing wetting.

3. *Glass fracture:* Stresses in the glass are sometimes relieved during thermal processing of the blank. The result can be a stress crack or fracture in the blank. Chips of glass can be left behind from this occurrence; chips of glass may also enter from rough handling of the plate edges or some abrasive fixturing in the production process. Also, placing the blank under pressure in a vacuum or similar fixture can cause a fracture.

4. *Glass seeds:* Seeds are imperfections in the glass substrate that have their origins in the glass-manufacturing operation. Seeds in the glass are not *always* printable defects, and the blank or mask can be tested for printability of this type of defect. Generally, seeds are seen as at least potential lithographic problems and are cause for plate rejection.

5. *Intrusion:* An intrusion is a narrowing of an opaque line edge or width caused by many possible problems. First, poor chrome (or other mask material) adhesion can result in excessive undercutting in etching, leaving an intrusion. Second, poor resist adhesion can cause the problem but generally will result in *many* intrusions on a mask since it occurs more generally. A particle either under the chrome or under the resist can cause chrome or resist lifting. Finally, poor exposure control will cause numerous intrusions at points where optical reflection causes unwanted resist exposure.

6. *Missing pattern element:* An entire pattern element will occasionally disappear in either the etchant or in resist removal. The cause of this infrequent problem can be complete loss of resist adhesion where the entire pattern image slides off in the resist developer. In subsequent etching, the chrome is etched completely away leaving a clear area where a chrome pattern should have been. A more remote possibility is the loss of chrome adhesion so that complete undercutting in the wet etch removes the pattern with the resist still on. This can happen more easily if an extremely small pattern is relatively isolated.

7. *Photoresist residue or spot:* Resists used in mask fabrication are very brittle and likely to shatter when contacted by a blunt object or any

tool that creates surface pressure nonuniformly. The resist breaks up like a glass plate, and chunks of resist will be left all over the plate area unless careful cleaning and re-imaging take place immediately. The consequence of resist flakes or chunks is opaque or semitransparent spots on the mask after etching. The resist film is only 7000 to 10,000 Å thick, and some coatings are only 4000 Å thick. Such a thin layer, when broken into very small parts, will adhere tenaciously to the glass surface or the chrome areas, both of which are very flat. Resist chunks can also be deposited by mask-plate handlers.

Another resist problem that leaves behind a layer or film is scumming or "veiling." This phenomenon occurs when the resist in the unexposed areas is attacked by the developer, and dissolved resist redeposits on the plate because of poor rinsing after development. The resist will leave a thin layer behind in a random fashion. Sometimes resist separates into two layers in developing, and the top section falls back onto the bottom layer as a veil, folding and sticking onto the resist layer already in place. Veiling can be caused by partial resist exposure in the center of the layer, caused by an antinode or exposure maxima in the standing wave pattern. Reduced developer strength or development time is one way to eliminate this problem. Another is to change the optical thickness to an odd multiple.

Finally, there can be elements in the resist that do not expose or develop out. These are often circular areas with fringed edges, suggesting a thickness gradient. This is a nondissolved area of resin and is difficult to remove, even from the resist as a liquid. One method to filter these out from a resist solution is to run the resist through diatomaceous earth or "filter-aid," a technique also used to remove resist contaminants.

8. *Pinholes:* Pinholes are small voids in the mask film or layer thickness caused by small holes occurring first in the resist layer or by poor adhesion of the chrome, leading to lifting in a small area. Particles in the chrome-deposition step can cause chrome lifting in small areas. Pinholes in the resist layer can be a result of poor resist filtration, dust or other contaminants getting lodged in the coating during the resist spin or soft-bake steps, or a defect in the pattern artwork original. Pinholes can be repaired by one of several proprietary processes or by well-defined opaque add-on processes. There are several materials that can be added to plug the pinhole. Some are special-viscosity, metal-containing inks.

9. *Pinspot:* A pinspot is a small island of chrome left behind after

ething. Pinspots are caused by incomplete etching, specks of resist left behind on the chrome in areas to be etched, dust or other contamination left during resist exposure that prevents complete resist removal, or a solid particle in the etch that deposits on the chrome during etching and keeps the etchant from wetting the surface properly.

10. *Protrusion:*   A protrusion is a small bulge in the resist or chrome pattern that can exceed the mask-design-rule specification and cause a part to be rejected. Protrusions are a result of some contaminant getting left on the resist layer that prevented resist removal in developing or of a wetting problem or contamination problem in the etchant. Another source of contaminants that will change the width of a line is the resist developer. Resist developer, thinner, and etch solutions should all be submicron filtered before use. In fact, all chemicals that end up touching the mask surface should be submicron (0.2 μm) absolute filtered. Small particles from many different sources are constantly getting into the process and finding their way to the mask surface.

11. *Opaque:*   An opaque spot is often just dirt or some contaminant sitting on the mask surface. Opaque spots can be dust, resist flakes, lint, hair sections, or glass chips. Good mask cleaning will often remove the randomly occurring and irregularly shaped opaque spots.

12. *Solvent spot:*   A solvent spot is a stain left on the clear field area of the mask that could print itself onto a wafer. Solvent spots are residual remains of an evaporated cleaning solution or other solvent material. Solvent spots, opaque spots, and general surface debris are all removable in a good cleaning cycle that uses some mechanical brushing or high-pressure jet-spray cleaning with or without ultrasonics. Ultrasonics alone will often jar loose these pattern-interfering contaminants. There are "zapper" and other methods to remove mask-surface irregularities that have not been removed in the cleaning cycle. Solvent spots are often left from poor drying or poor alcohol rinsing after a standard cleaning cycle.

All these defects can and do occur on a completely unused mask, and the number of these problems increases as the mask is put into the production line. Dust, dirt, resist particles, and other random contaminants increase as the mask is exposed to the semiclean process area. Repeated cleaning cycles will wear away at the chrome mask, causing an increase in the number of pinholes and intrusions as the chrome layer is eroded. Attack of the chrome by the cleaning solutions is another source of increased pinholes and general degradation of the chrome layer.

Scratches and fractures also increase with mask handling in the production line. The need for frequent and repeated inspections is real and is based on the number of pattern-interfering phenomena that are generated when a mask is placed in the imaging process environment.

MASK QUALITY AND YIELD

The increase in the die size is the single largest factor requiring such strong attention on mask quality. A simple mathematical yield equation shows why this is so:

$$Y = \frac{1}{1 + D_0 A}$$

where D_0 = density of random defects on wafer
A = die area on wafer
Y = yield

A plot of die or circuit area in square mils versus yield-per-mask level (at several defect densities) is shown in Fig. 7-3. Note that the yield decreases rather quickly as die area increases *and* as defect density increases. The data in this figure are applied to a single mask level, and

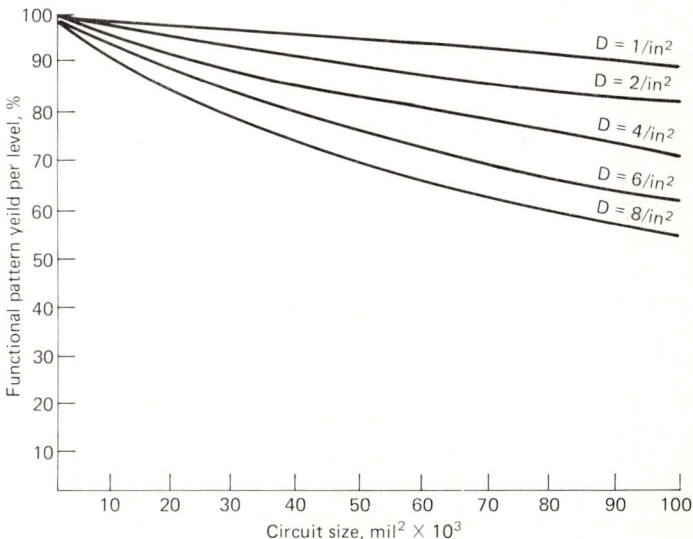

FIG. 7-3 Functional pattern yield versus circuit area for several defect densities.

yield for a mask set or a 5 to 10-mask-level process is calculated as follows:

$$Y = \frac{1}{(1 + D_0 A)^n}$$

In Fig. 7-4 the relationship between yield required per masking step and final yield is plotted for several mask-level sizes. Note that in order to get even a 50 percent final yield for any of the multilevel examples, any single level must yield over approximately 88 percent.

The number of defects we have discussed and their impact on the process economics can now be more fully appreciated.

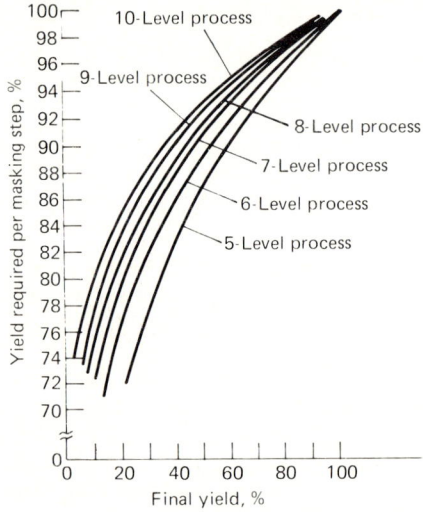

FIG. 7-4 Functional pattern yield required per masking step versus desired final yield for processes requiring 5 to 10 mask steps.

EXAMPLES OF MASK DEFECTS

The following series of photographs serves to illustrate common mask defects and problems that affect mask yield. All these will be picked up in a complete 100 percent inspection process, hopefully with an automatic mask inspection system.

In Fig. 7-5 an example of resist shattering is given. Note the large number of individual sections created by a single break in the resist film. Figure 7-6 is an example of an opaque spot printed onto a wafer from the defective mask. Note the short circuit caused between metal

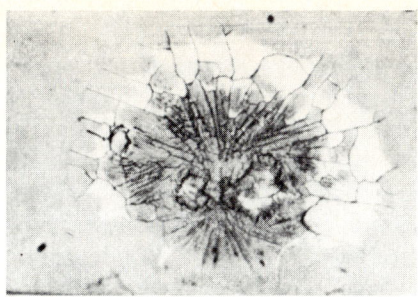 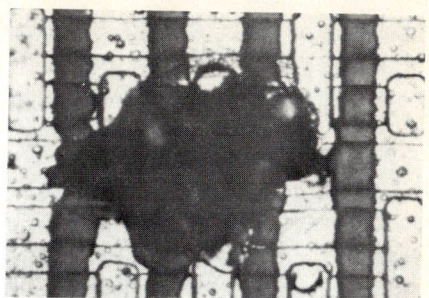

FIG. 7-5 Example of resist shattered on a surface. *(Shipley.)*

FIG. 7-6 Opaque spot printed from a mask onto a wafer. *(Shipley.)*

traces in the photograph. This could have been residual resist, dirt, or some large solid contaminant not removed from the mask in one of the cleaning operations. The solvent stain or residual-contaminant stain from cleaning is shown in Fig. 7-7, printed from the mask onto the wafer. The opacity of the stain was sufficient to cause a break in metallization where the darkest edge of the stain was coincident with the metal trace. If these defects are not caught by inspection, they "move on" to create full-fledged defective chips.

The common bridge defect is shown in Fig. 7-8. In the example shown, three good bridges have been built to cause three separate shorts in the aluminum metallization. Bridging is still a problem when metal traces are very closely spaced (design rule problem) and exposure control is poor in resist processing.

The circular defect called a "resist gel," or dewetted area surrounded by a series of resist rings, is depicted in Fig. 7-9. These occur frequently on chrome plates when the resist has not been filtered or has been contaminated.

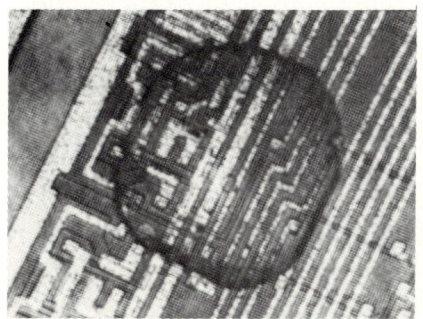 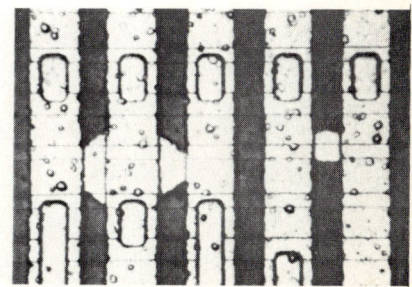

FIG. 7-7 Stain image printed onto a wafer. *(Shipley.)*

FIG. 7-8 Metal bridging defect. *(Shipley.)*

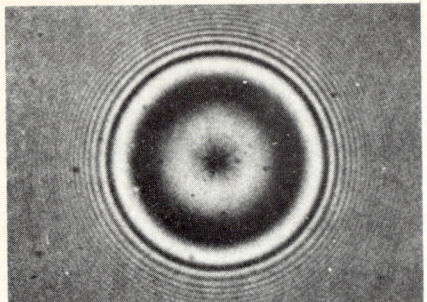

FIG. 7-9 Dewetted area of resist on chrome. *(Shipley.)*

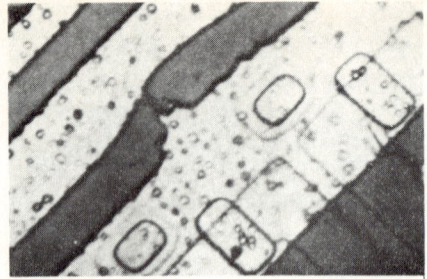

FIG. 7-10 Protrusion defect printed on a wafer. *(Shipley.)*

Figure 7-10 is a good example of the protrusion defect discussed earlier. This particular example nearly becomes a bridge when printed onto the wafer. Note that the width of the lines changes considerably in the area near the protrusion.

A good, clean break in the pattern is shown in Fig. 7-11. This is a particularly large break and one that should have been picked up by inspection before the mask was released to production. This certainly will reject the device.

Figure 7-12 shows an intrusion defect probably caused by a large piece of lint that printed in the wafer. The large size of this intrusion is more than enough to cause a rejection, being way beyond the 30 to 35 percent intrusion tolerated on some devices. In use, a chip with this type of defect would fail early in its life.

Resist between pattern elements that is not cleaned out in development will lead to sizable protrusions and eventually bridges. Figure 7-13 shows the extra metal left behind where resist was not completely removed between traces. This could be transferred directly from the mask or could have originated at the wafer level in the resist-developing step. A possible solution to this problem is more complete exposure and/or

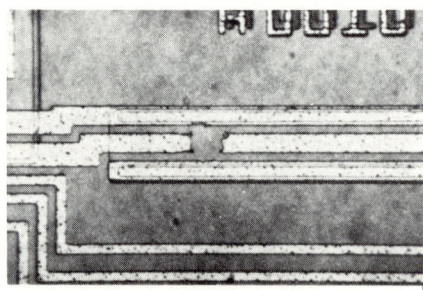

FIG. 7-11 Break defect on a wafer. *(Shipley.)*

FIG. 7-12 Intrusion defect. *(Shipley.)*

additional development. There are many other types of defects that occur on mask and wafer surfaces, and inspection is reaching the point of being able to catch most of these before they become wafer-yield problems. The trend away from sampling toward 100 percent automatic inspection makes this possible. However, defects can and still do become a part of the real production world, regardless of how many times you inspect a mask. The smart process operator or engineer identifies and carefully documents typical problems, causes, and solutions.

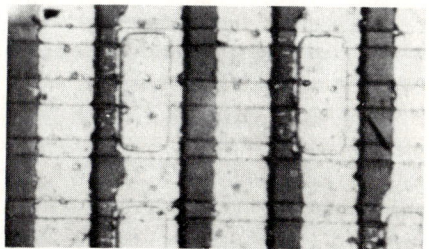

FIG. 7-13 Extra metal caused by incomplete resist removal in exposed areas. *(Shipley.)*

INSPECTION TECHNIQUE

Long before VLSI masks appeared on the scene, inspection was performed by sampling methods. A given manufacturer would select an allowable yield loss for given steps of the mask fabrication process. This approach of using sampling plans worked well since there were many dice per wafer, and the selection of certain numbers of sites for inspection resulted in a reasonable statistical yield. Also, defects were allowed to exist, and the reject dice that resulted simply dropped out as an expected part of overall process economics. Sampling plans still provide a usable method of inspection in processes where there still remain a large number of dice per wafer. VLSI designs have changed this criteria by virtue of having very large dice. Defects considered tolerable are either one or two on a typical high-density design, and most defects exceeding the allowable number must be sought out and repaired if possible. The small number of dice per wafer no longer permits getting good statistical results by sampling plans. All of this means VLSI masks are 100 percent inspected, and every possible problem eliminated by whatever means possible. A good example of the magnitude of inspection at 100 percent is the number of individual locations to be checked on a 5×5 in mask: 1.6×10^{10} for 1-μm or larger defects. Obviously, manual visual inspection would not be economically feasible with these kinds of numbers.

Simplification of the inspection task for thousands of individual "peeks" at a VLSI pattern is accomplished several ways. The types of inspection covered here are optical comparison, image enhancement, and adjacent-die comparison.

Optical Comparator Method

This method uses the principle of comparing two masks for differences. The masks are placed on a common stage as shown in the schematic diagram in Fig. 7-14. The masks are illuminated with light that is filtered to give complementary colors. The superimposition of the patterns results in dark- and clear-field matching areas, and any pattern or object deviations show up as a color. The eye is very sensitive to image

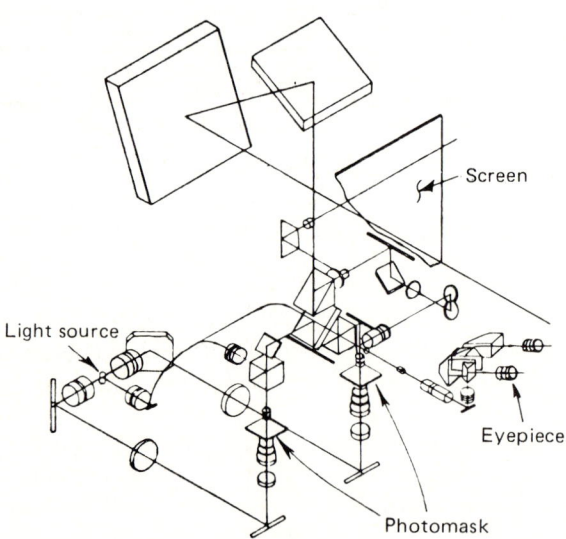

FIG. 7-14 Schematic diagram of an optical comparator.

differences, and defects or pattern anomalies can be readily seen. However, the cost of finding defects with this method is high due to the following difficulties:

1. Alignment must be perfect, which is time-consuming.
2. The process is difficult to automate.
3. Extremely high mechanical precision is needed.

These problems are not trivial, and the optical comparator is generally relegated to the still-important task of checking mask-set overlay and CD and line variation.

Image Enhancement

Image enhancement uses a primary difference between pattern geometries and defect geometries as the means to spot problems. The plotted IC patterns are all orthogonal, but defects are almost always random. This fundamental difference is the basis of a system shown by Tokyo Shibaura Electric in 1976 at a Kodak microelectronics seminar. The system automatically reduces the image intensity of the IC-pattern elements that occur in horizontal and vertical planes. Images occurring at angles other than these are passed through the optical system at relatively higher intensities and show up as defects.

The principle of the Toshiba system is based on the diffraction of coherent light caused by illumination of an object. The Fourier spectrum of the object, shown in Fig. 7-15, is created at the back focal plane of the lens. In the figure, a simple periodic mesh pattern is used as an example, with its Fourier spectrum as shown behind the imaging lens. Since the periodic structures are considered normal and not of interest, spatial filters are added to this system and block most of the intensity from the orthogonal images. This leaves the nonorthogonal images from random mask defects as primary energy carriers to the focal plane, where they show up as image points. The predominant amount of light energy coming from diffraction of light by random defects occurs mainly in planes other than those blocked by the spatial filters. Shown in Fig. 7-15 at the bottom are the xy grating and an unmodified energy distribution from this grating at the back focal plane of the imaging lens.

A low-cost application of this principle for detecting mask defects is placing the spatial filters in an optical microscope with noncoherent illumination. The loss of image resolution by using noncoherent light is a drawback, and this type of inspection is still largely manual and not easily automated.

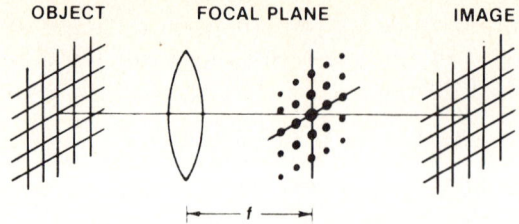

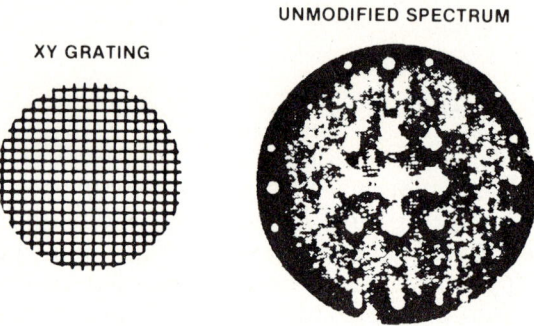

FIG. 7-15 Formation of Fourier spectrum of object at back focal plane of imaging lens (at distance f), when object is illuminated by coherent light. Also shown are a periodic mesh (*xy* grating) and the energy distribution at the back focal plane of the imaging lens (unmodified spectrum).

Adjacent-Die Comparison Method

The adjacent-die comparison method has several inherent advantages for automatic inspection. The conclusion has already been reached that individual inspection using manual techniques is simply too laborious and that automation of this task is essential. The adjacent-die comparison method is automatable because

1. All dice are identical.
2. Reference masks are not required (one mask used).
3. Focus is simple on one mask.
4. Relatively loose mechanical tolerances for mask scanning can be used.
5. Automatic-focus capability is used to compensate for mask sag and bow.

Several systems have been developed to provide automatic inspection by this method. Some use laser-scanning systems with computerized information storage and printout. Others utilize a color TV camera where defects are found by illuminating three die patterns simultaneously, each with a primary color. After recombination of the three die images, a black-and-white image of the patterns is formed. However, a defect on one or two or all three dice will not have the fully recombined color scheme and will appear as one or two of the primary colors, signaling a defect.

The general requirements for any of the adjacent-die comparison methods are stage precision and accurate placement of the two sets of optics over the die. If the alignment is off by 1 μm, the computer logic can only measure defects larger than 1 μm in order to differentiate them from registration errors.

The KLA-100 series automatic photomask inspection system avoids this problem in a unique way. The operator visually aligns the dies to make sure the optics are imaging nominally identical pattern elements. As the system scans the mask surface, it digitizes the images into matrices. These matrices are then positioned to obtain a "best fit" situation between two dies. The KLA system then uses proprietary algorithms to process the matrix data, and it automatically signals when differences occur and also stores the difference information in system memory. At the end of a complete mask scan, the operator calls up all the stored data, reviews the results, and makes decisions about defects that are found.

The resolution of the KLA-100 is a function of the area (pixel) digitized on the mask. This figure is 1.25 μm for the KLA-100 and 500 nm for the KLA-101. The KLA-101 can locate 900-nm defects 95 percent of the time and will locate 400-nm defects with lower probability. The KLA-100 system diagram is shown in Fig. 7-16. The actual system is shown in Fig. 7-17. Figure 7-18 shows an expanded version of the KLA-100 that includes an off-line review station for comparison of masks and reticle arrays against printed wafers.

PELLICLES FOR IC MASK PROTECTION

The economic pressure for higher yields in IC fabrication at the VLSI density level is high. All means to improve device yield are pursued beginning with purity improvements in all of the raw materials and ending with the final stages of testing and packaging.

The most yield-sensitive area of IC device manufacturing is lithography. Figure 7-19 breaks down the typical yield values for major areas of the IC process. Since the highest leverage exists in the masking areas, we should logically spend a disproportionate percent of the yield-improvement dollar in this area.

260 INTEGRATED CIRCUIT MASK TECHNOLOGY

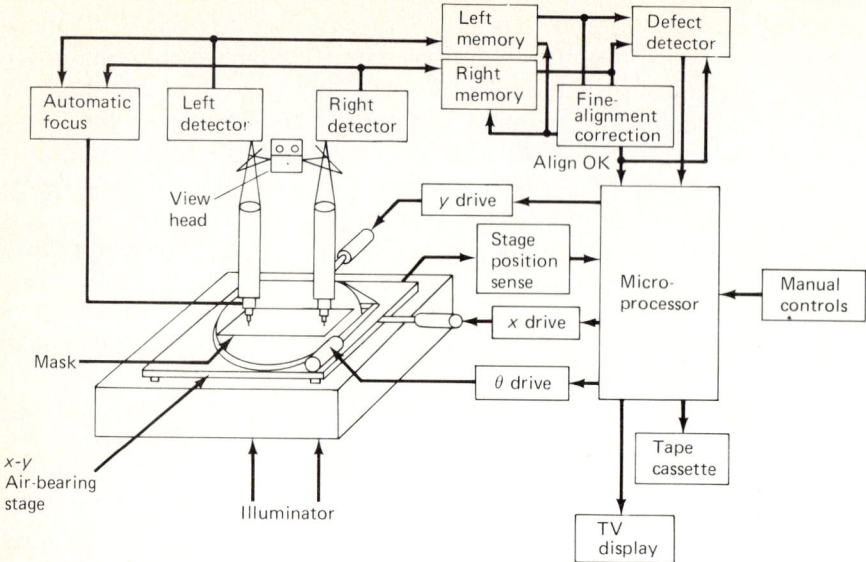

FIG. 7-16 Block diagram of the KLA-100 series automatic inspection system that employs a pixel size of 1.25 μm. *(KLA Instruments.)*

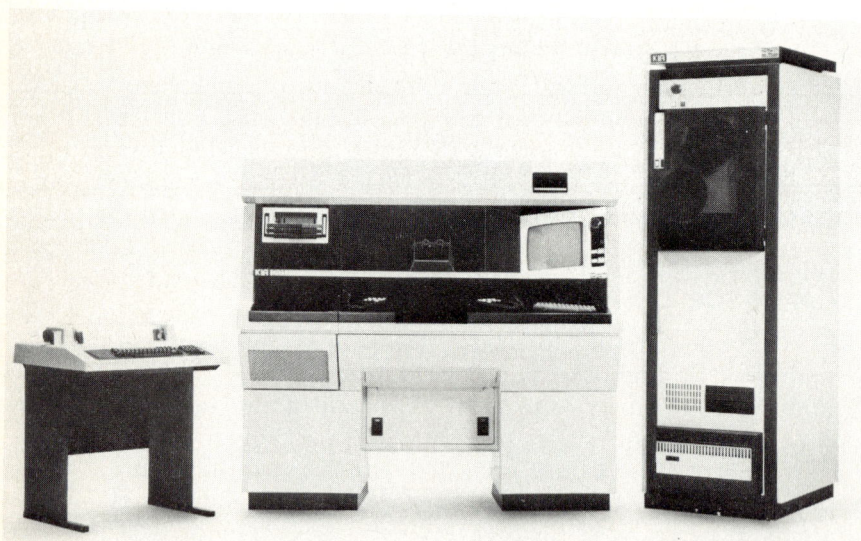

FIG. 7-17 KLA-100 automatic mask inspection system. *(KLA Instruments.)*

MASKS IN PRODUCTION **261**

FIG. 7-18 Complete system using KLA ADD/100 series inspection equipment. (ADD denotes automatic defect discrimination.) *(KLA Instruments.)*

85-90% typical yield

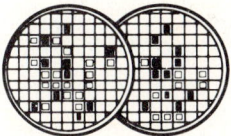

3-85% typical yield

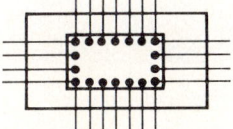

85-90% typical yield

65-90% typical yield

FIG. 7-19 Typical yield values for IC fabrication steps.

The image-transfer steps are particularly sensitive to defects in the production line. A large reticle at 10× is meticulously processed to be defect-free, and yet several micrometer-sized contaminants can undo much of the effort and create reject chips as a result. The concept of putting a protective covering over these large reticles to maintain their near-perfect image quality is a powerful idea. The manifestation of this concept is a pellicle.

A pellicle is a very thin membrane that is used on top of IC masks to insulate them from airborne particles and other environmental contaminants. Pellicles are transparent so as not to interfere with the exposing energy on its way through the mask onto the resist coating. The pellicle membrane is stretched over a frame and placed directly onto the imaged side of a mask. Figure 7-20 shows a mounted pellicle placed over a mask as it would be in the production environment. Pellicles are made out of Mylar and nitrocellulose materials. The membrane thickness of a pellicle ranges from as thin as 0.7 μm to over 12 μm.

FIG. 7-20 Pellicle for reticle protection mounted and unmounted. *(Advanced Semiconductor Products, Santa Cruz Calif.)*

Transmission Properties of Pellicles

The first key consideration in the use of pellicles is their impact on lithography. Since the pellicle has a finite thickness and reflecting surface, it detracts from the resolution in any imaging system. The spectral transmission properties of commercial pellicles are shown in Fig. 7-21. The transmission versus wavelength, plotted in nanometers, shows that high transmission exists at wavelengths above 350 nm for Mylar and nitrocellulose materials at thicknesses between 2.9 and 12 μm. The

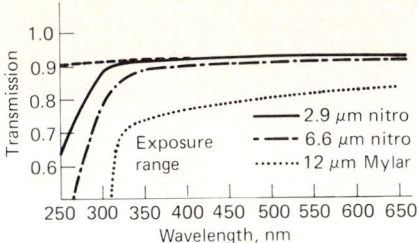

FIG. 7-21 Spectral transmission properties of commercial pellicles. *(Advanced Semiconductor Products, Santa Cruz, Calif.)*

major resist exposure lines for mid-uv and longer uv wavelengths are safely under the transmission curve for these pellicles. On the deep-uv region, only the Mylar pellicle material shows high transmission down into the 200-nm range. In summary, the transmission properties of Mylar and nitrocellulose pellicles both are compatible with the primary spectral output energy lines of resist exposure systems and also pass sufficient energy so as not to extend resist-exposure times significantly.

The refractive index of nitrocellulose is about 1.5, causing a loss of light by reflection of approximately 8 percent. The refractive index of Mylar is higher, about 1.65, and causes light reflection of approximately 12 percent. Mylar is less desirable for this reason even though the energy loss is only 4 percent more. Positive optical resists used to pattern most high-density devices are already slow photographically, and additional reductions in exposure throughputs on wafer aligners are expensive. Capital equipment is very expensive, and resist and equipment people alike work very hard to improve the number of wafers that can be exposed per unit time. New resist developers for positive resist have helped improve this situation, as have some intensity gains made in optical steppers. In the future, even greater pressure than now exists to raise wafer throughput will be exerted as sizable consumer markets demand much greater numbers of chips.

Mylar does not compare favorably with nitrocellulose in another area that directly impacts resist exposure, namely, light loss by internal scattering. The most advanced and highest-quality pellicles made of nitrocellulose will consume up to 2 percent of the exposure energy passing through them. The same loss for Mylar is as high as 10 percent. These losses are measured in the portion of the energy spectrum where resist exposure takes place, typically between 280 and 450 nm. Light-energy loss by pellicle membranes from scattering within the membrane is caused by reflections from internal surfaces that are part of the nonuniform structures of the membrane. The diagram presented in

Fig. 7-22 includes all the light losses, including absorption, reflection, and scattering losses.

Evaluation of pellicles from various commercial sources should include careful optical screening tests, including uv-spectrophotometer measurements, empirical resist-exposure tests to measure actual increases in exposure time, resolution testing to measure the impact or loss of resolution caused by the membrane, and resist-contrast change, if any, caused by the use of a pellicle.

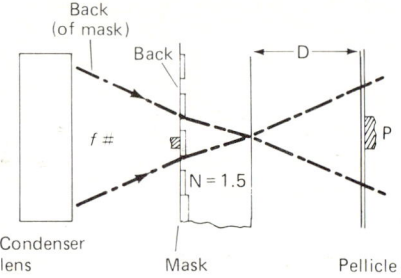

FIG. 7-22 Obscuration of illumination by particles on the back of the mask and pellicle surface. Intensity variation $\propto \dfrac{p^2}{(D/f)^2}$.

Midultraviolet Technology and Pellicle Use

Pellicles are by their very nature a tool for use in advanced technology areas of microlithography. The greater the density and the higher the resolution of a reticle or mask, the more expensive it is to clean and the greater the need for pellicle protection. Cleaning is the only way to remove particles from masks used in production lines, and repeated cleaning degrades the images on the mask, as does the handling that accompanies the cleaning. Thus, leading-edge-device designs are natural pellicle application areas.

Mid-uv lithography is resist-imaging technology between 280 and 365 nm and has emerged as one of the next frontiers for obtaining smaller image dimensions. Pellicles must be highly transmissive at mid-uv wavelengths to be effective, and only nitrocellulose appears to be a candidate material for this spectral region. The 2.9-μm-thick membrane shown in Fig. 7-20 has sufficient transmission to work in the mid-uv area.

Resists for mid-uv imaging to accompany this technology are also available, including Shipley XP-2138 positive photoresist, Azoplate 4000 series positive resist, and Hunt positive resist. Exposure equipment for mid-uv imaging is available in the Perkin-Elmer Model 500 used in the uv-3 mode.

Shorter wavelengths naturally favor obtaining higher resolution, and the combination of high-quality pellicles, scanning projection printing in the 280- to 340-nm range, and high-contrast positive resists with good sensitivity at mid-uv wavelengths constitutes a viable imaging technology. The resists cited will also withstand most commonly used dry-etching environments, permitting complete process capability without additional process steps. In this case shorter-wavelength imaging is a very simple way to obtain higher resolution in VLSI device fabrication processes.

Pellicle Particle Protection

The reason for pellicle existence is to "catch" the particles and other airborne contaminants that would ordinarily land on a reticle or mask surface. Pellicles are thereby practically eliminating the need to clean a reticle or mask except when a pellicle is damaged and needs to be taken off the mask and replaced.

The other causes of mask degradation are damage from microscopic or other methods of inspection and from breakage or other process-related accidents. The pellicle is attached to the mask and remains with it during all standard exposure operations. The question of pellicle cleaning and insulating the mask from particles raises the issue of clean attachment. Pellicles can be blown off with filtered dry nitrogen or rinsed with ultrapure deionized water to remove dust, dirt, or any relatively loose contaminant falling on the pellicle surface. Contamination of a more serious nature *or* physical damage to the pellicle will necessitate removing the pellicle and replacing it again after cleaning or putting on an entirely new pellicle.

Pellicle attachment is probably best performed by the company supplying the mask in order to minimize surface contamination. Perfectly clean (near-zero- or zero-particle surfaces and zero-defect reticles or masks) masks from an independent mask shop or from the mask shop within a given company can be "pellicized" during the final packaging steps normally used for the mask. The complete assembly would then be shipped and opened, under the cleanest possible conditions, immediately before insertion in the equipment. This would reduce the problems of particle entrapment between the mask, or reticle, and the pellicle. Masks that are pellicized in the production area most certainly stand a chance of including several particles between the underside of the pellicle and the face-up surface of the reticle. While the job of pellicle attachment is relatively simple and does not require expensive or complicated equipment, it must be performed in an extremely clean (Class 10 preferably) environment and with masks or reticles that have been cleaned immediately prior to use. Pellicles can be attached to *both* sides of a reticle or mask and thereby give double protection against excessive cleaning and the contamination that makes it necessary.

Once the pellicle is properly attached to the reticle or mask, it can be placed in the exposure equipment. Since most exposure aligners were developed without consideration for the need of pellicle space in the reticle or mask housing, minor modifications may be needed to allow the pellicized substrate to fit easily.

Once clean mask and pellicle surfaces have been provided and inserted in the exposure system, the periodic monitoring of reticle and mask cleanliness is really all that remains. During the exposure process, particle contamination is inevitable since air can never be kept completely free of particles when operators are close to the equipment. Even a completely robotic operation will result in particle contamination from wear on moving parts in the equipment. As these particles land on the optical surfaces in the imaging path, they can create disturbances in the intensity and shape of the aerial image. Typically, particles need to be sizable (greater than 10μm) before their optically disturbing effects are measurable. Downstream from a condensing-lens element, large particles can obstruct the image when landing on the pellicle or reticle and mask surfaces.

The primary means to minimize the effects of particles in the optical path is to provide sufficient distance between the pellicle and the reticle mask so that the particles cannot form images or significantly disrupt the aerial images. The increased distance will, unfortunately, allow more space for particles to find their way to the reticle and mask. A formula for determining a sufficient standoff distance has been proposed by Ron Hershel of Hershel Consulting Inc., Albany, Oregon.[1] The formula is as follows:

$$D = \frac{NFP}{280}$$

where D = minimum standoff, mm
P = particle size, μm
N = refractive index (1.0 for air, 1.5 for glass)
F = condenser f number at mask or reticle

The data presented in Fig. 7-23 show the required particle standoff for 10 percent variation in illumination. The air gap in millimeters (y axis) is plotted against the standoff distance, also in millimeters. The $f4$ curve represents a no. 2 aperture on a Perkin-Elmer aligner, while

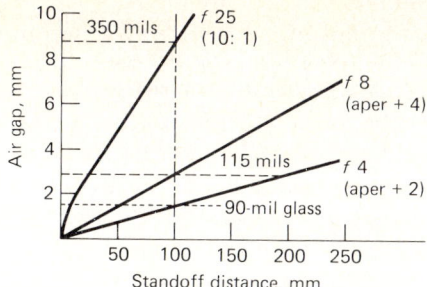

FIG. 7-23 Required particle standoff for 10 percent variation in illumination. [Ref. 1.]

the $f8$ curve represents a no. 4 aperture, also on the Perkin-Elmer aligner. The 100-mm standoff is thus good for particle immunity with particle sizes of 100 to 200 μm on the pellicle surface. The 90-mil mask thickness also provides relief from particle imaging for 50- to 100-μm-sized contaminants on the mask backside. The Ultratech Model 900 also fits on the $f4$ curve, using a 50-mil-thick pellicle and a 90-mil-thick reticle. The optical stepping aligners are better suited for pellicles due to their greater depth of focus, allowing particles to "fuzz out" within the optical path and be less of a disturbance to the transmission of microimages.

There is a spatial relationship between the pellicle, mask or reticle, and the condenser lens. The presence of particles on the various optical surfaces affects this relationship. This demonstrates the need for working in especially clean environments, even *with* pelicle protection on both sides of reticles or masks. In the future, pellicle technology will certainly advance to help reduce the problem of contamination entering between the pellicle and the mask. Special fixtures are conceivable that can act as barriers to the entry of particles in the standoff areas.

The problem of optical interference must also be considered with thin pellicles. Studies of the spectral transmission properties of these membranes have been conducted, and the control of pellicle thickness in manufacturing provides the most significant reduction of resist-exposure variation caused by optical interference. Improved manufacturing techniques for pellicle thicknesses control have been reported, and pellicles are available with less than 1 percent thickness deviation for thicknesses of 2.9 μm. In addition to thickness control, pellicles can be coated with special films to reduce optical reflections. Magnesium fluoride is one such material tested for this application. The use of thin coatings on pellicle membranes is still in a research stage, and future improvements in optical transmission can be expected. An immediate way to at least reduce optical effects is similar to standing-wave reduction in resist imaging in chrome, namely, selection of optimal imaging parameters to average out differences of known frequency. The overall optical parameters can be specified for any given system, including resist thickness and absorbence and optical transmission of the exposure source (intensity and wavelength breakdown, pellicle thickness, refractive indexes of the surfaces, and others). Calculations are then made to arrive at an optimal pellicle thickness for the exposure and resist system.

In the previously cited work by Hershel, calculations are presented to arrive at the solution to the interference problem or to obtain optimizations that eliminate much of the optical disturbance that directly impacts uniform resist exposure time and intensity. One obvious way of reducing or avoiding optical problems created by pellicles is to use them in exposure systems that have polychromatic illumination. Exposure systems with monochromatic illumination are always more sensitive to any changes or disturbances in the optical path due to the absence of wave-canceling effects that average out or cancel the peaks of unwanted images, such as standing waves.

Optimization of pellicle thickness to fit the optical parameters (an even integer of quarter wavelengths) has been demonstrated in very thin membranes (0.72 μm) that still maintain sufficient physical strengths to withstand 30 lb/in^2 pressure from blow-off guns. These improved membranes have up to 99 percent transmission to 436 nm as well as good transmission at 546 nm for visual or automated aligning.

The more recent pellicle configurations for use on reticles and masks are shown in Fig. 7-20. These materials incorporate the low-reflectance properties as well as good transmission, physical strength, and uniformity of membrane thickness, all significant functional parameters needed for current VLSI device fabrication.

MASK DEFECTS AND REPAIR

The combination of defects in resist films due to airborne particle contaminants, solid contaminants in rinse waters, and particles of resist that break off and redeposit on mask and reticle surfaces is part of the mask production situation. The best efforts to limit all forms of contamination are at best control oriented and cannot eliminate the realities of a contaminating environment. Techniques used to continually upgrade the mask fabrication environment include

1. Air filtration
2. Humidity control
3. Submicron filtration of all chemicals, gases, and other filterable materials

4. Antistatic devices
5. Operator particle control via protective clothing, hygenic procedures, and traffic-flow patterns
6. Ongoing monitoring of all critical environmental parameters (temperature, humidity)

These measures can be tightened as the process needs dictate, and current trends in VLSI mask and reticle fabrication indicate the strong need for superclean (less than Class 10) environments for future chip designs. Current leading-edge processes and future advanced design processes will no doubt continue to face the age-old reality of *defects*. Given that we accept the continuing presence of mask defects as part of any economic model, the question of treating them must be addressed.

Zero defects is an unlikely possibility without the retouching and post-fabrication techniques designed to patch voids and spots on reticles and masks. Several commercially available process methods and chemistries are used to remove or add portions of pattern elements to help arrive at a zero- or near-zero-defect level. In keeping with environmental and operator safety guidelines, mask-defect control techniques need to be as safe and nonpolluting as possible and at a minimum conform to local and state ordinances. Future planning strategies will anticipate trends in this area and incorporate materials and equipments that exceed any current environmental limitation.

Defect Removal by Laser

The laser as a tool for defect removal on reticles and masks is well-established. Lasers are ideal for this application for several reasons, including the collimated nature of the beam, relatively low cost, adaptability to production line equipment and processes, operator safety, elimination of repair processes requiring the use of polluting chemistries, and small area of plant space needed to perform the repair operations. Laser "zapper" systems are used in conjunction with high-quality optical microscopes and are engineered to give the best mask and reticle throughput (or minimum repair time). Such a system is shown in Fig. 7-24.

Production use of lasers for mask and reticle repair requires rapid magnification changes to locate the defect, "zap" or vaporize it away, and move quickly to the next die location or next mask. Turret-lens capability is therefore essential on the companion microscope. Since VLSI masks and reticles are specified to the highest obtainable flatness in order to hold critical-dimension tolerances, they require an equally flat surface to be used in a laser or any mask and reticle repair system.

FIG. 7-24 Xenon laser system for vaporizing opaque defects. *(Florod.)*

Stages of inspection and zapping microscope systems that are not as flat as the reticle will result in flatness deformation, such as gravitational sag. An example of a laser-zapped structure is shown in Fig. 7-25.

Repair of Transparent Defects

In addition to removing opaque and clear defects, laser photodecomposition can also be used to plug pinholes. Laser photodecomposition

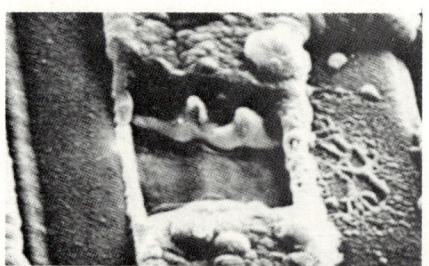

FIG. 7-25 Scanning electronmicrograph of an opaque defect vaporized by a xenon laser. *(Florod.)*

involves illuminating a defect in the reticle or mask using focused light from a low-power uv laser. The reticle or mask is contained in a gas cell that has a mixture of an inert gas (e.g., helium) and a metal alkyl at atmospheric pressure. The decomposition in the gas phase of the metal alkyl generates a spot of the metal on the area illuminated. This is all accomplished in a single step, making it a simple, production-oriented operation. The resolution limit of this technique is about 1 μm. The apparatus used to perform the operation is shown in Fig. 7-26.

The laser is a frequency-doubled argon uv laser generating 1 mW at 257 nm. Photodecomposition has also been achieved using CW (CO_2) lasers at longer wavelengths, pulsed eximer lasers, and other types of laser systems. In use, the beam is focused beyond the front window of the gas envelope so as to avoid metallizing its surface. The use of soda-lime, quartz, and other substrates is compatible with the 2λ argon uv laser. Photodeposits of 2 to 3 μm have been made, and after deposition of the material, a laser trim may be needed to sharpen the edges.

The reticle or mask, after placement on a superflat stage, can be traversed via a rapid inspection motion system. A second "crawl" setting for slower stage motion is used for zapping. The reticle or mask is positioned over the defect, and the operator turns on the laser and observes as the beam vaporizes the defect. There are typically four positioning knobs in the x and y planes, two for each stage speed.

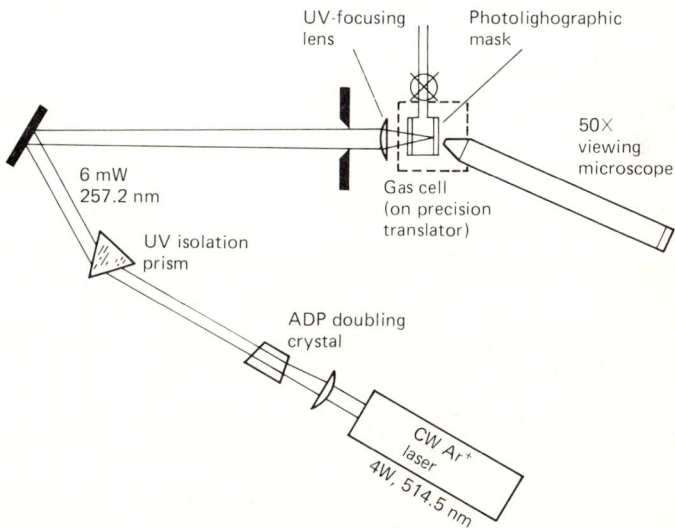

FIG. 7-26 Schematic diagram of system for laser repair of defects.

Movement of the plates in and out of the scope is facilitated, in the example of Florod lasers, by dovetail paddles that do not damage the mask.

Repair Equipment

Safety is always a key concern when high-intensity energy beams are close to operators. The systems used typically have the laser oriented vertically down, traveling along the operator's line of sight, which is known as "collinear viewing." The variety of microscope options is also important, since inspection should be done with high-quality optics to ensure high-quality repair. A key feature to have is a wide viewing area considering the 5 × 5 in area needed for inspection. Lasers should be used that will vaporize most mask materials. The xenon-type lasers are capable of vaporizing emulsion, black chrome, shiny or bright chrome, iron oxide, gold, tantalum, silicon, ferrite, aluminum, and nickel-iron materials. Since masks are made of most of these materials, and since there may also be a need to remove some of the substrate to get rid of a defect, the wide range of vaporization capability is important.

In operation, a laser is operated by a hand or preferably a foot switch. Defects are sometimes simple chrome spots in the field or protrusions on the edges of lines. The size of these defects can range from 0.5- to 0.7-μm spots to 25-μm defects where a large particle kept the etchant from removing the chrome. Many systems have the resolution capability needed to remove defects between closely spaced lines. High-density memories, CCD, and CMOS designs will typically present geometry situations where lines are spaced 1 μm apart and a defect gets lodged between the lines. Cutting out or vaporizing to this resolution level is a current production need.

Florod manufactures a production-ready system. Its coarse- and fine-focus knobs are easy to access and the laser microscope is out of the way at the back of the unit. Overall dimensions of the base plate are 22 × 46 in, and complete specifications for the Florod Model LMT are given as follows:

Item	Specification
Mask materials	All hard surfaces—chrome, iron oxide, chrome oxide, silicon.
Mask paddles	Choice of three: 5 × 5 in, 4 × 4 in, 3.5 × 3.5 in, 3 × 3 in, 2.5 × 2.5 in, 2 × 2 in.
Stage travel	5 × 5 in (greater travel on special order).
Spot size	For opaque defect removal, adjustable spots 1 to 20 μm.
Aperture	Rectangular with xy controls.
Spot maker	Red spot in microscope to outline size, shape, and location of laser zap. Images the laser aperture for automatic visual display of changes in spot size.

Stage vertical travel	⅜ in (1 cm) to handle all plate thicknesses.
Laser path and safety	Down through microscope top objective. Provides safe viewing while lasing. No laser radiation visible in microscope.
Optics	Binocular microscope head, Leitz Dialux. $10\times$ eyepiece Leitz high eyepoint. Leitz objectives $50\times$ and $10\times$. Trinocular optional.
Xenon gas laser	Stable command pulse laser. Green and blue output for easy visual alignment and photoresist exposure. Five pulses per second and single pulse.
System mounting	Table top (46×22 in) with welded steel frame and optional stand.
Shipping weight	375 lb (170 kg).
Power requirements	117 Vac, single-phase, 2 A, 50/60 Hz.

In addition to opaque spot removal, clear spots are also removable with accessories to the xenon system described above. Interface with a KLA mask inspection system provides video display and computerized location selection. The communications interface is a powerful feature to keyboard defect locations and obtain data output.

The removable thickness is generally 1000 to 1500 Å for antireflective or shiny chrome without damaging the borosilicate or quartz substrate. Spot markers are an additional feature used to outline the size, shape, and location of laser removal patterns. The repair resolution is certainly good enough for $10\times$ reticle repair.

The main parameters surrounding metal deposition are gas pressure, laser power, and beam size at the mask. Typical rates of removal are greater than 100 Å/sec. After deposits are made, reticles and masks are cleaned, and the durability of the deposit should be checked. Most metal depositions performed with uv decomposition methods withstand scrubbing with alcohol, cotton swabs, and Scotch tape tests and are opaque for subsequent exposure energy blockage. Improvements in the spatial resolution will permit applications on $1\times$ and $5\times$ masks and reticles.

Patching Clear Defects

A special process directed at repairing clear defects is used on masks in production under the trade name of Master Patch (from Master Image Inc., San Jose, California). The process works on most substrates to repair broken lines, pinholes, and other clear defects in the 5- to 160-μm-size range. The specifications for this method are given as follows:

1. Capability
   a. Clear defects from 5 to 160 μm in diameter may be repaired.

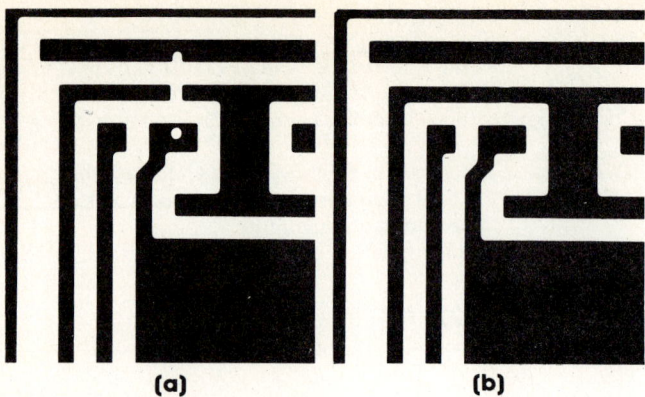

FIG. 7-27 Defects repaired with the Master Patch process. Above left: reticle photographed at 800× contains three 4–5 μm defects (pinhole, broken geometry, and intrusion). Above right: Same reticle after repair. *(Master Image, Inc.)*

    b. Clear defects may be repaired in 15 min or less.
    c. Repairs may be made on soda-lime, white-crown, borasilicate, and quartz substrates.
2. Durability
    a. The repair will withstand firm scrubbing with lens tissue.
    b. The repair will withstand 2 hr immersion in 10% chromic/90% sulfuric acid at room temperature.
3. Opacity: The repair will withstand a uv exposure twice that required to reduce the 10× reticle geometry width 10 times, before exposure through the repair causes penetration of the positive photoresist and subsequent etching of the underlying film.

Figure 7-27a shows a mask with three defects before using the Master Patch process; the right-hand portion (Fig. 7-27b) shows the mask after repair. This illustrates the type of repair possible.

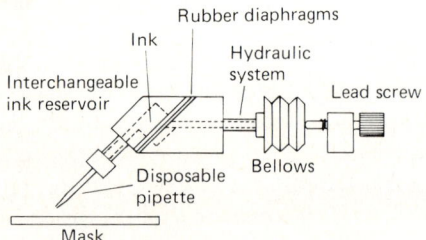

FIG. 7-28 Schematic of ink-dotting microscope for repairing mask defects.

Ink-Dot Repair of Defects

Pinholes, "mouse bites," and breaks in the opaque area of the masks can be repaired with an ink-dotting microscope. A schematic is shown in Fig. 7-28. Called the Ultra Dot, this is simply a microscope fitted with a controllable micropipette that places small droplets of an opaquing ink on the defect. The application of appropriate pressure to the ink reservoir causes a droplet of ink to form at the tip of the pipette. The reticle is raised with the coarse-focus knob, and when the droplet touches the plate, ink transfer occurs.

The ink is supplied in heavy, medium, and light viscosities, and ultra pipettes are graded into coarse, medium, fine, and superfine. After ink has been applied to all of the defects on the mask or reticle, the plates are baked at 90°C for 30 min. When the ink extends beyond the defect area, laser zapping is used to trim excess ink. Figure 7.29 shows an operating ink-dot microscope.

After complete repair, the following cleaning procedure is used to check the durability of the ink repair and simultaneously prepare the mask for production use.

Washing Procedure for Repaired Reticles

Prior to each use of a repaired reticle, it must be superwashed, and the ink must withstand this cleaning in order to be of any value at all. The following wash procedure has been thoroughly tested and has proved very satisfactory.

The reticle is totally immersed in acetone and gentle swabbed on both sides with a Texwipe foam swab, rinsed in running deionized water for 30 sec, removed, and allowed to drain for 3 to 5 sec. It is then

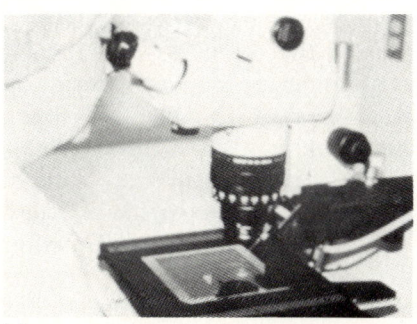
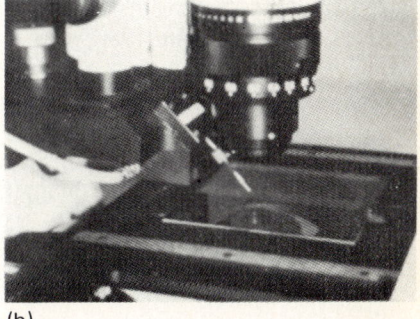

(a)   (b)

FIG. 7-29 (a) Operator using ink-dotting microscope to repair mask defects. (b) Ink-dotting microscope. *(Phototronics Labs.)*

placed in a chromic acid solution (9 lb sulfuric acid plus 1 oz chromic acid) at a temperature of 60 to 70°C for no more than 3 to 5 sec, removed from the bath, and allowed to drain for 3 to 5 sec. Next the reticle is placed, image side up, on the chuck blades of an Ultratech plate washer for a 45-sec wash and 45-sec dry cycle, with a pump pressure of 1600 to 2000 lb/in^2 (11.0 to 13.8 MPa).

MASK CLEANING IN PRODUCTION

Masks are constantly being contaminated in production, and repeated cleaning is used for all types of mask. Cleaning for emulsion and hard-surface masks and reticles is also needed after repair operations and when resist imaging is not acceptable and reimaging is required. There are many types of contamination that require removal before the masks can be returned to production, and several cleaning methods are suggested for various types and levels of contamination. Chemical- and mechanical-cleaning techniques are reviewed here, including recommended process parameters.

Forces Affecting Particle Contamination

Cleaning is necessary both as the plate is imaged and periodically as the plate is used. Even if plates are freshly deposited and exposed to clean-room conditions for several hours, contamination can occur. Particle adhesion to photomask plates is caused by molecular forces (van der Waals–London forces), capillary forces, and electric forces. The van der Waals forces can become extreme, particularly as the interaction between atoms and molecules increases by closer proximity. As separation occurs, these forces decrease very rapidly.

Electric forces play a large role in mask contamination and cleaning. Most (greater than 85 percent) airborne particles are electrically charged, and because of different work functions of the electrons in different materials (glass and dust), a potential is generated between the mask surface and the particle. For example, an electric force of 1 dyn has been calculated for a 50-μm glass particle contacting a nonconducting surface. Coulomb interaction, more difficult to measure than other electric forces, is also responsible for particle adhesion to surfaces. These electric forces of attraction are very difficult to measure, being a function of numerous physical and environmental factors. Particle contaminants are removed by simply overcoming these adhesion forces. Most studies indicate the need to create bursts of energy on the surface that introduce a quasi-steady updraft. The "burst" of air or fluid must overcome the surface-adhesion energy, and then the aerodynamic lift force of air bursts (or hydrodynamic lift force of a liquid) will carry away the contaminant.

Cleaning after Deposition

In many processes there is a tendency to overclean. Masks taken directly from a vacuum or CVD environment should be very clean and, if quickly protected from the environment, will remain clean enough to be processed directly into photo-imaging areas. The only minor contaminant to be removed before any resist operation, regardless of the level of packaging after deposition, is dust. A simple cleaning procedure for masks not yet subjected to production-line contamination and damage is

1. Ultrasonic clean in Freon TF for 10 min.
2. Dry blank in clean air.
3. Dry-nitrogen purge.

Proceed to resist-coating operation or hold in dry-nitrogen desiccator. Cleaning steps, especially in corrosive hot acids and alkalies, may often add more defects and contaminants than they remove. This is particularly true for plates that have not yet seen the exposure-aligning process.

Dry Cleaning of Masks and Reticles

Dry cleaning of $10\times$ reticles and $1\times$ masks has been described by H. R. Rottmann of IBM, Hopewell Junction, New York.[2] Dry cleaning is desirable since it eliminates the need for toxic and contaminating chemicals, which also create pinholes in masks and reticles. Dry suction (versus dry pressure) is known for its effective particle-removing capabilities and can be used in conjunction with wet chemical cleaning if nonparticle contamination (chemical residuals) are present.

The use of a mechanical brush with bristles, together with airflow, has proved to be very effective for removing particles in both photomask and silicon-wafer cleaning. Adding vibration increases the removal efficiency of the brushes. Thus the process for mask cleaning can be a completely dry one, eliminating the need for potential staining with liquid solutions. A special type of air device, described by Rottmann,[2] uses a vacuum nozzle and, from the test data, is very effective in removing surface-particle contamination. Placing the vacuum nozzle 7 mils from the surface generated a 5-in vacuum pressure, and this was the maximum distance recommended. A gap of 2 mils generates a 22- to 25-in vacuum force, wherein the rapidly moving air molecules "grab" particles and remove them swiftly. This type of system, using either a series of nozzles, or a vacuum air knife under which plates are conveyed, permits automatic mask cleaning with good throughput time and high reliability. The system could also incorporate a vibrating, rotating bristle brush to first remove layer particles.

The dry cleaning of new or reprocessed masks is effective for particles down to about 50 μm in size. Particles around 100 μm across and larger weigh more than the adhesive bonding them to the mask surface. However, a 10-μm particle will have an adhesive force (van der Waals, electric, and capillary combined) over 35 times its weight, and the bonding force increases significantly for increasingly smaller particles.

Chemical Cleaning

Both chemical and mechanical methods can be used successfully to clean new and reprocessed masks that have been contaminated in printing operations. Chemical methods range widely from solvent-vapor (or solution) to alkaline-soak cleaners, oxygen-plasma-acid cleaning, and water rinsing. In addition to the brushing, ultrasonic, and gas-flow methods already mentioned, abrasive cleaners are used to remove mask-surface contaminants.

Chemical mask cleaning in a wet-processing area using only solutions in an immersion mode is lengthy but may be the only practical method in the absence of equipment. The recommended method for new and reprocessed chrome masks is given in Table 7-1.

Air drying will permit a small amount of chromic oxide growth, which will aid in bonding positive resist to the surface. One should be careful to not grow an oxide thick enough to radically affect etching

TABLE 7-1 Chemical chrome-mask cleaning

Solution	Time	Temperature
How soak cleaner	5–10 min	Ambient to 175°F, as required
DI water rinse	5–10 min	Ambient, not below 21°C, preferably 25–30°C
Isopropyl alcohol	15 sec	Ambient to 21°C
Dry forced nitrogen	30 sec	Ambient
Chromic-sulfuric acid	2 min	Ambient to 120°F, as required
DI water rinse	5 min	100°F
Triple-cascade (overflow) DI water rinses	3 min each	Ambient
Oven dry (nitrogen or air ambient)	20 min	100°C

parameters, or one should simply use the nitrogen. A shortened procedure for plates with little or no soil or contamination is simply an ultrasonic cleaning in Freon TF for 10 min followed by dry-nitrogen purging. These procedures are used for new masks that inevitably receive some form of particle contamination in the 0.5- to 10.0-μm range, the most common particle-size range.

Masks that have been used for exposure and contain not only particles but chunks of positive or negative resist need to be first processed through a proprietary resist stripper according to the type of resist contamination. Most positive-resist-contaminated masks can be immersed in Shipley Remover 1112A at 120 to 160°F for 2 to 5 min. This solution is highly compatible with chrome and iron oxide mask surfaces and is free of metal ions, phenols, phosphates, chlorides, and fluorides. In addition, it is a clear aqueous solution, permitting observation of the cleaning process. These proprietary strippers are recommended over acetone for reasons of flammability and waste disposal. While the chemical-immersion process described earlier is very effective for removal of all organic particles and films, it will not remove the small (less than 10 μm) inorganic-particle contamination that is a large source of rejects during mask inspection. The solutions are, however, more effective than gaseous removal. For example, airflow of 100 m/sec will not overcome the adhesive force of a 1-μm particle, whereas only several meters per second of water flow will remove the same particle. The data of Zimon[3] show particle size versus water velocity required for removal (Table 7-2).

The use of high-velocity streams of water is especially effective in overcoming the adhesive forces between small particles and mask surfaces. Average jet velocities of 100 to 170 m/sec were generated at pressures ranging from 100 to 3000 lb/in^2, as reported by Kroeck of Bell Laboratories.[4] The mask-cleaning system reported in this work uses pulsing high-pressure (approximately 2500 lb/in^2) deionized-water streams through oscillating nozzles positioned about 2 in above a spinning mask.

TABLE 7-2 Particle size versus water velocity required for particle removal*

Particle size, μm	Water velocity, m/sec
500	0.108
250	0.08
80–100	0.07
30–40	6.17
5–10	0.41

* From Zimon, ref. 4.

The parameters with this system are as follows:

Parameter	Specification
Water pressure	2500 lb/in^2
Mask spin speed	3000 rpm
Nozzle pivot angle	90°
Nozzle orifice	0.008 in
Nozzle-to-mask distance	1.5–2 in
H$_2$O impingement angle	30–45 degrees
Nozzle traverse	7 min
Drying	Infrared spin
Elapsed time per mask	1.5 min/side

A special feature of this system is a sheet of magnesium metal that allows magnesium ions to enter the water stream from the pump and neutralize static charges caused by water moving across the mask surface. These metal ions prevent an erosion of chromium edges, occurring from electric discharge. The yield data for this method are impressive for both positive- and negative-resist masks.

Another mask-cleaning technique is mechanical scrubbing with a nylon brush. Designed by Oswald of Bell Laboratories (U.S. Patent 3,585,668),[5] a nylon retractable rotating brush scrubs the spinning mask surface while deionized water feeds the mask. Water or other mask-cleaning solutions are dispersed at a rate of 0.2 to 0.4 gal/min. The top and bottom surfaces may be cleaned in this fashion. Operating parameters are as follows:

Parameter	Specification
Deionized-water flow (chrome side)	0.4 gal/min
Deionized-water flow (glass side)	0.2 gal/min
Brush speed	260 rpm
Turntable spin speed	200 rpm (clean)
	1800 rpm (dry)
Filtered-nitrogen flow	10 L/min
Capacity per cycle	Six 4 × 4 in masks
Elapsed time	1.5 min/side

The filtered dry nitrogen is dispensed after the water or mask-cleaner rinse cycles for drying. A 9 percent yield gain was reported using this method compared to the high-pressure water method. The mask-cleaning applications are different for these methods, the high-pressure water technique being recommended for stored masters or working plates just before they are put into aligners. The rotating-brush method should be used on new mask products or after an acid soak on all plates that are being recleaned after printing operations. The main advantage of high-pressure gas and water cleaning, as well as mechanical brush cleaning (with deionized-water flush simultaneously), is a dramatic increase in throughput. The old immersion techniques may have an advantage in being able to remove stubborn organic contamination, but the slow cleaning cycle and disposal and handling problems are severe compared to the newer methods.

Masks should always be stored in containers that prevent glass-to-glass contact and should be covered to prevent environmental contamination. Masks should be oriented vertically to prevent sag in storage or transit, and all packing and unpacking should be done under Class 100 minimum clean-air conditions. The outside containers should indicate "This Side Up" and carry an instruction regarding careful handling and opening only under clean-room conditions.

Cleaning Low-Expansion Glass

Special cleaning procedures are often used for highly resistant substrates that can tolerate more aggressive cleaners. Glasses low in chemical resistance, for example, cannot be cleaned with hydrofluoric acid. The cleaning solutions below are suggested for low-expansion materials such as Hoya LE-30 glass.

- HF cleaning
    0.1% HF, ultrasonic for 1 min
    Deionized water, ultrasonic for 1 min (4 times)
    IPA, ultrasonic for 1 min (2 times)
    Freon vapor dry
- Alkali cleaning
    1% RBS (50°C) ultrasonic for 1 min (3 times)
    Deionized water, ultrasonic for 1 min (4 times)
    IPA, ultrasonic for 1 min (2 times)
    Freon vapor dry

REFERENCES

1. Hershel, Ron: "Pellicle Protection of IC Masks," *Semiconductor International*, Aug. 1981, p. 97.
2. Rottman, H. R.: "Dry Cleaning of 10× Reticles," SPIE Conference, 1982.
3. Zimon: "High Velocity Water Cleaning," internal technical publication, Bell Labs.
4. Kroeck, W. H., R. Doll, and E. Stokes: "Removal of Particulate Contamination from Hard-Surface Photomasks by Various Cleaning Techniques," Kodak Microelectronics Conference, 1977.
5. Oswald: U.S. Patent 3,585,668.

Index

Adjacent-die comparison method of inspection, 258–259
Array design technique, 17–18
Artwork:
   computerized, 3–4
   hand-drafted, 13–15
Automatic routing design technique, 20

Backscatter, 139–140
Baking, postexposure, 176–177
Beveling, edge, 67
Blanks:
   coatings for, 69–92
   hardness of, 54, 58
   protection of, 55–58
Borosilicate glass, 37–42, 48–49
Building-block design methods, 26–27

CAD (computer-aided design) system, 1–2, 4, 6–7, 16, 29
Cathode-ray tube (CRT), 3
Channel spectra thickness measurement, 238
Chemical-vapor deposition (CVD), 84–87
Chromium (chrome), 59
   coating of, on glass, 190
   etching of, 170–171, 179–182, 185
   reflectivity of, 81–83, 166
Cleaning:
   of glass, 44–45, 50–58, 83–84
      low-expansion, 281

Cleaning, of glass (*Cont.*):
      mask blanks, 83, 84
   mask, in production, 276–281
      chemical, 278–281
      after deposition, 277
      dry method of, 277–278
      forces of particles in, 276–277
      with nylon brushes, 280
      of particulates, 279
      with water pressure, 279
   ultrasonic, 54–55
Coatings:
   chrome on glass, 190
   iron oxide, 77–81
   for mask blanks, 69–92
   resists as [*see* Resist(s)]
Comparator, optical, 256–257
Comparison microscope, 213–216
Computer-aided design (CAD) system, 1–2, 4, 6–7, 16, 29
Contact printing, 123–128, 134
Contacts, design rules for, 11
Coordinatograph, 14
COP negative electron resist, 138–140
Critical-dimension (CD) checking, 245–246
CVD (chemical-vapor deposition), 84–87

Defects:
   cleaning of, 276–280

283

Defects (*Cont.*):
   definition and sources of, 247–251
   examples of, 252–255, 270, 273
   in glass, 42–45
   inspection of, 244–255
   vs. mask level, 244
   patching of, 274–275
   quality control of, 251–252
   removal of, 268–270
   repair of, 268–276
   specific, 252, 255
   vs. yield, 261
Deposition, 277
   glass-blank, 84–91
Depth of focus, 155–157
Design:
   array technique, 17–18
   automatic routing approach, 20
   building-block methods, 26–27
   CAD system, 1–2, 4, 6–7, 16, 29
   fixed-grid layout method, 24–26
   hierarchical method, 20–23
   historical overview of, 2–6
   lithography in, impact of, 9
   process of, 30–31
   production steps, 5, 6, 30–31, 59
   silicon compilers, 18–20
   symbolic-logic method, 23–25
Design rules, 7–13, 23
Development:
   exposure following, 177–178
   processes following, 169–170
   resists and, 131–138
Device modeling, 28–31
Diazo resin coatings, 75–76
Dry cleaning of masks and reticles, 277–278
Dry etching (*see* Etching, dry)

EBES writing strategy, 102, 109–114
Edge beveling, 67
Electron-beam imaging (*see* Imaging, electron-beam)
Electron-beam resist (COP; PBS), 138–140
Electron microscope, scanning (SEM), 222–227, 231, 235, 236
Ellipsometry in thickness measurement, 237–239
Emulsions, 70–76
Etch-resistance testing, 176

Etching:
   dry, 188–202
      advantages of, 188–190
      overetching, 200–201
      rate vs. oxygen gas concentration, 193–194
      rate vs. power, 192–195
      rate vs. pressure, 192
      reverse etching, 201–202
      temperature-time function, 191–192
      time vs. pattern change, 195–197, 199
      undercutting, 197–200
      vs. wet, 187–188
   resists removal after, 202–207
   wet, 178–189
      batch equipment, 187
      of chrome, 170–171, 179–182, 185
      vs. dry, 187–188
      formulas for, 182–184
      of iron oxide, 183–184, 186
      process steps, 185–186
      types of etchants, 181
Evaporation, vacuum, 89–91
Exposure:
   parameters, 125–127, 146
   postdevelopment, 177–178
   postexposure baking, 176–177
   of resists, 129–131, 155, 158

Fixed-grid layout design method, 24–26
Flatness of glass, 59–66
Focus, depth of, 155–157

Glass, mask-quality, 33–67
   borosilicate, 37–42, 48–49
   chemical resistance of, 53–54
   chrome coating on, 190
   cleaning of, 44–45, 50–58, 83–84, 281
   composition of, 45
   defects of, 42–45
   flatness of, 59–66
   forming of, 34–37
   gravitational sag of, 64–66
   handling resistance of, 44
   hardness of, 54, 58
   low-expansion, 38–40
   melting of, 34–37
   optical transmission of, 37–38, 49–51
   pinholes in, 42–44, 54–55
   processing of, 36

Index **285**

Glass, mask-quality (*Cont.*):
  production steps, 59
  properties of, 46
  quartz, 37, 39–41, 49–50
  runout/run-in, 39–41
  soda-lime, 37–42, 45–48
  stabilization time, 40, 41
  thermal expansion, 38–41
  thickness of, 60, 67
  types of, 37–50
Gravitational sag of glass, 64–66

Hand-drafting, 13–17
Handling resistance of glass, 44
Hardness of glass, 54, 58
Hierarchical design method, 20–23

Image enhancement, 257–258
Image hardening, 173
Image profile, optical, 210–212
Image-shearing microscope, 216–217
Imaging:
  electron-beam, 98–123
    capabilities, 104–109
    dose profile, 106
    EBES writing strategy, 111–114
    equipment, 104, 115
    facilities, 107–110
    MEBES writing strategy, 116, 118
    optical column, 108
    vs. optics, 100–102, 106–107
    raster vs. vector, 102–104
    resists [*see* Resist(s)]
    scattering effects, 120
    sources, 107
    throughput, 100, 105–106
    writing strategies, 102, 109–114, 116–122
  optical, 100–102, 106, 107, 123–138, 146–167
    contact printing, 123–128, 134
    depth of focus, 155–157
    exposure parameters, 125–127, 146
    modulation transfer function (MTF), 153–155, 159–161
    pattern generation, 146–161, 165–166
    photorepeaters, 161–164
    postdevelopment processing, 169–170
    resist processing, 128–146, 171–178

Imaging, optical (*Cont.*):
    spectral reflectance, 167
  of reticles, 96–98, 114, 164–167
Ink dotting, 274–275
Inspection:
  criteria for, 246–247
  for critical dimensions, 245–246
  for defects, 244–253
  equipment for, 260–261
  of raw glass plate, 59, 60
  registration errors, 245
  of specific defects, 252, 255
  techniques of, 255–259
    adjacent-die comparison method, 258–259
    image enhancement, 257–258
    optical comparator method, 256–257
Interferometry, 231–233
Intrusions, 255
Ion-implant regions, 10
Iron oxide:
  coatings of, 77–81
  etching of, 183–184, 186

Laser mask repair, 269–274
  equipment, 270–274
  parameters, 272
  principle of, 271
  technique, 269–272
  of transparent defects, 270–271
Laser measurement, 219–222
Lithography, impact of, on design, 9
Logic, symbolic, in design, 23–24
Low-expansion glass, 38–40

Market trends in mask design, 29
Measurement pattern (*see* Metrology)
MEBES writing strategy, 116, 118
Metal layers, 11–12
Metrology, 209–241
  applications of, 239–241
  laser-based, 219–222
  optical microscopy, 212–217
    comparison microscope, 213–216
    image-shearing microscope, 216–217
  photosensing, 217–218
  profile of optical image, 210–212
  SEM, 222–227, 231, 235, 236
  thickness measurement, 231–239
    channel spectra, 238

286 Index

Metrology, thickness measurement (*Cont.*):
   ellipsometry, 237–239
   interferometry, 231–233
   prism-coupler, 236–237
   stylus profilometry, 233–236
  TV scanning microscope, 218–219
Microdensitometer, 218
Microscopes:
  comparison, 213–216
  image-shearing, 216–217
  scanning electron (SEM), 222–227, 231, 235, 236
  TV scanning, 218–219
Mid-ultraviolet (mid-uv) technology, 264–265
Modeling, device, 28–31
Modulation transfer function (MTF), 153–155, 159–161

Nylon brushes in cleaning, 280

Optical comparator, 256–257
Optical image profile, 210–212
Optical imaging (*see* Imaging, optical)
Optical microscopy (*see* Metrology, optical microscopy)
Overetching, 200–201

Particle removal (*see* Cleaning)
Particle standoff calculation, 266–268
Pattern generation, 146–161, 165–166
Pattern layout, 13–27
Pattern measurement (*see* Metrology)
PBS positive electron resist, 138–140
Pellicles, 259–268
  attachment, 265–266
  definition of, 262
  in mid-uv technology, 264–265
  optics of, 264, 267
  particle protection and, 265–268
    particle standoff calculation, 266–268
  in production, 265–268
  transmission properties of, 262–264
Photorepeaters, 161–164
Photosensing in metrology, 217–218
Pinholes in glass, 42–44, 54–55
Plastic flow, 63–64
Polysilicon regions, 10–11
Postbaking, 170, 174–176

Postdevelopment exposure, 177–178
Postexposure baking, 176–177
Prism-coupler measurement, 236–237
Processing:
  postdevelopment, 170
  resist, 128–146, 171–178
Production steps in design, 5, 6, 30–31
  for glass, 59
Profilometry, stylus, 233–236
Protrusions, 254

Quality control and yields, 251–253
Quartz, 37, 39–41, 49–50

Raster vs. vector imaging, 102–104
Reflectance, spectral, 167
Registration error, 245
Repair of defects, 268–276
Resist(s), 75–78, 128–146
  absorption profiles, 78, 166
  COP negative electron resist, 138–140
  developing, 131–138
  and electron microscopy, 222–227
  exposure of, 129–131, 155, 158
  image hardening of, 173
  images as masks, 171–173
  images from SEM, 226
  in imaging, 138–140, 142–147
  multilayer, 140–142
  PBS positive electron resist, 138–140
  postbaking, 174
  postdevelopment exposure, 177–178
  postexposure baking, 176–177
  processing of, 128–146, 171–178
  removal after etching, 202–207
    criteria for, 203
    dry, 204–207
    wet, 203–204, 206
  selection of, 143, 145–146
  sensitivity, 131
  shrinkage, 174–175
  thermal flow, 174–175
  thickness measurement (*see* Metrology, thickness measurement)
  troubleshooting, 142–145
Reticles:
  dry cleaning of, 277–278
  imaging of, 96–98, 114, 146–167
  washing of, 275–276
Reversal processing, 71–73

Index

Reverse etch, 201–202
Rubylith, 2–3, 14–15
Runout/run-in, 39–41

Scanning electron microscope (SEM), 222–227, 231, 235, 236
Scattering effects in imaging, 120
Sensitivity, resist, 131
Shrinkage, resist, 174–175
Silicon compilers in design, 18–20
Silver halide, 70–76
Soda-lime glass, 37–42, 45–48
Stabilization time for glass, 40, 41
Standards in metrology, 228–230
Stylus profilometry, 233–236
Substrate imaging (see Imaging)
Symbolic logic in design, 23–25

Thermal expansion in glass, 38–41
Thermal flow and resists, 174–175
Thickness measurement (see Metrology, thickness measurement)
Throughput, 100, 105–106

Transmission of pellicles, 262–264
Troubleshooting in electron-beam resist work, 142–145
TV scanning microscope, 218–219

Ultrasonic cleaning, 54–55
Ultraviolet (uv) technology, 264–265
Undercutting in dry etching, 197–200

Vacuum-chuck distortion, 64
Vacuum deposition, 87–88, 91
Vacuum evaporation, 89–91
Vector vs. raster imaging, 102–104
Very large-scale integration (VLSI) integrated-circuit design, 1–2

Warpage of glass, 63
Washing of reticles, 275–276
Water pressure, cleaning by means of, 279
Wet etching (see Etching, wet)

Yield and mask quality, 251–252, 261

About the Author

With over fifteen years' experience in the field of semiconductor technology, *David J. Elliott* has an in-depth knowledge of semiconductor photolithographic problems and needs. He has developed marketing plans and strategies for photoresist products worldwide as well as presented papers, conducted seminars, and taken on other special assignments around the globe. Presently the Strategic Planning Manager, Microelectronic Products, for Shipley Company, he has worked at all levels of the organization to manage both people and projects, resulting in successful products in the marketplace. A member of the Electrochemical Society, among other organizations, Mr. Elliott has written numerous technical papers for various professional journals and is the author of *Integrated Circuit Fabrication Technology*. He obtained his M.B.A. from Boston College.